WHAT COMES TO MY LIPS

AMBREEN BUTT

■■■ black dog press

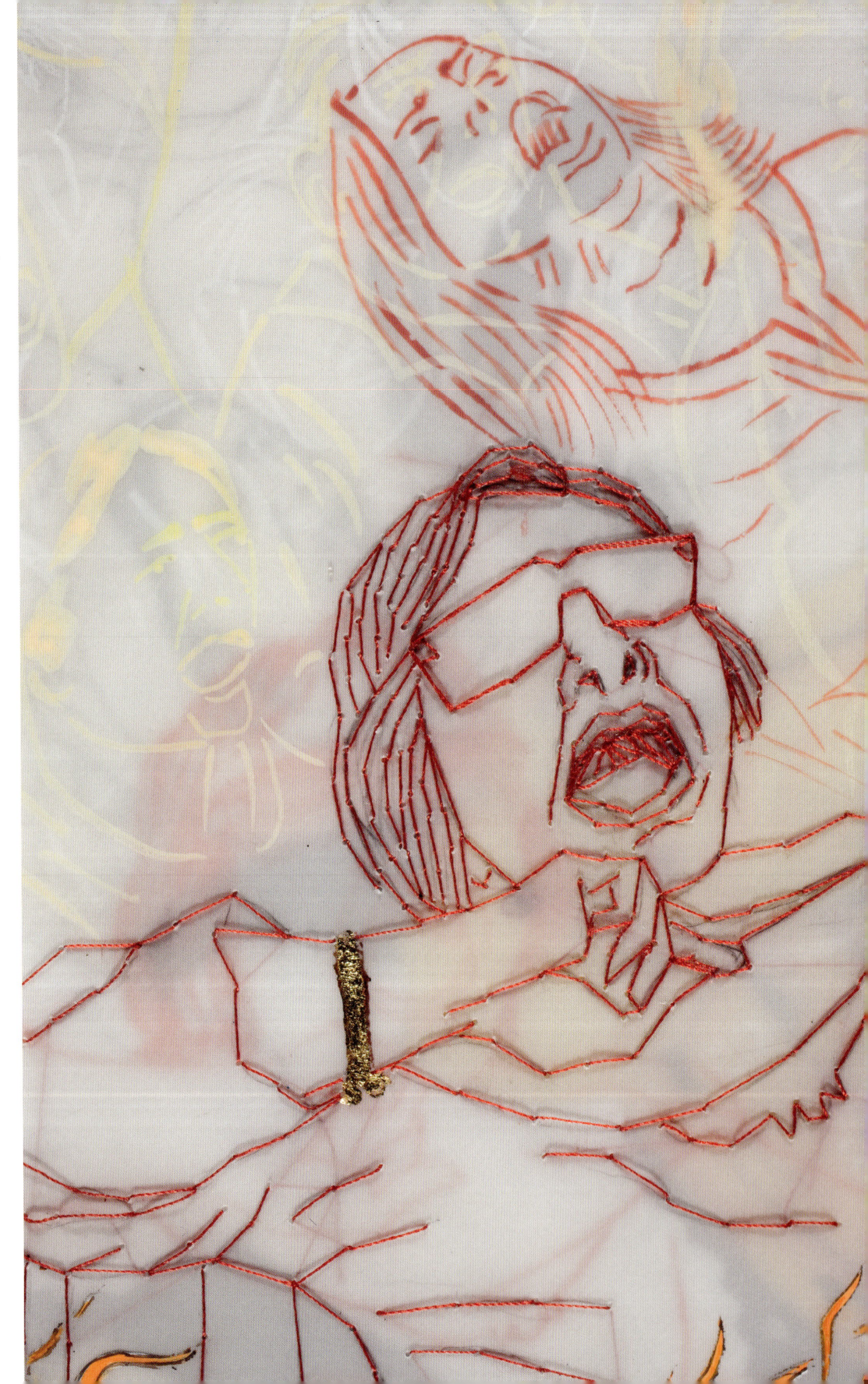

مُونہہ آئی بات نہ رہندی اے

سچ آکھیاں بھانبڑ مچدا اے
جھوٹھ آکھاں تے کچھ بچدا اے
جی دوہاں گلاں توں جچدا اے
جچ جچ کے جیبھا کہندی اے

مُونہہ آئی بات نہ رہندی اے

I must utter what comes to my lips.

Speaking the truth creates chaos.
Telling a lie saves one scarce.
I am afraid of both these.
Afraid I am both here and there.

I must utter what comes to my lips.

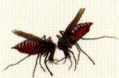

Bulleh Shah
Translation by Kartar Singh Duggal

To Shahnaz, my mother, the anchor of my
life, who bears the weight of my being.
To Saima, my sister, for her unconditional
support in both my dark and bright days.
To Noor-E-Saher, my daughter, for being
the Noor of my life, the source of my
continuous learning.

And to all the incredible women who have
stood by my side in solidarity and support
throughout my creative journey.

CONTENTS

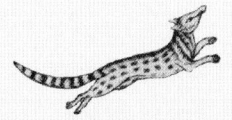

FOREWORD

MARÍA MAGDALENA CAMPOS-PONS

There is fruitful tension in the work of Ambreen Butt that manifests as a sort of dance between the exquisite, delicately-rendered surfaces and the complex narratives presented through the story-telling impulse that is so vivid in her pieces.

Since the 1990s, Butt has commented—with subtlety and unrestricted beauty—about some of the most compelling and challenging stories of the confrontations within the Muslim world and its complex relations with the West. As a Muslim woman living in the U.S., her work claims substantial territory with captivating feminist commentaries that both describe the difficulty of assimilating into a new country and celebrate the wealth and richness of the tradition from which her own work arises.

Trained in miniature painting at the National College of Arts in Lahore, Pakistan and instructed in Western modernism and contemporary practices at Massachusetts College of Art in Boston, her oeuvre emanates from the formal propositions and thematic ideas central to the formidable heritages of Pakistan and the U.S. It is through this cultural hybridity that Butt weaves her ancestral lineage with her own artistic pursuits.

Present in Butt's work is the preciousness of miniature painting. Evident in her preparation of surfaces, creation of pigments, application of brushstrokes, and execution of compositional structures and narrative space, Butt embraces many of the symbolisms, representations, and methodologies of the idiosyncratic miniature painting traditions of Pakistan and India.

The attention to detail, precise description of subjects, and mutation of forms—all of which take a surprising turn when the artist imbues them with radical propositions—respond to everyday issues and contemporary political events. The implication here is that of a woman artist using her voice to command a position of power. Butt's feminist stance imbues miniaturist techniques with empowering messages of resistance through and with beauty.

Butt has masterfully created mythical representations of some of the most profound historical events of our time. For instance, immediately after the tragic events of September 11, 2001, Butt created the series *I Must Utter What Comes To My Lips,* through which she expresses, with singular clarity, the sentiment of loss, the limbo state of otherness, the uncertainty of acceptance, and the negotiation of difference that arose from that dreadful day. In one of the images from her project, Butt depicts a petite woman teetering across a tightrope that spans the blazing Twin Towers. The rendition of this colossal and catastrophic clash of cultures with quiet power and beauty is disarming to the eyes and to the soul. Viewing the miniature requires proximity and close observation, thereby requiring the viewer to get as close as possible to this narrative of discomfort and distress and to contend with its scale.

An early piece from 1997 summarizes the central ideas in Butt's work. Titled *Why Do You Stay In Prison When the Door Is So Wide Open*, this work is the result of her careful destruction of letters she had received from home. Butt takes these textual fragments and disperses them across a grid in a process of disembodiment that makes way for renewal. A metaphor for her diasporic experience, through which the quest for belonging renders the self looted, butchered, exorcized, and incorporated into new knowledge systems in the adopted geography, the topography in these pieces reverberates as meta-strata of the ineffable condition of exile, migration, and transculturation. Roots emerge from the body and become trees growing sprouts of a new, yet-to-be-named species.

The works Ambreen is producing are the vibrant, twisting growths of this new art specimen.

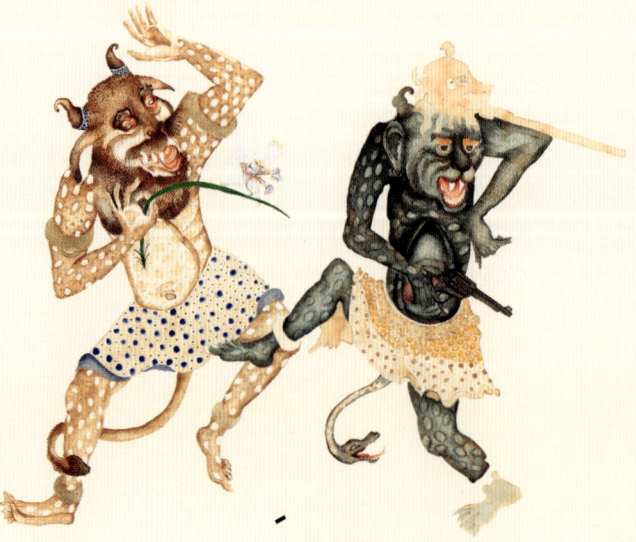

P. 2 (DETAIL) **The Great Hunt I** 2008 FROM THE SERIES Dirty Pretty Pigments, gouache, text, thread, gold leaf on Mylar and tea-stained paper, 45 × 30 inches

OPPOSITE (DETAIL) **Why Do You Stay In Prison, When The Door Is So Wide Open** 1997 Acrylics, gesso, collage of text on wood, 24 × 24 inches

Nashville, Tennessee
June 2023

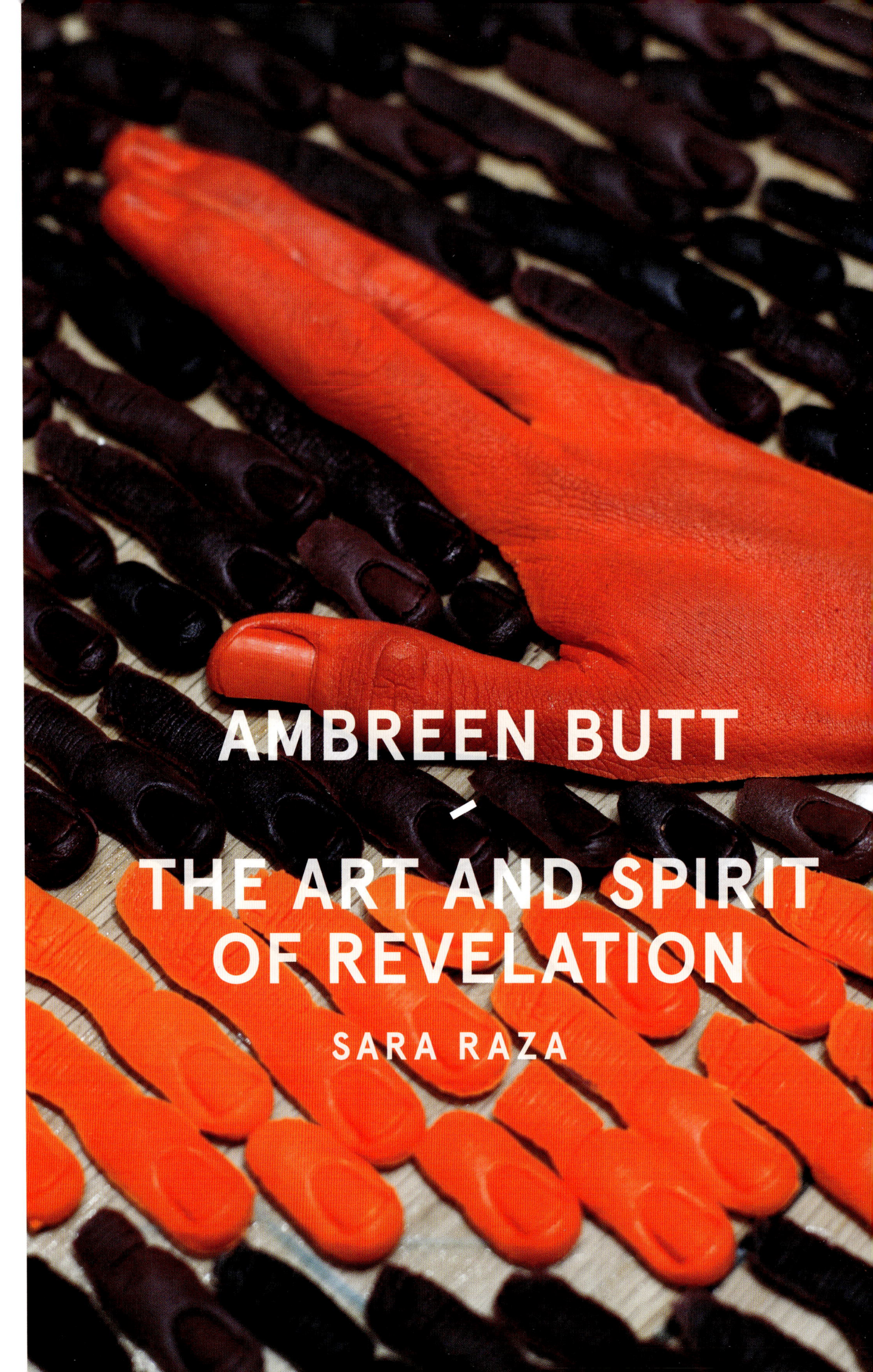

AMBREEN BUTT

THE ART AND SPIRIT OF REVELATION

SARA RAZA

THE END OF ALL KNOWLEDGE IS THAT OF PURE BEING AND THE RELATION OF PARTICULAR BEINGS TO THIS BEING WHICH IS THEIR OWN ORIGIN AND PRINCIPLE.[1]

Operating as a kind of manifesto on universal themes related to "truth" and "knowledge", Ambreen Butt's art practice has for over two and half decades poignantly interwoven the legacy of Islamic cosmology alongside contemporary Indo-Persian inspired visual cultures to explore post-migratory aesthetics and their association with ethics, gender, race, and decolonial thought. Honoring a nuanced approach, Butt's critical set of inquiries derive from a non-didactic position and present a multifaceted understanding of "otherness" that is intentionally unburdened by apologist attitudes and representational principles and ideals. Instead, Butt's art and ideas are grounded in the creative and intellectual pursuit of "truth" which is applied as a plural method for addressing the theme of unity and absolute reality to reveal a crisis of consciousness, brought on by the disordering effects of colonialism and imperialism formed during and after the making of the modern world, which she explores from both a local and global context.

The manifestation of ideas related to truth that reside within Butt's practice are closely connected to the Arabic word *hikmah* which is the given term for the study of higher philosophical forms of spiritual and intellectual knowledge and ways of being connected to the cosmos and natural sciences.[2] As such, Butt's ideas are guided via the universe's common core attributes of "nature", "element", "existence", "intellect", "man", "matter" and the "soul". These attributes have a tendency to overlap, highlighting concepts of unicity and pure being, and can be conceptually traced throughout the contours of Butt's poetic oeuvre. The foundations of these concepts have been cultivated by scholars, scientists, philosophers, and thinkers during the Golden Age of Islam from the 7th to the 14th century. As a system of knowledge *hikmah* drew from ancient sources developed by the ancient Egyptians, Greeks, Hindus, Persians, and Kabbalists, who contributed to esotericism and the mathematical thinking sciences which existed prior to the advent of Islam and were later built upon. Central to Butt's application of *hikmah* is her quest to locate unicity and a universal common form of consciousness. Therefore, knowledge seeking as a form of wayfinding serves as nourishment for Butt's allegorical multimedia art practice that consists of collage, drawing, painting, printmaking, and sculpture, and oscillates between the celestial and terrestrial, center and the periphery, cryptic and unambiguous, logic and illogic, and illusion and reality.

Butt's multilayered works unveil complex conflicting moralities that are obviously inherent within the study of ethics, truth, human patterns, and contracts of social interaction. She does so by deliberately bypassing judgment and the correction of flawed beliefs in favor of open-ended questions that can be accessed from multiple entry points, echoing philosopher Michel Foucault

and his extensive writing on ethics and truth. Foucault asserts, "To take care of the self is to equip oneself with these truths: this is where ethics is linked to the *game* of truth."[3] Symbolically, virtues associated with enlightenment and value can be imagined within the embodiment of a diamond—which can itself be thought of as an allegory for "truth" in that it is cut, chiseled and polished. In Butt's *I Am My Lost Diamond 1 & 2*, 2011–12, a pair of interconnected wall- and floor-based installation works created from resin casts of human scale hands, fingers, and toes rendered in pink, red, orange, cream, and black colors, Butt uses these abstract remnants of the human body—which are frequently used as tools for a numeral metric system for counting and generating mathematical value and function as digits in their own right—to create complex geometric patterns. The roots of numeral systems are attributed to the scholarly work of 9th-century Persian mathematician and polymath Muhammad ibn Musa al-Khwarizmi, who expanded upon the ancient Hindu numeral system to explore the formation of Arabic numbers which were later adopted in Europe. These numerals were based on ten marks and were presented in his influential treatise *On the Calculation with Hindu Numerals*.[4]

In *I Am My Lost Diamond, 1,* Butt employs 25,000 of these cast fingers and toes in pink and red hues which are pinned on the wall to form a monumental and complex tapestry of 13 geometric patterns. The patterns allude to flora, and can also be thought of as visually reminiscent of dynamic fireworks that are suspended mid-explosion in the sky. Each individual cast resembles a single digit, and is imbued with its own set of conceptual forensic DNA data. This data is used for identification, but also functions as a marker still used today as a substitute for a signature (known in Urdu as a *chap*), employed by non-literate individuals to sign official documents. In Butt's installations these "digits" are displayed akin to a series of fragmented cords that are pinned, and suggest a type of stigmata whereby fingers and toes are dislocated from the physical body to create an abstract portrait of the figurative. The works can also be read along the metaphorical lines of symptoms related to the medical condition known as phantom-limb syndrome, where the body experiences a lingering sensation for a limb that no longer exists.

Correspondingly, *I Am My Lost Diamond 2,* a floor-based installation, evokes a decorative picnic floor furnishing (known as a *sofra* in Persian or *dastarkhawn* in Urdu and Turkic languages), which is an embroidered or printed textile that is placed upon a rug on the floor, atop which food and dishes are placed. Composed of decorative diamond and rectangular shapes, Butt's unconventional table setting is entirely composed from resin fingers and hands in shades of red, orange, black, and cream, and suggests a more macabre kind of feast that hints at the

[1] Nasr, Seyyed Hossein, *An Introduction to Islamic Cosmological Doctrines*, London: Thames and Hudson, 1978, p 5.
[2] *Hikmah* is the highest form of Islamic philosophical knowledge rooted in the thinking sciences.

[3] Foucault, Michel, *Michel Foucault, Ethics: Subjectivities and Truth*, edited by Rabinow, Paul, New York: The New Press, 1997, p 285.
[4] Al-Khwarizmi, Muhammad ibn Musa, *On the Calculation with Hindu Numerals*, c. 820 AD.

OPPOSITE (DETAIL) *I Am My Lost Diamond 2* 2012
Resin cast digits, 98 × 152 inches
Installation view, Tufts University Art Galleries, Massachusetts

practice of cannibalism. The artworks were in fact created in response to a harrowing account in which the artist's friend marginally escaped a fatal suicide bombing incident at a local market in Lahore. The works reveal a stark reality connected to the sensational explosive chords of domestic and international terror that can be thought of as another type of cannibalistic activity. At the same time, Butt comments on cycles of trauma that have arisen from fundamentalist religious forms of indoctrination, neo-imperialist violence, repression, and inequality, exploring the socio-psychological effects of terror enacted by desperate individuals and the subsequent human toll. Butt's installations meditate on the idea of sensory guilt and cultural memory through an abstract study of the sacred (the human body) and the profane act (violence) and solicits the urgent call for repair and reform to address a universal crisis in thinking stemming from extreme forms of polarization.

The act of smuggling as a subversive exercise also permeates Butt's practice and unveils her ability to poetically encode her works with hidden value. This practice bears its roots in the mystical properties of the *ghaib,* the Arabic Islamic term for concealed wisdom that resides in the unseen and the unknown. In *I Am All What Is Left of Me,* 2015 Butt presents large decorative sculptural panels akin to the fresco floral tiles that adorn the exterior and interior walls of shrines and religious buildings throughout the Islamic world and operate as a metaphor for the garden. In Islam, the garden is thought of as a manifestation of paradise; it functions as an interlocutor between heaven and earth based on a quadrilateral layout composed of four gardens referred to as *Charbagh* in Persian:

> ### *And whoever is in awe of standing before their Lord will have two Gardens*[5]

> ### *And besides these two there shall be two other Gardens*[6]

In Butt's garden, the floral inspired patterns are created from locks, hooks, and keys which are cast from resin and imply enclosure and entrapment. However, Butt doubles the negative connotation to create a positive charge by suggesting that the keys gesture toward gateways for other unworldly portals, contesting ignorance, with the aid of the metaphor of a walled garden—historical spaces of serenity where flora, fauna, and fountains could be cultivated and protected from external elements in mainly desert climates.

The symbolic assessment of weights and measures pertaining to value systems is also explored in *Pages of Deception,* 2012, a large-scale diptych work on paper. The artist collected one year's worth of materials related to the well-known Boston federal court trial and conviction of U.S. born pharmacist Tarek Mehana who was charged with supporting Al-Qaeda terrorists. Butt collected the documents relating to both the defense and prosecution's closing arguments of the trial from the American Civil Liberties Union and tore up over 160,000 pieces of

text before collaging it upon tea-stained paper. The pages resembled traditional Islamic manuscripts that mirrored one another to reflect the paradox of polarity relating to the first amendment and the inability to decipher the sets of two "truths" put forth by the prosecution and the defense. The intentional illegibility of this work is underscored by the idea that there is no separation between the so-called sacred and the profane, and the thin veil that exists between the two. In this emotionally charged work, Butt deliberately straddles the two perspectives in order to explore and dispel the paradoxical nature of modern civilization.

Posing the open-ended question of what constitutes an act of terror is explored in Say My Name, 2015, a series of works on paper that are an abstract portrait and ode to the unknown child victims of conflict in Pakistan and Afghanistan. This fraught series corresponds with civilian deaths caused by the U.S.-led "War on Terror" which was launched partly in response to the 9/11 terror attacks and has complex roots that go back to the Cold War era and the Soviet-Afghan War. During this time, Pakistan served as a base for Saudi-American backed Mujahideen fighters in Afghanistan as part of a proxy conflict that pitted Soviet communism against fundamentalist Islam whilst concealing Western interests. In Butt's series, the child casualties she highlights have no known legacy assigned to them at the time of their deaths and are usually referred to as a simple statistic. To research these works, Butt assembled data from a variety of different sources in an attempt to create dignified human-centric portraits and reverse engineer the inhumane practice of assigning individuals a faceless and nameless number. Butt's research highlights that the figure of deceased children who have been caught in the crossfire of drone attacks is close to 1,500 and counting. In the artwork *Namaloom,* 2019, the title of which translates to "unknown" in Urdu, Butt creates an outline of a figure using black paper with black text, applying it with glue to a tea-stained surface to juxtapose—and measure against one another—concepts of life and matter. In *Shoaib (6),* 2018, Butt painstakingly created a serene, wave-like seascape, shredding blue paper by hand to document the name and age of the deceased child and the cause of their death. In a similar vein, *Muhammed Yunus (16),* 2018 was also created using hand torn fragments of paper which featured the teenager's name and age. The piece includes red-bellied mosquitos descending upon the victim's body, which provide a piercing analogy for the parasitic nature of war that is part of a vicious capitalist paradigm fueled by the sale of military weapons. The practice of cutting, tearing, stitching, and piercing takes on a repetitive and meditative gesture anchored in the Indo-Persian miniaturist tradition of mark making called *pardakht,* in which Butt is trained. Pardakht loosely and somewhat ironically also translates from Urdu to English as the act of care or correction in one's search to achieve perfection.

Say My Name connects with the collage series In God We Trust, 2012–17, a work that directly explores capitalism and monetary systems in reference to the operations of "church" and "state". To make this work, Butt created

[5] Quran, Surah Ar-Rahman, 55:46.
[6] Quran, Surah Ar-Rahman, 55:62.

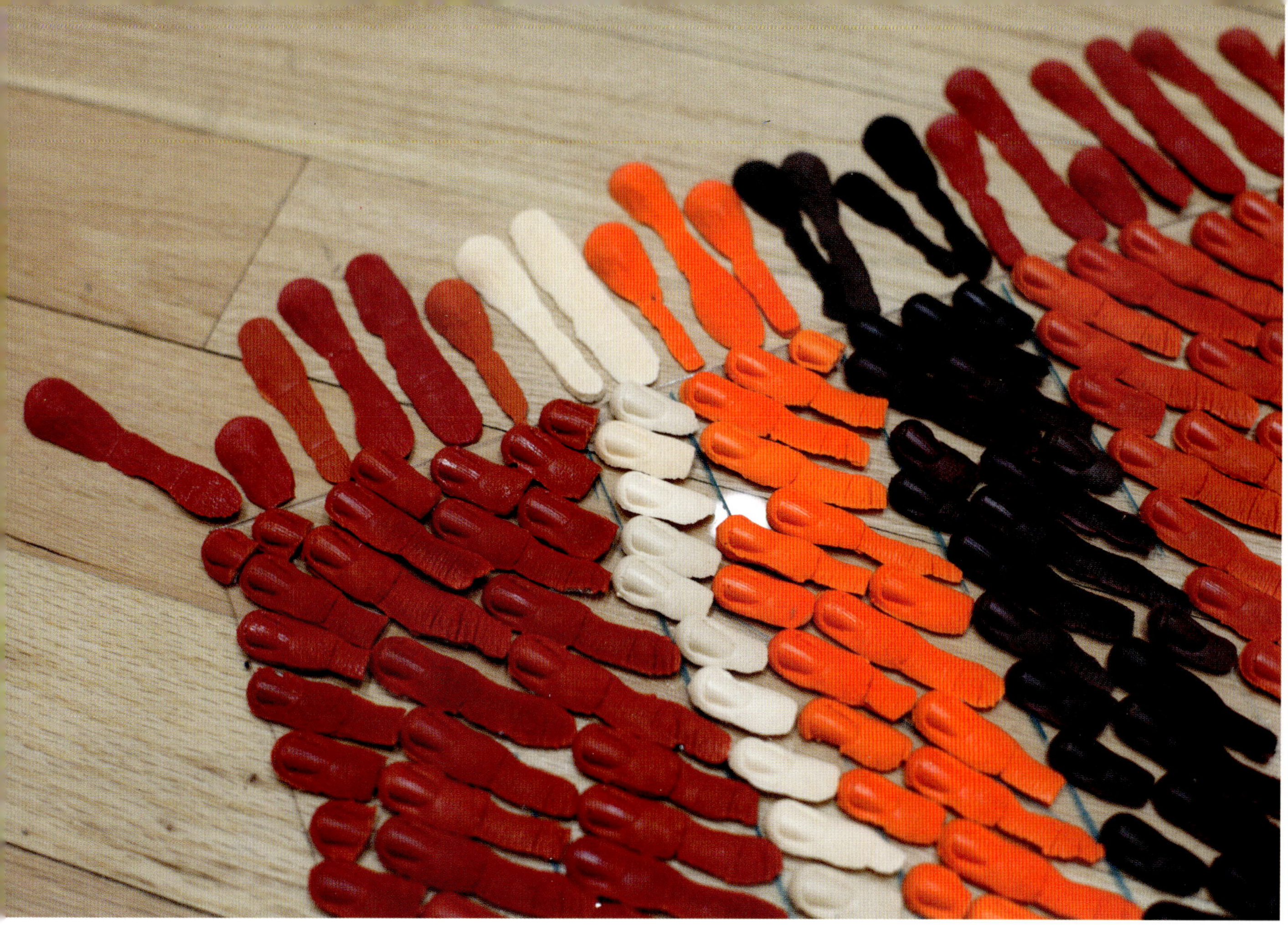

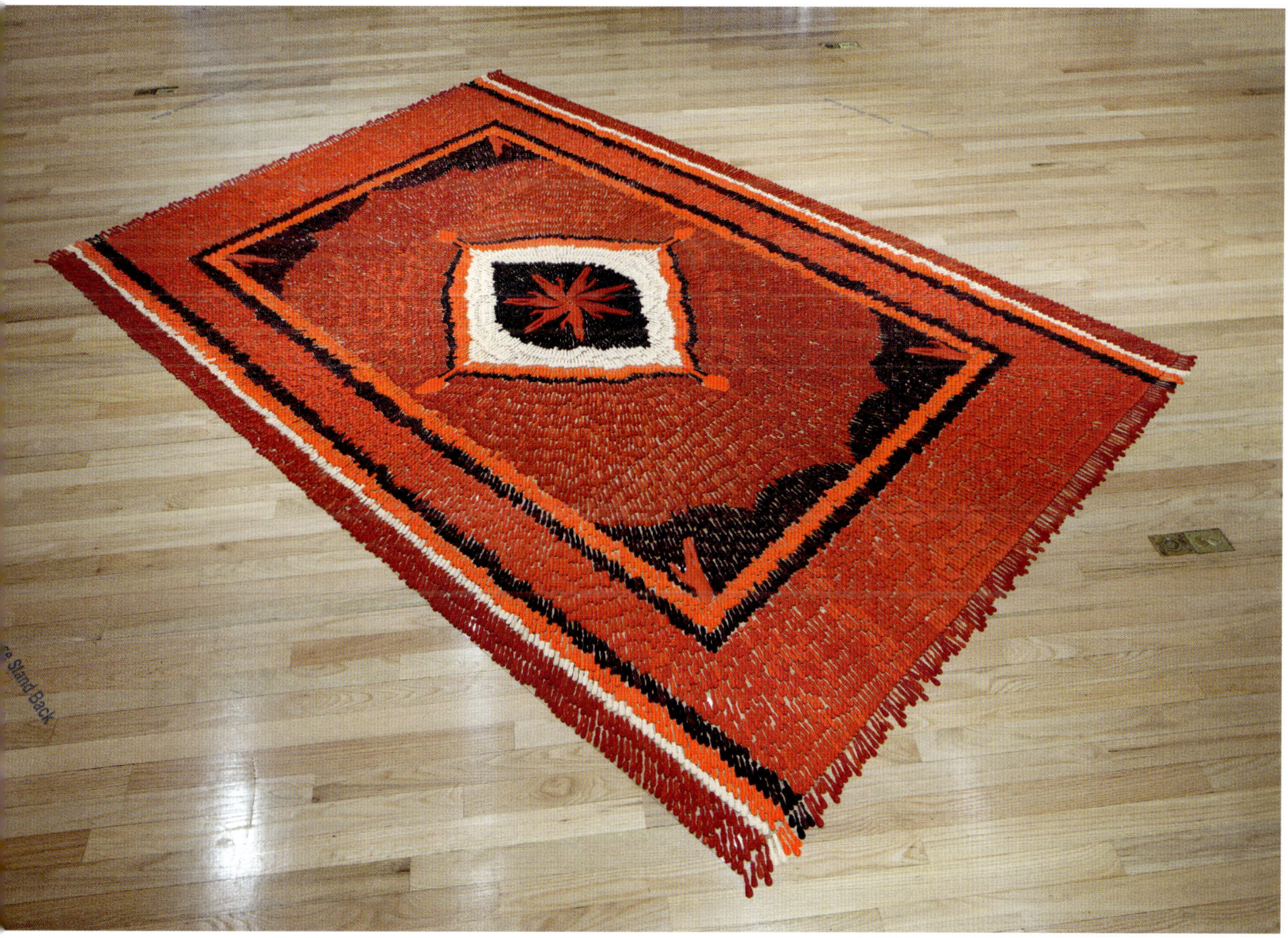

TOP (DETAIL) AND BOTTOM *I Am My Lost Diamond 2* 2012
Resin cast digits, 98×152 inches
Installation view, Tufts University Art Galleries, Massachusetts

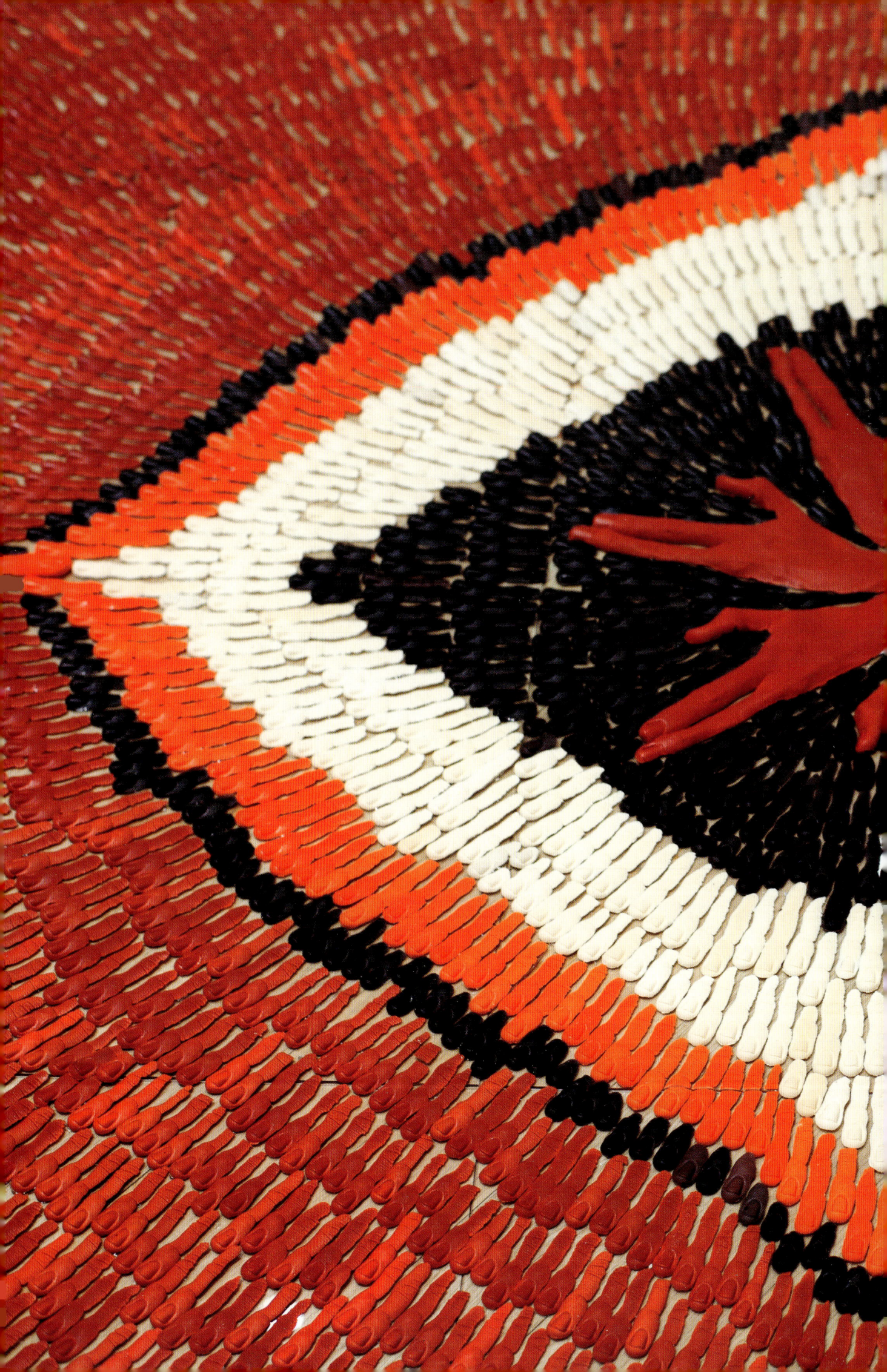

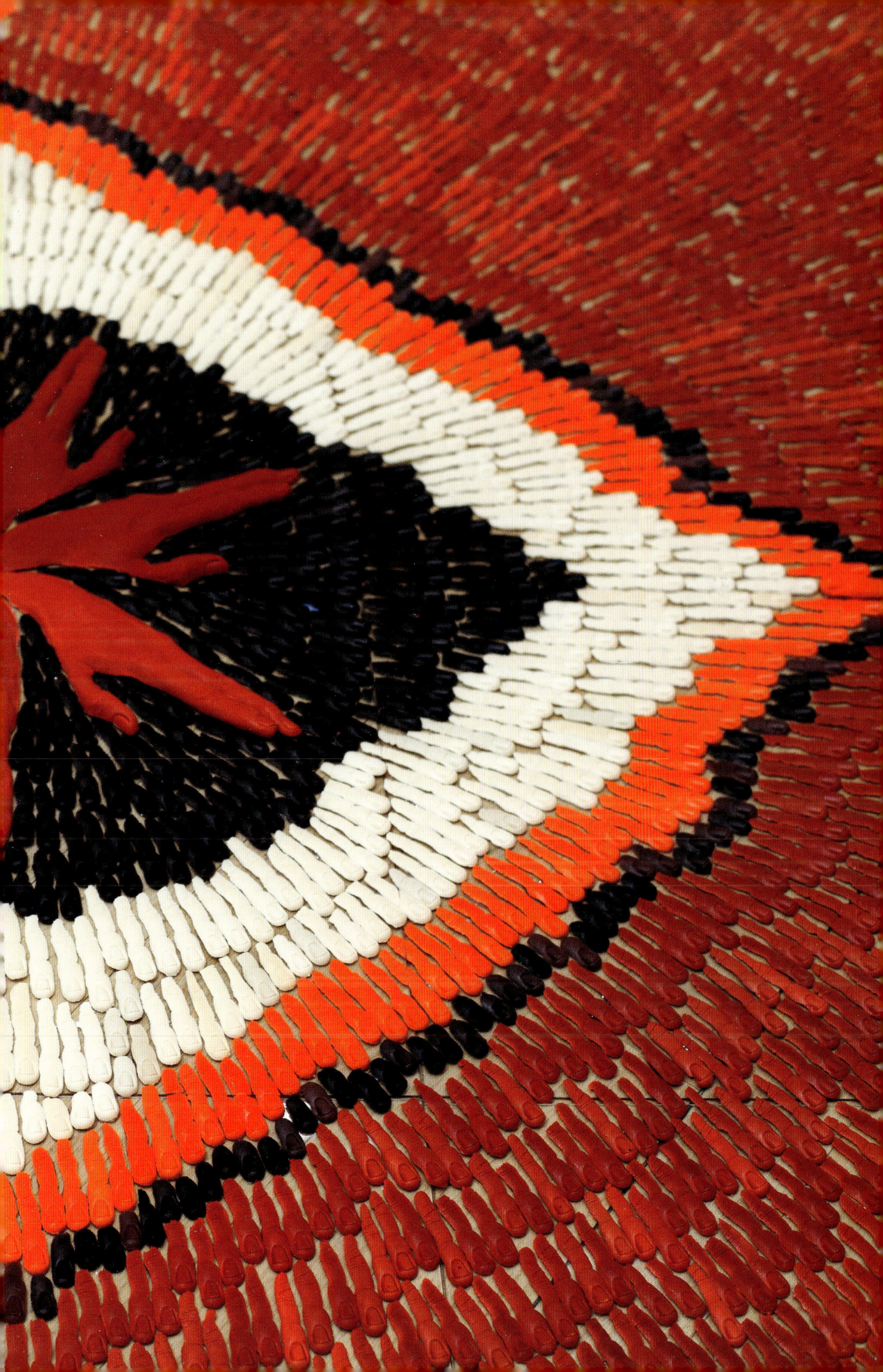

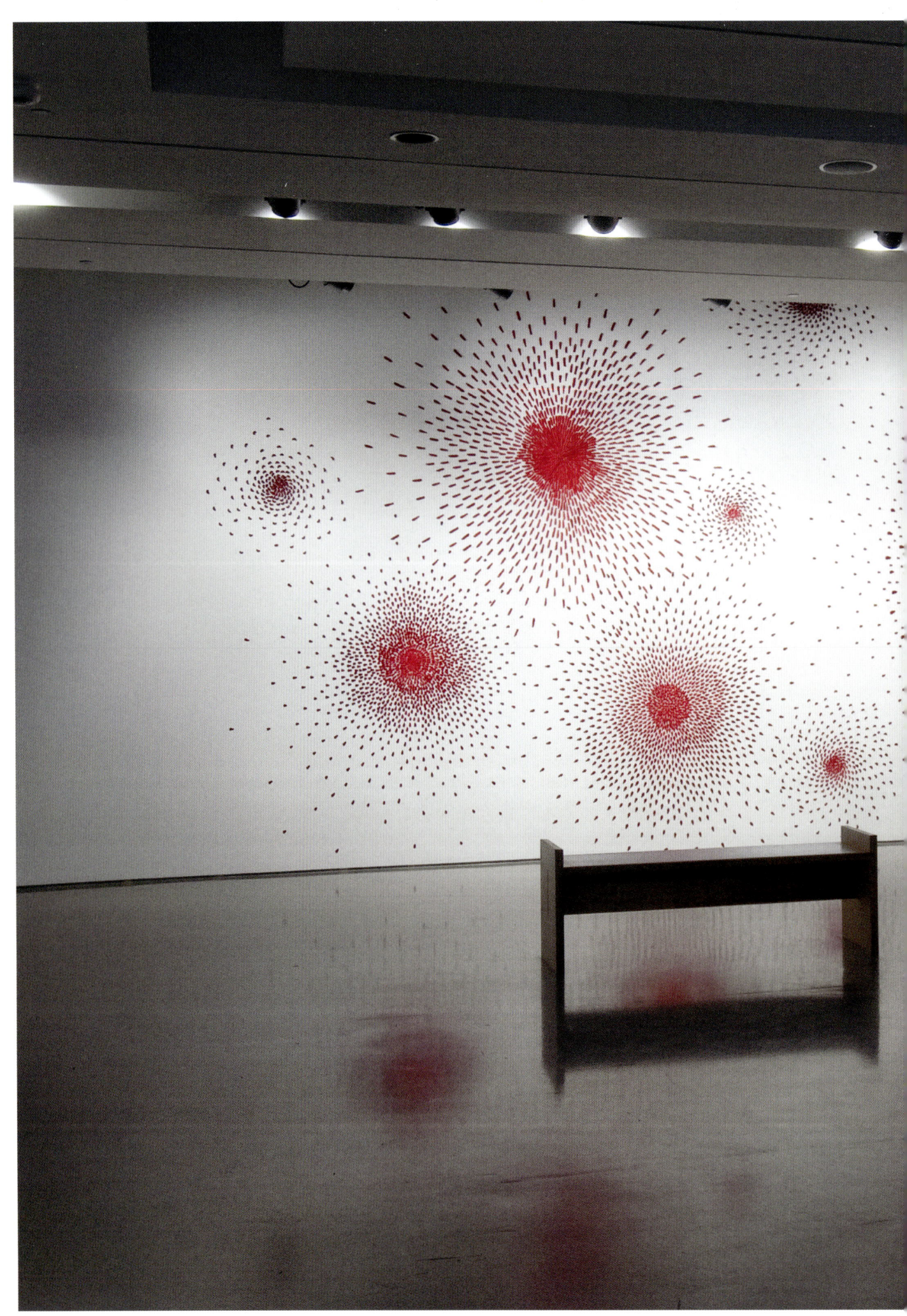

PREVIOUS PAGE (DETAIL) *I Am My Lost Diamond 2* 2012
Resin cast digits, 98 × 152 inches
Installation view, Tufts University Art Galleries, Massachusetts

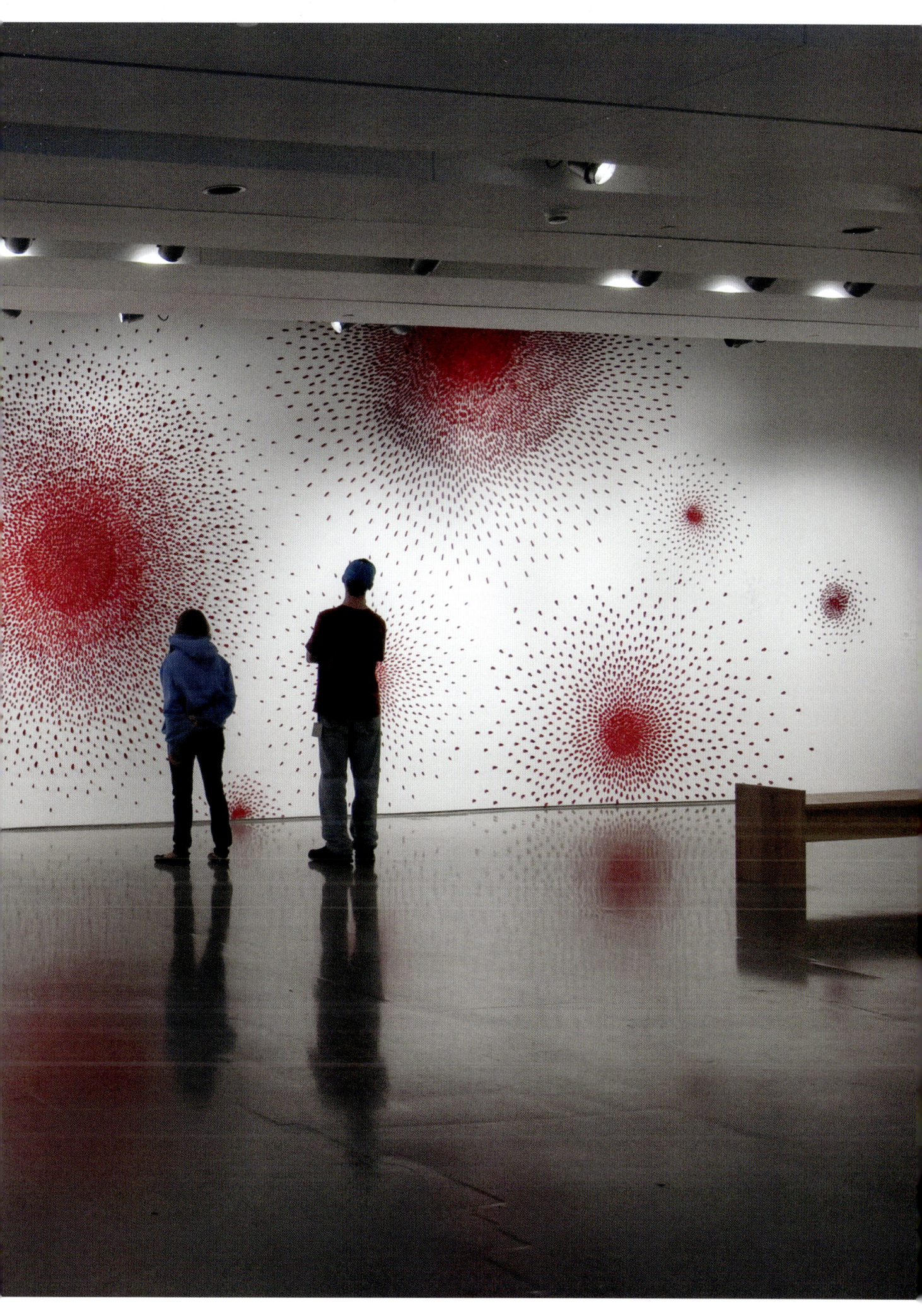

ABOVE *I Am My Lost Diamond*, 2011
Resin cast digits, dimensions variable
Installation view, Contemporary Arts Center, Cincinnati

15

detailed large-scale paintings from redundant shredded five- and ten-dollar bank notes that she purchased from the U.S. Department of Treasury. The work ironically examines the chasm that exists between religion and money and profit and loss, juxtaposing value systems as the treasury is responsible for making and un-making the notes' worth. The work also touches upon capitalism's complex relationship to neocolonialism and the mimicry of colonial mechanisms that have been used as a method for oppression.

Butt's approach to disentangling complicated social narratives in a post-factual world comment on the viral nature of biased news and information sources that threaten the free and unbiased circulation of factual news accounts. She satirically explores this topic in Dirty Pretty, 2008. In this series of works Butt employs the mixed media practice of etching, silkscreening, and lithography to create a vivid and fantastical tableau featuring a mix of flora, fauna, 16th-century Mughal-era warriors, romantic couples, dancers, animals, and contemporary images from the news media of individuals embroiled in various suspended hyperbolic interactions from fight scenes to intense arguments. These highly vivid and brightly colored works combine high and low registers of public assembly, and borrow from Indo-Persian fable tradition of the book arts, such as the ancient book of fables Khalila and Dimna. The origins of Khalila and Dimna can be traced to the ancient Sanskrit Hindu fable Pancatantra, which was translated into Middle Persian in the 6th century and allegorized animals to illustrate moral tales. Historically, due to the small size of these circulating manuscripts they could only be viewed by two persons at a time as part of an intimate visual experience. In Butt's paintings she subverts this notion, toying with scale as well as creating a direct confrontation between the figures and the viewers. This marks a departure from traditional Persian painting as renowned Islamic art curator Sheila R. Canby notes "... [b]efore the nineteenth century the figures in Persian painting almost never look directly at the viewer. Later when they do, they keep their emotions to themselves."[7] Contrary to this tradition, Butt draws from pop cultures and melodramas to allegorize the media's ability to create viral materials which amounts to a concoction of homegrown fanaticism and geopolitics.

Similarly, the series Cirque Du Monde, 2007, which translates to circus of the world, also probes the idea of the spectacle and combines both the contrasting idiom of the grotesque and the seductive. Through this multilayered project, Butt examines the nefarious nature of "entertainment" via the metaphor of the circus where various characters participate in "acts" that inform another in the name of entertainment on the global stage. Here she explores ideas related to terrestrial curiosities associated with the absurd to conjure up the spirit of the carnivalesque. Hybrid figures, part human and part animal, along with birds, dragons, lions, serpents, and zebras, serve as complex connected scaffolding. In many of these painterly compositions several characters exist atop one another or overlap to suggest complex and fragile acts of balance, conflict,

harmony, and strife. Untitled 16, 2007, features a part horse, part human couple crawling amidst a landscape strewn with eyes. The landscape nods to the hyper-surveillance state and big brother's watchful eye, whilst a bird resembling the ancient and revered Persian mythical bird known as Simurgh, who is believed to possess great wisdom, circles above. In this work, the bird flies upside down—an act that is suggestive of an awry dystopian environment.

The surreal dream-like world that Butt creates is highly fantastical and transports viewers into a theatrical Dadaist space which her bold art inhabits. By contrast, in Untitled 3, 2005, two zebras verbally assault one another. The words "pig" and "bitch" populate the composition like speech bubbles created from small pieces of text pasted atop the canvas. Butt's use of text here and elsewhere highlights the foundational principles of language, power, and position, along with the concept of "linguistic vulnerability," a term attributed to Judith Butler's seminal text Excitable Speech, where she poses the following questions:

> *Could language injure us if we were not, in some sense, linguistic beings, beings who require language in order to be? Is our vulnerability to language a consequence of our being constituted within its terms?*[8]

Butt's practice, striated by necessarily mutable conceptions of "truth" and "intellect", uses both symbolism and abstraction to explore real and fictional accounts and unearth covert and overt patterns of human consciousness. Her practice poetically moves between various epistemological methods to reveal disparate yet interconnected realities that are mutually interdependent. She does so by exposing a fragmented and complex space of alterity where political, social, and religious factions compete, exploit, and magnify the contradicting conditions of contemporary cultures.

[7] Canby, Sheila R., *Persian Painting*, London: The British Museum Press, 1993, p 12.

[8] Butler, Judith, *Excitable Speech: A Politics of the Performative*, New York and London: Routledge, 1997, p 1.

OPPOSITE (DETAIL) **I Am All What Is Left Of Me** 2015
Resin with pigments, 120 × 240 inches

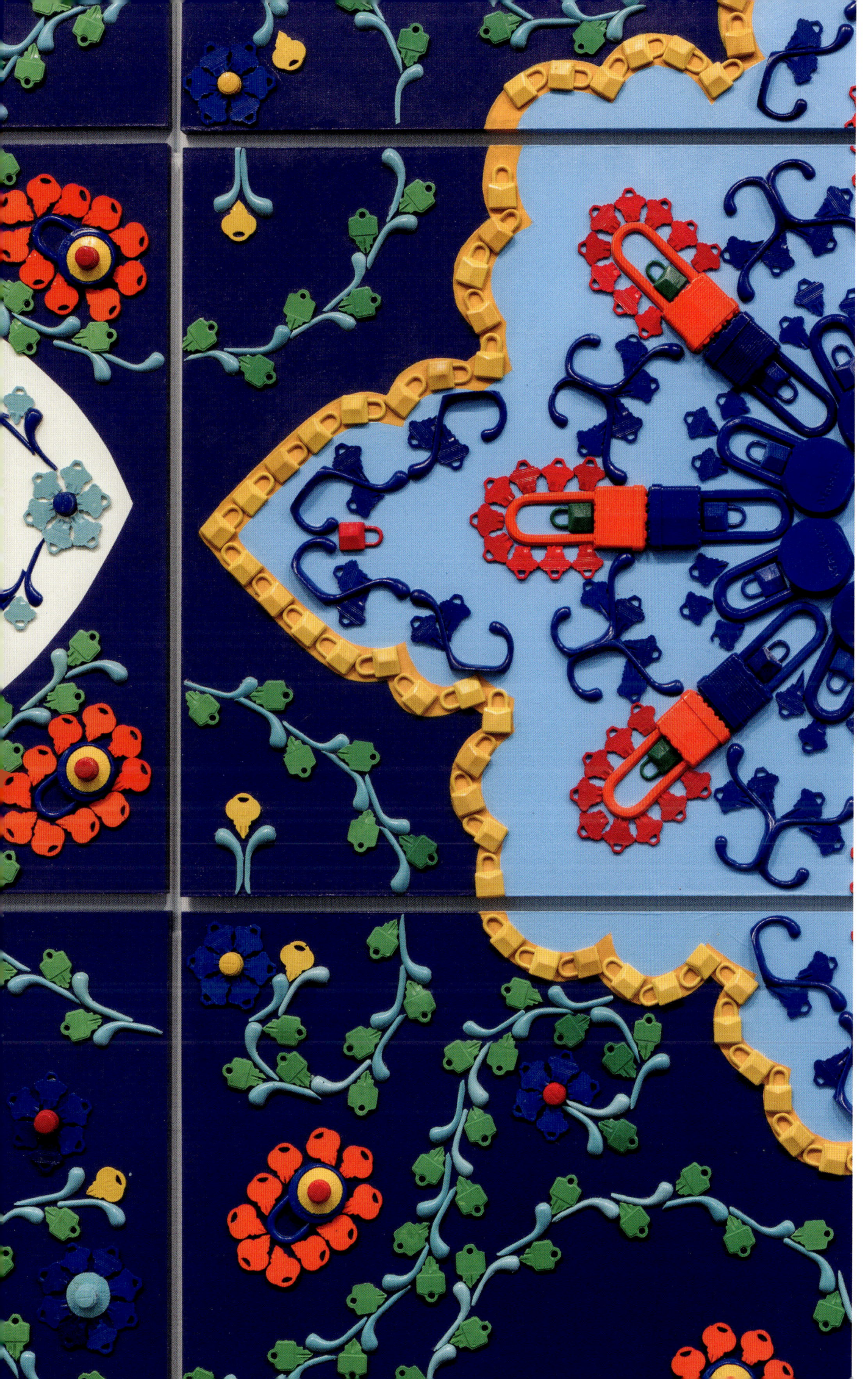

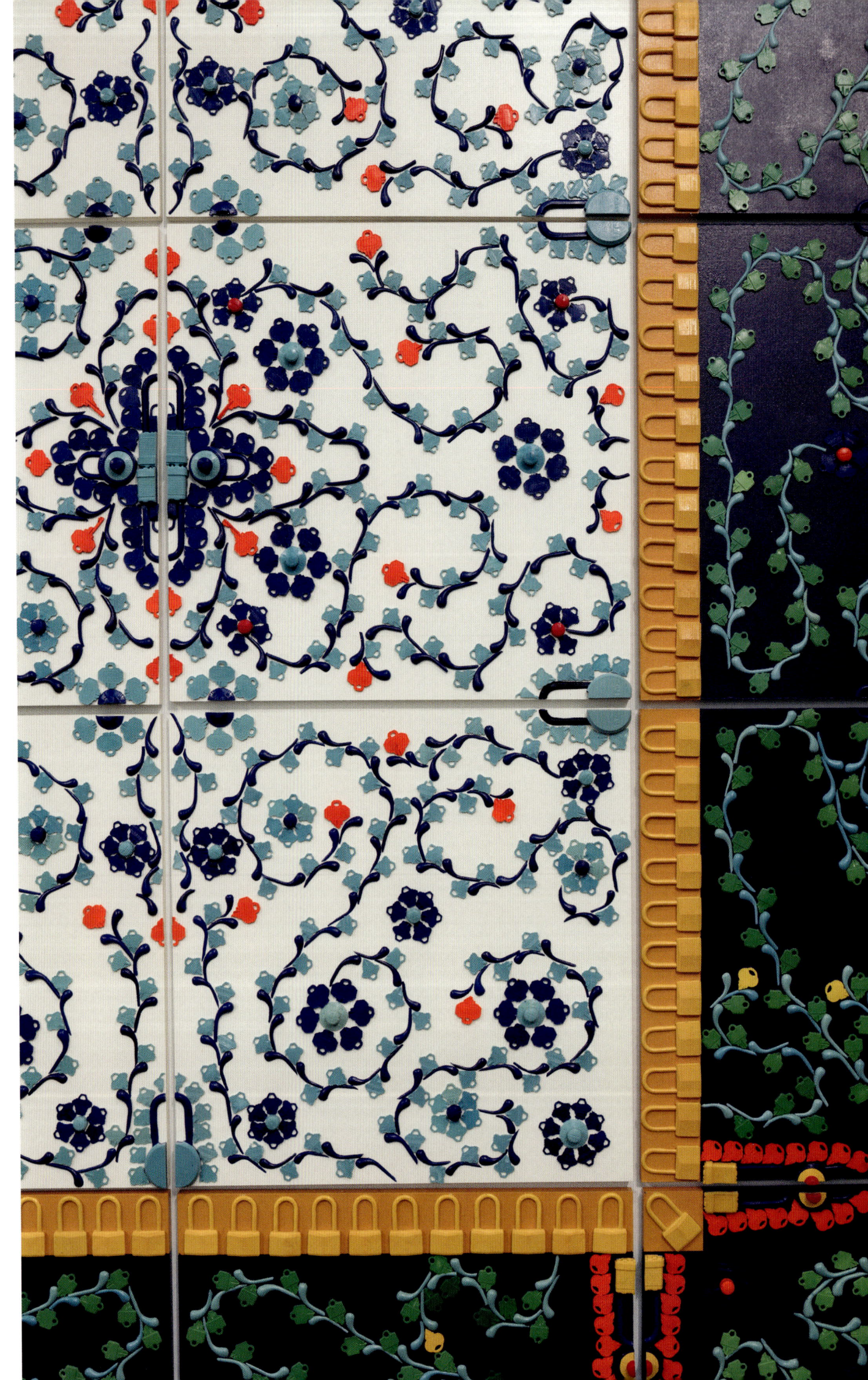

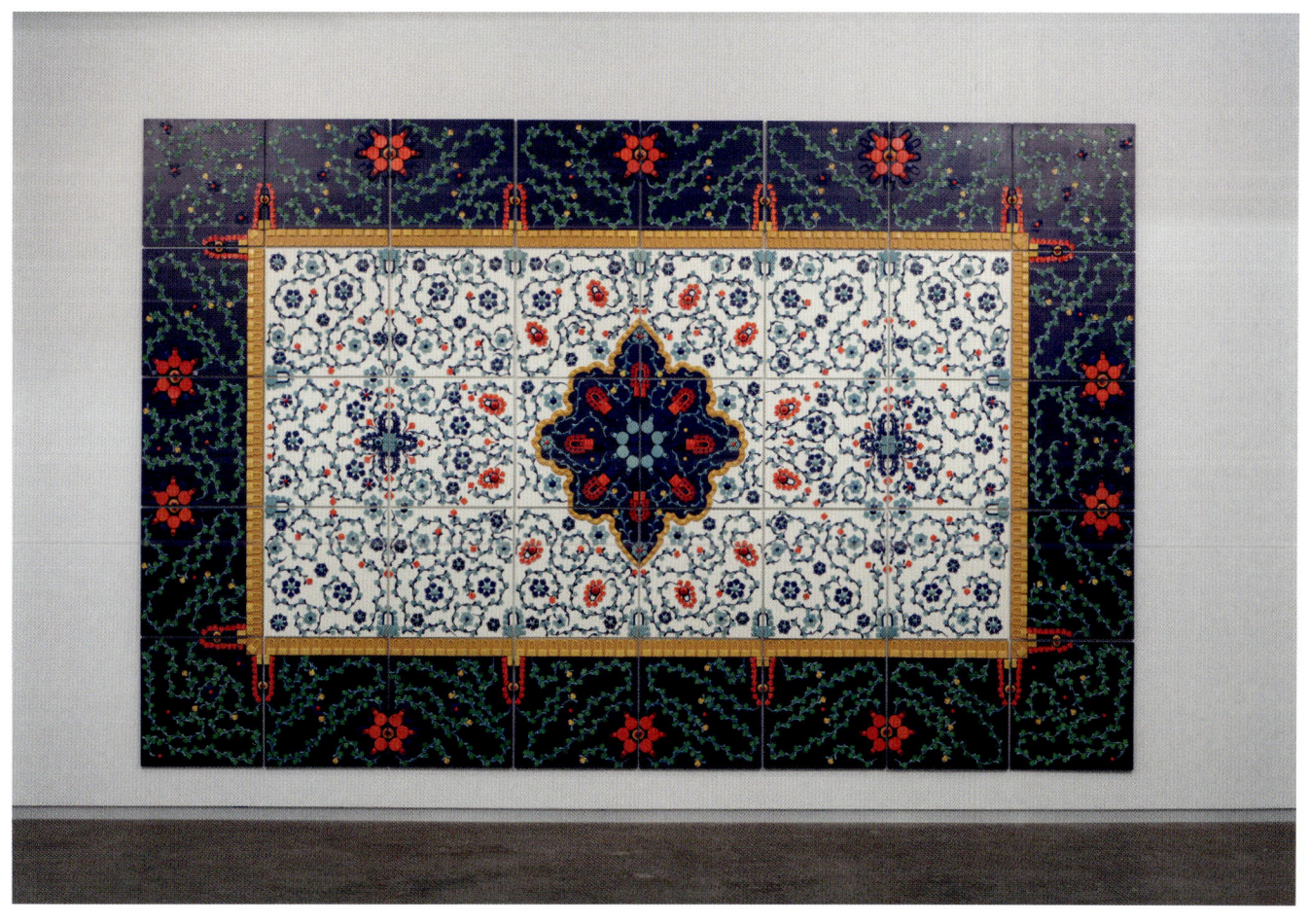

OPPOSITE (DETAIL)/ABOVE *I Am All What Is Left Of Me* 2015
Resin with pigments, 120 × 240 inches
Installation view Dallas Contemporary, Dallas, Texas

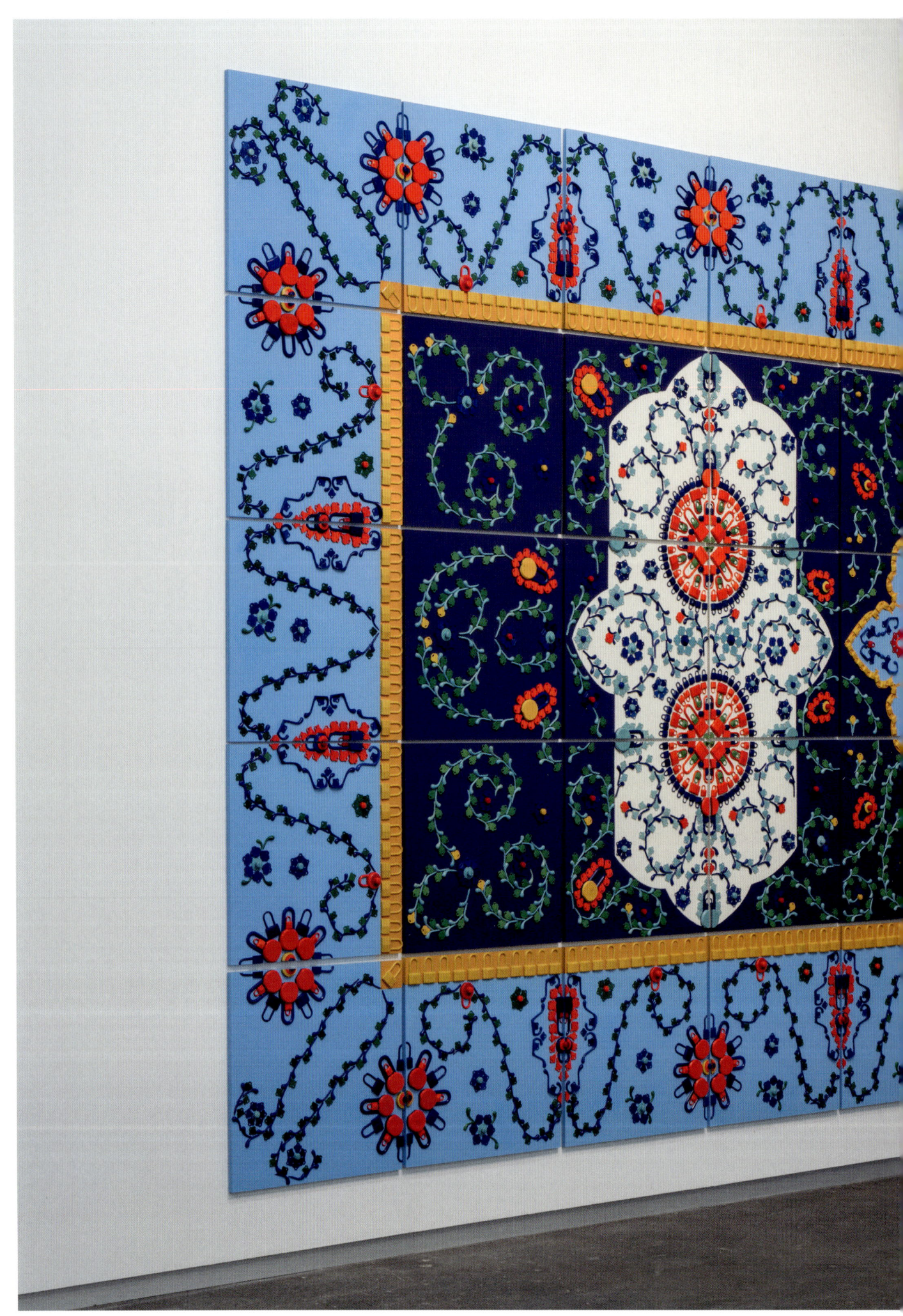

I Am All What Is Left Of Me 2015
Resin with pigments, 120 × 240 inches
Installation view Dallas Contemporary, Dallas, Texas

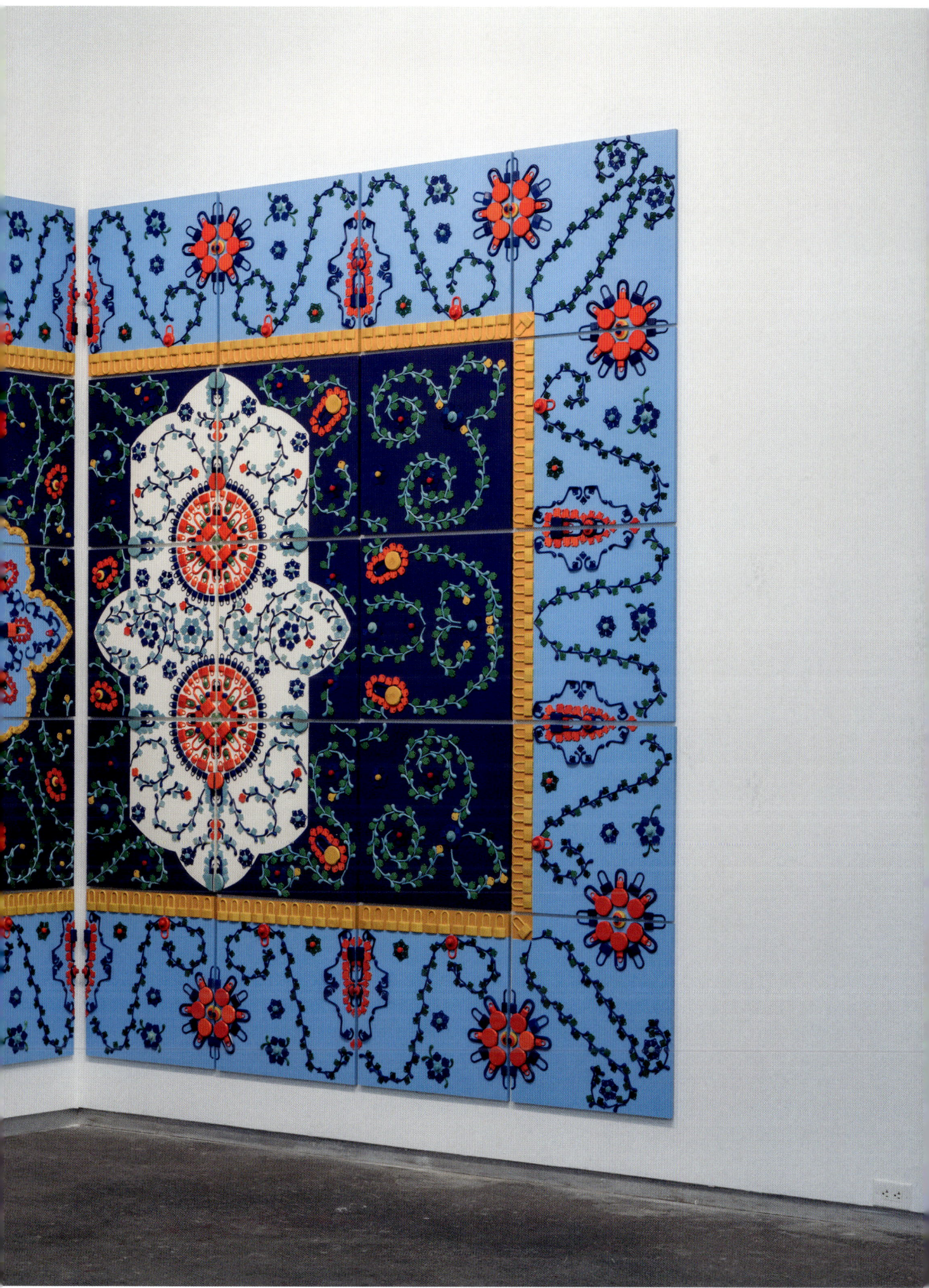

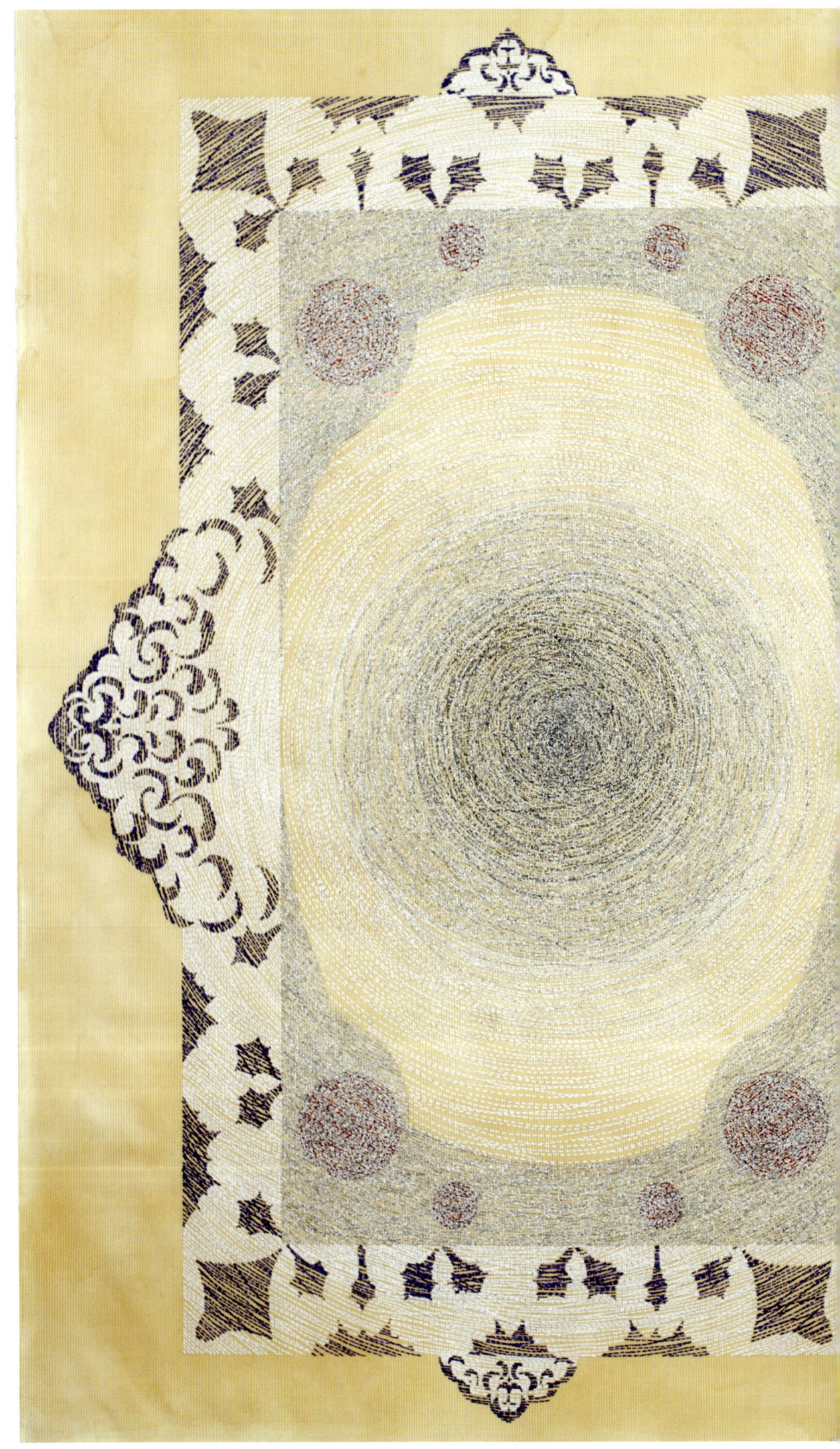

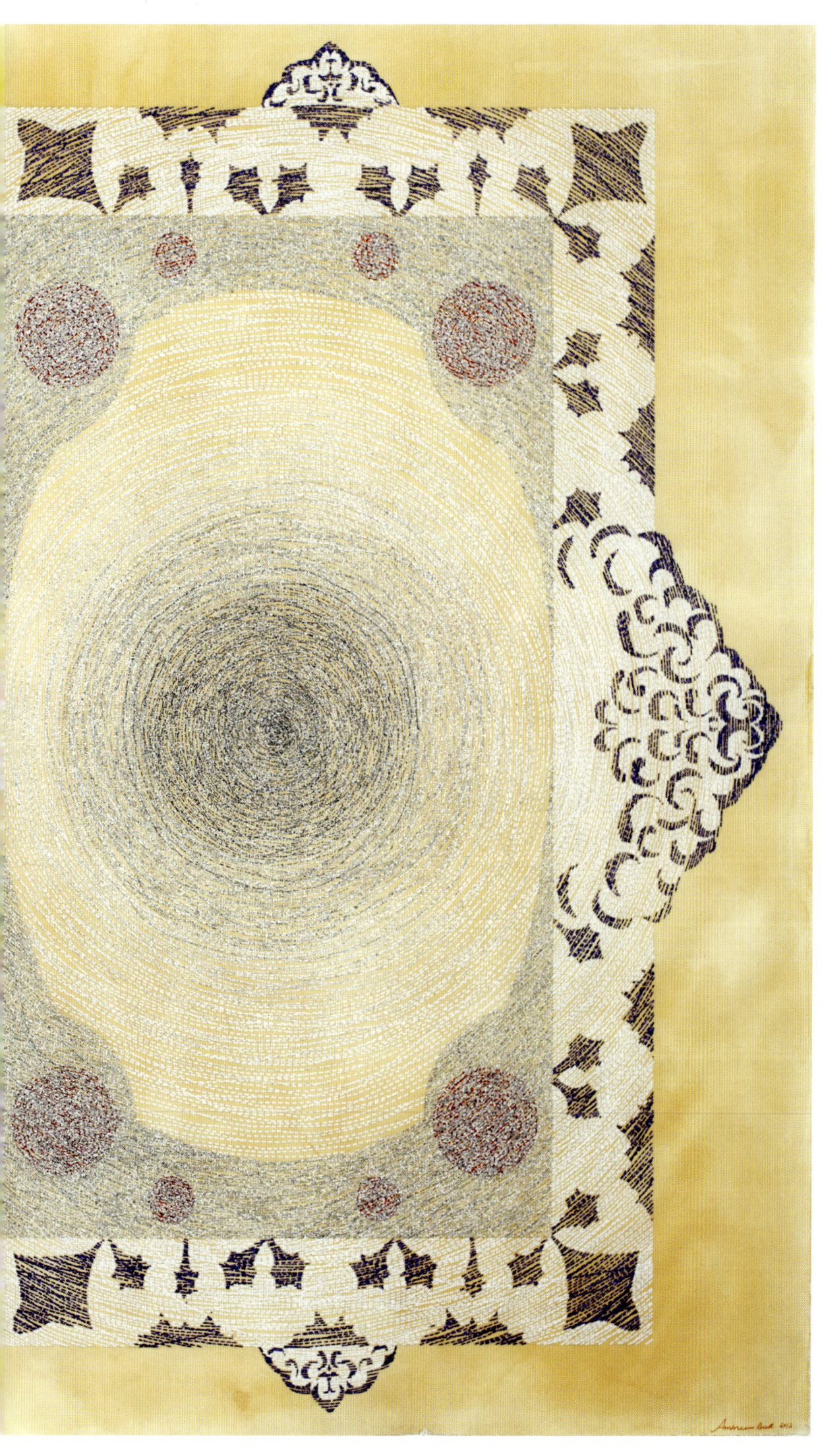

LEFT/OVERLEAF (DETAIL) *Pages Of Deception* 2012
Collage of torn text on tea-stained paper, diptych,
each 70½ × 45 inches

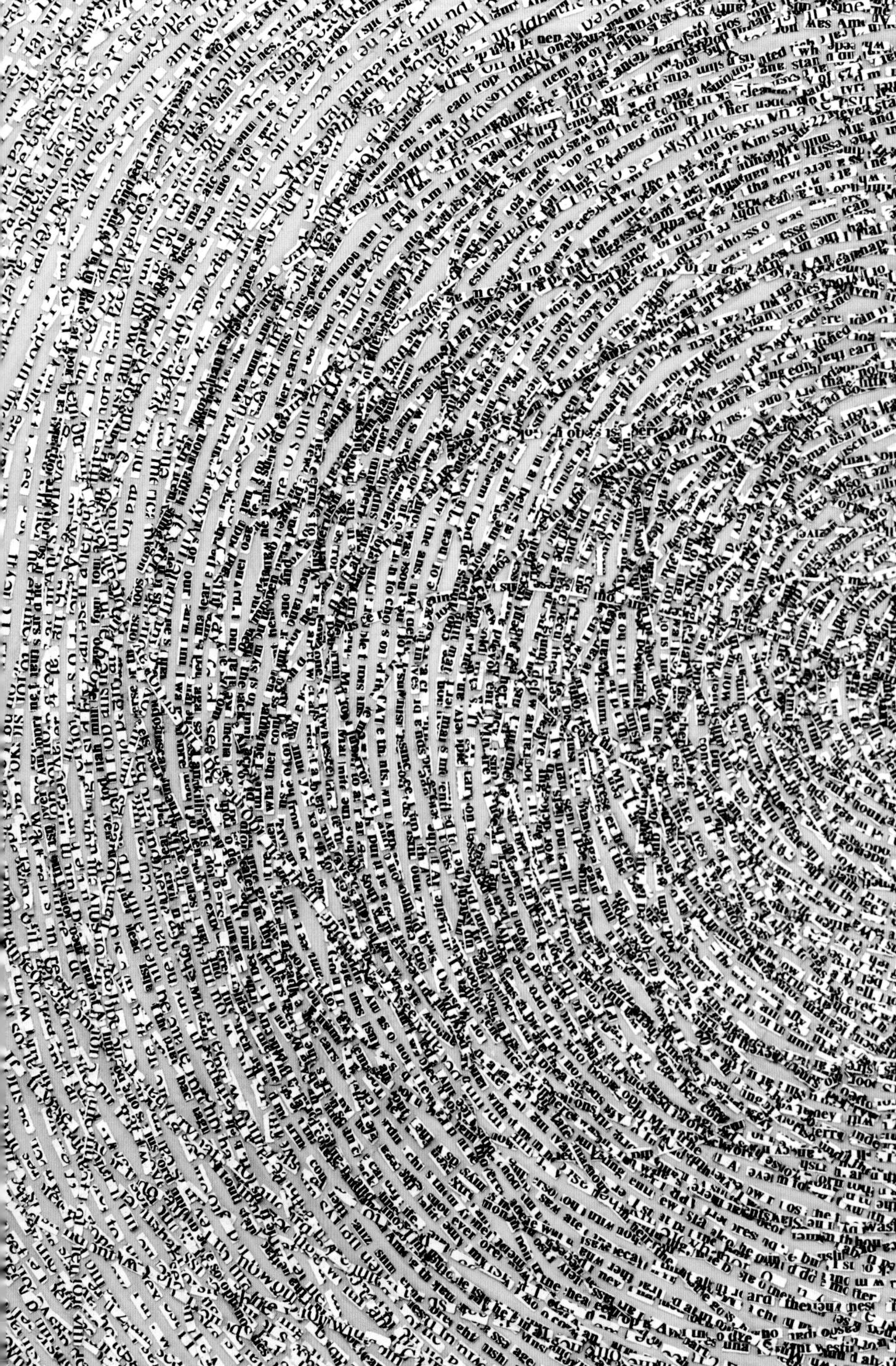

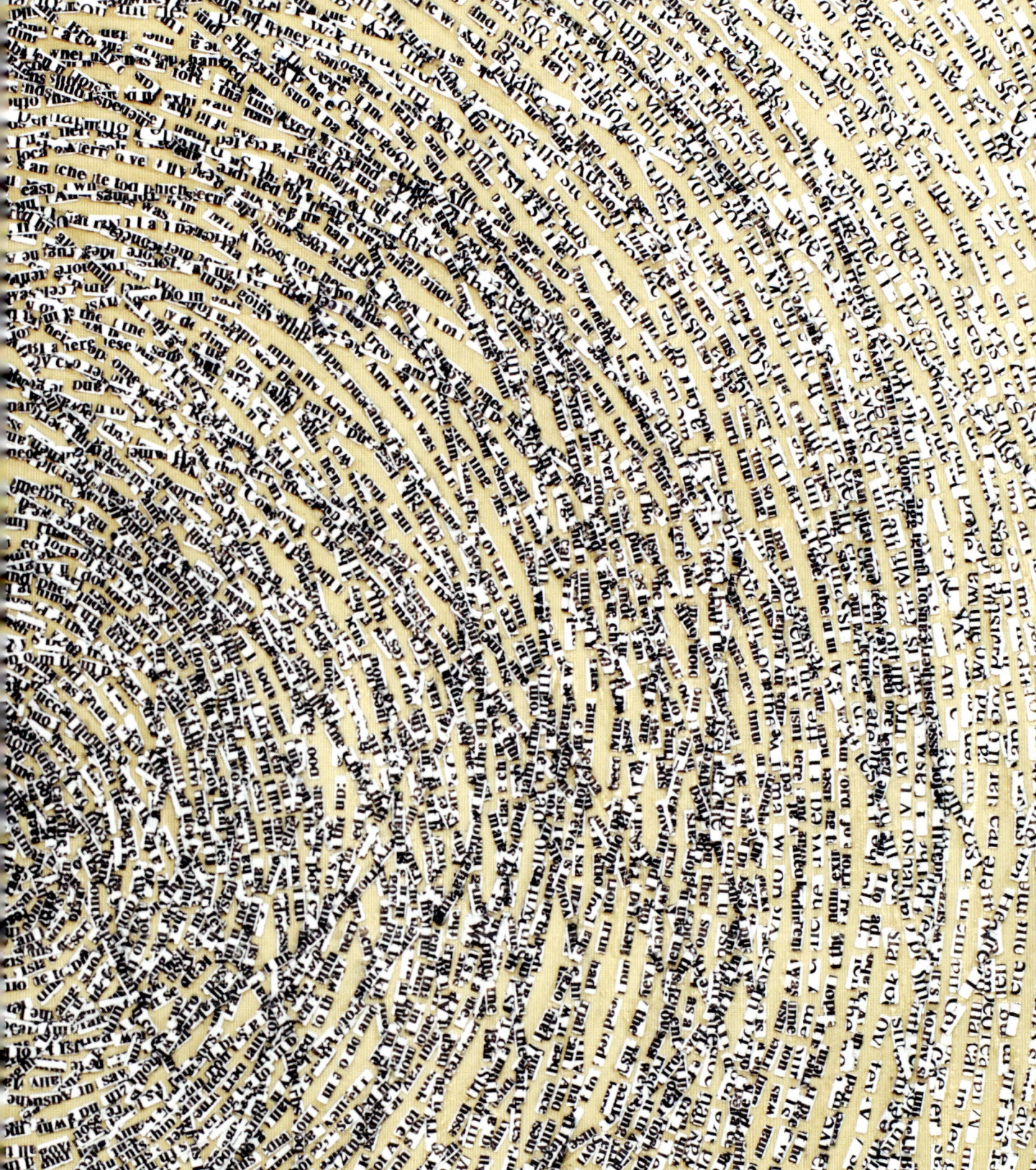

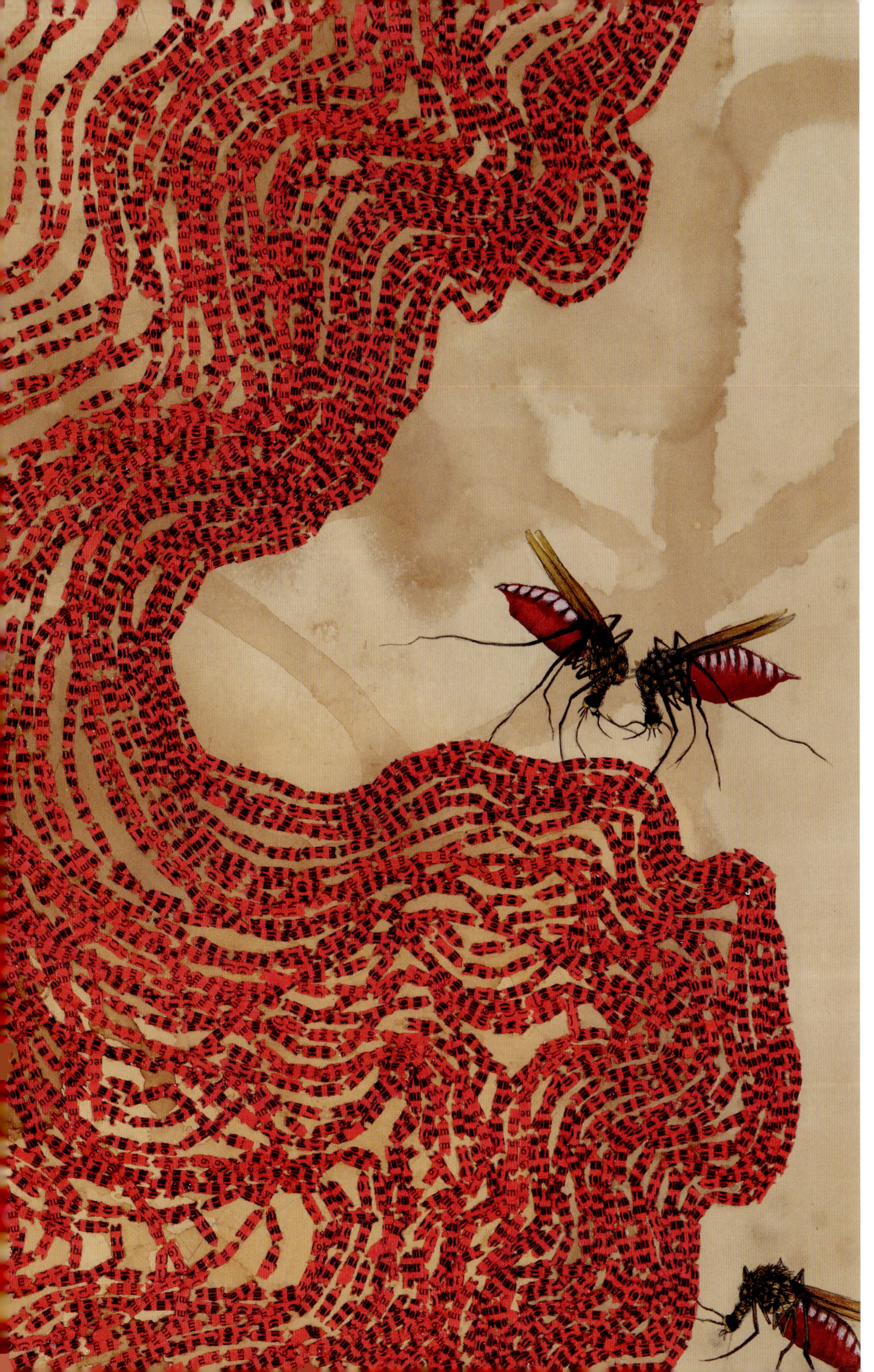

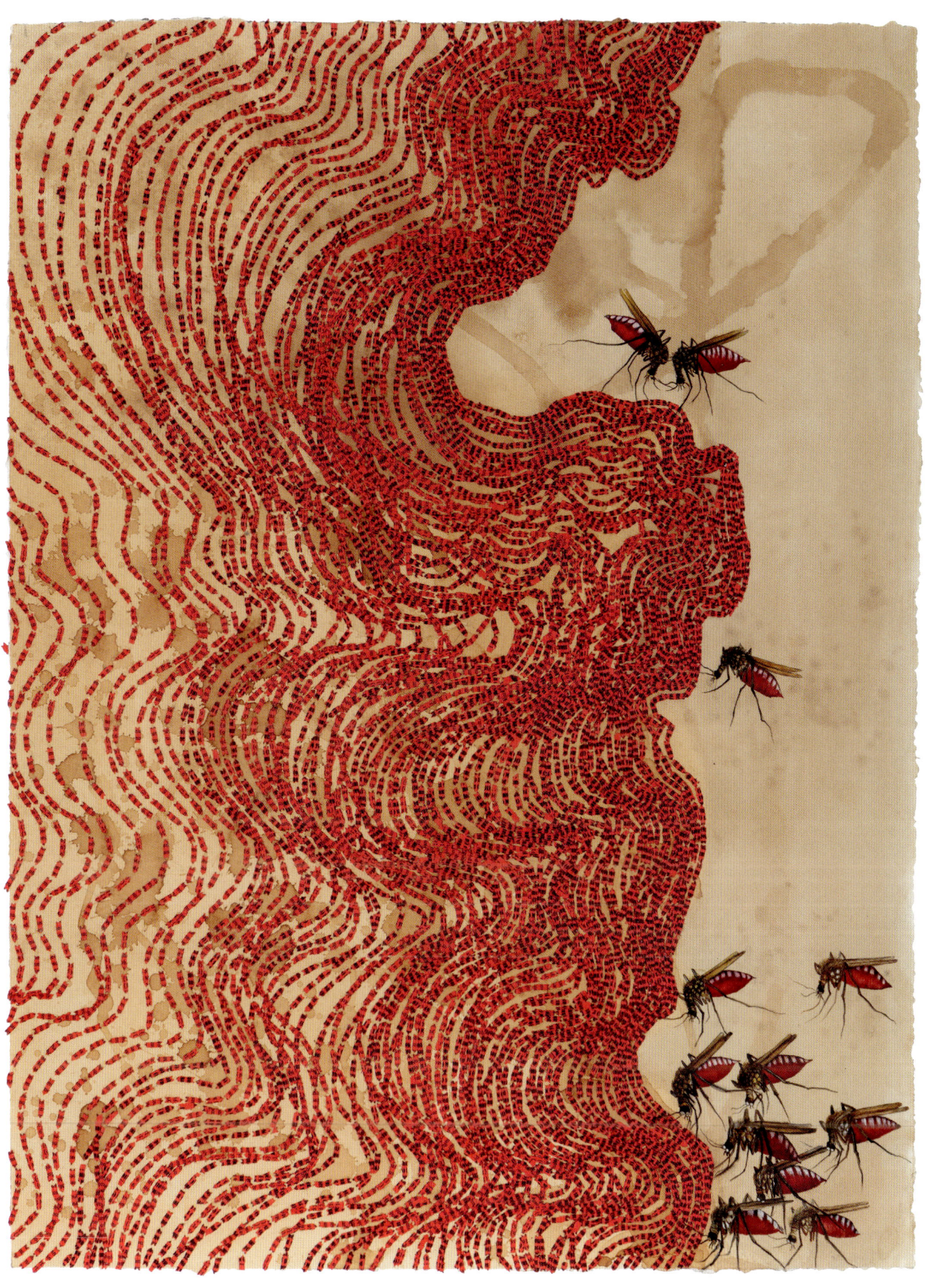

OPPOSITE (DETAIL)/ABOVE **Mohammed Yunus (16)** 2018
FROM THE SERIES Say My Name
Watercolor, collage of torn text on tea-stained paper,
29 × 21 inches

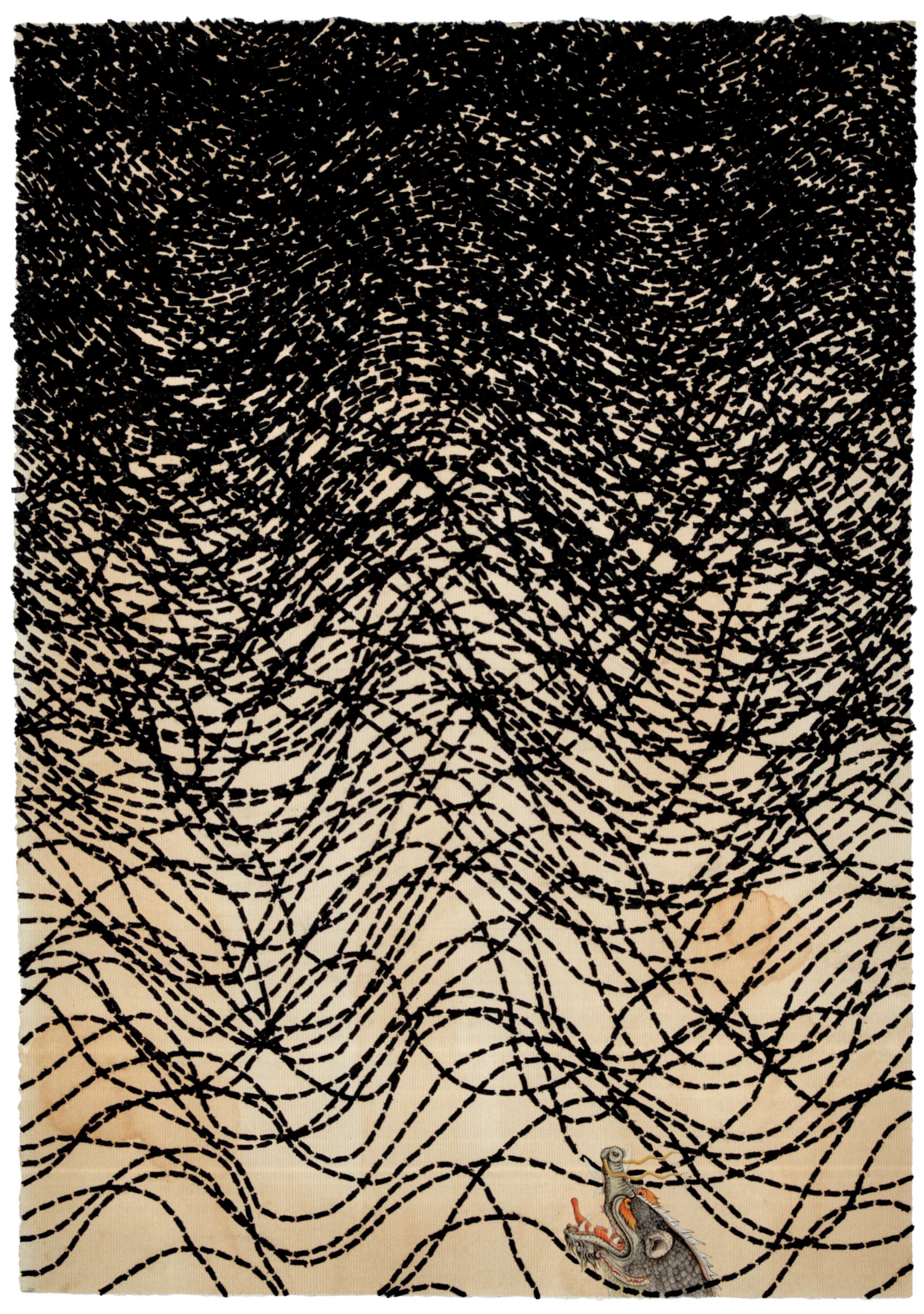

ABOVE/OPPOSITE (DETAIL) *Namaloom (Unknown #1)* 2019
FROM THE SERIES Say My Name
Watercolor, collage of torn text on tea-stained paper,
29 × 21 inches

28

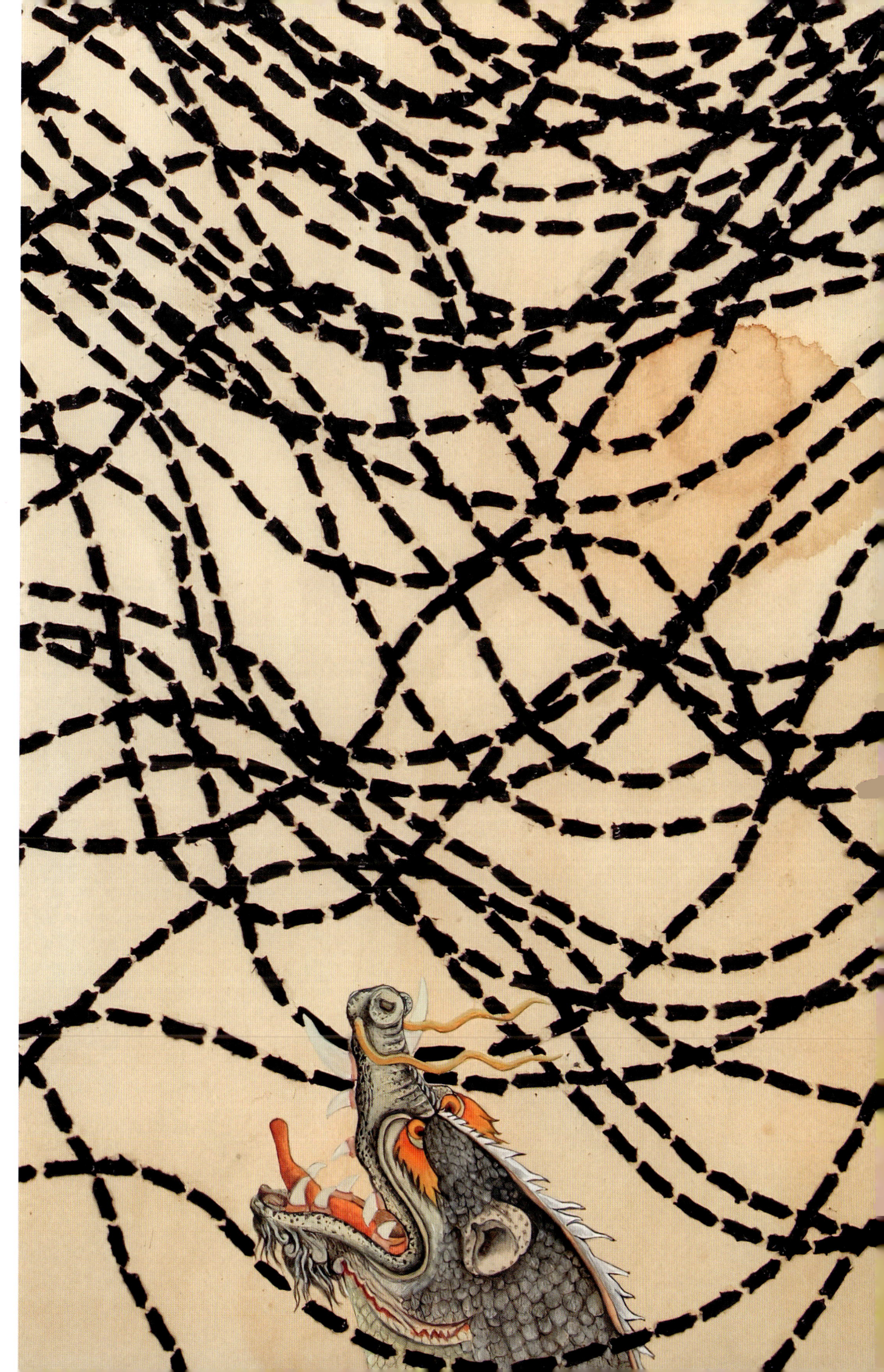

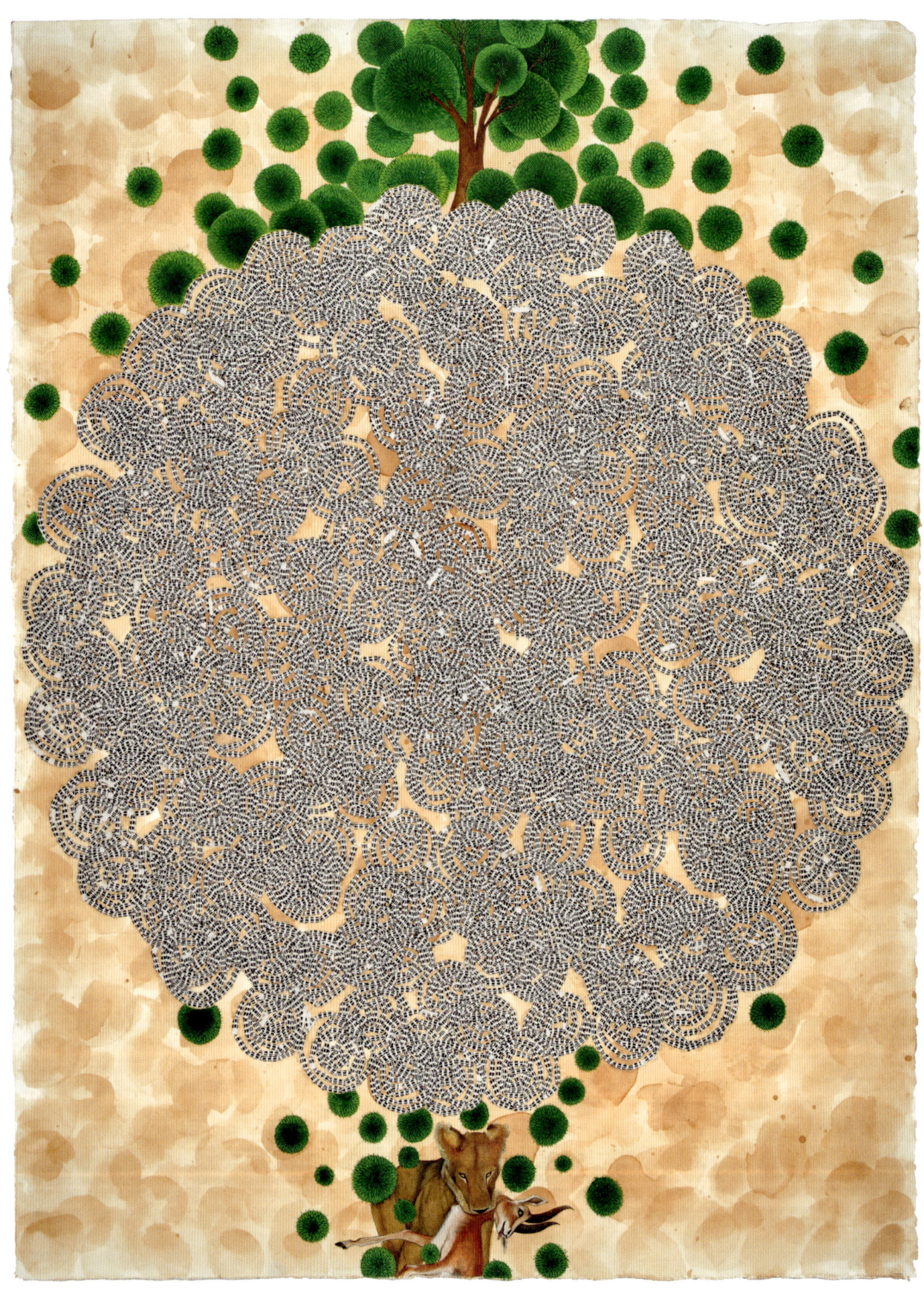

ABOVE/OPPOSITE (DETAIL) *Asadullah (9)* 2019
FROM THE SERIES Say My Name
Watercolor with white gouache and collage of torn text
on tea-stained paper, 30×22 inches

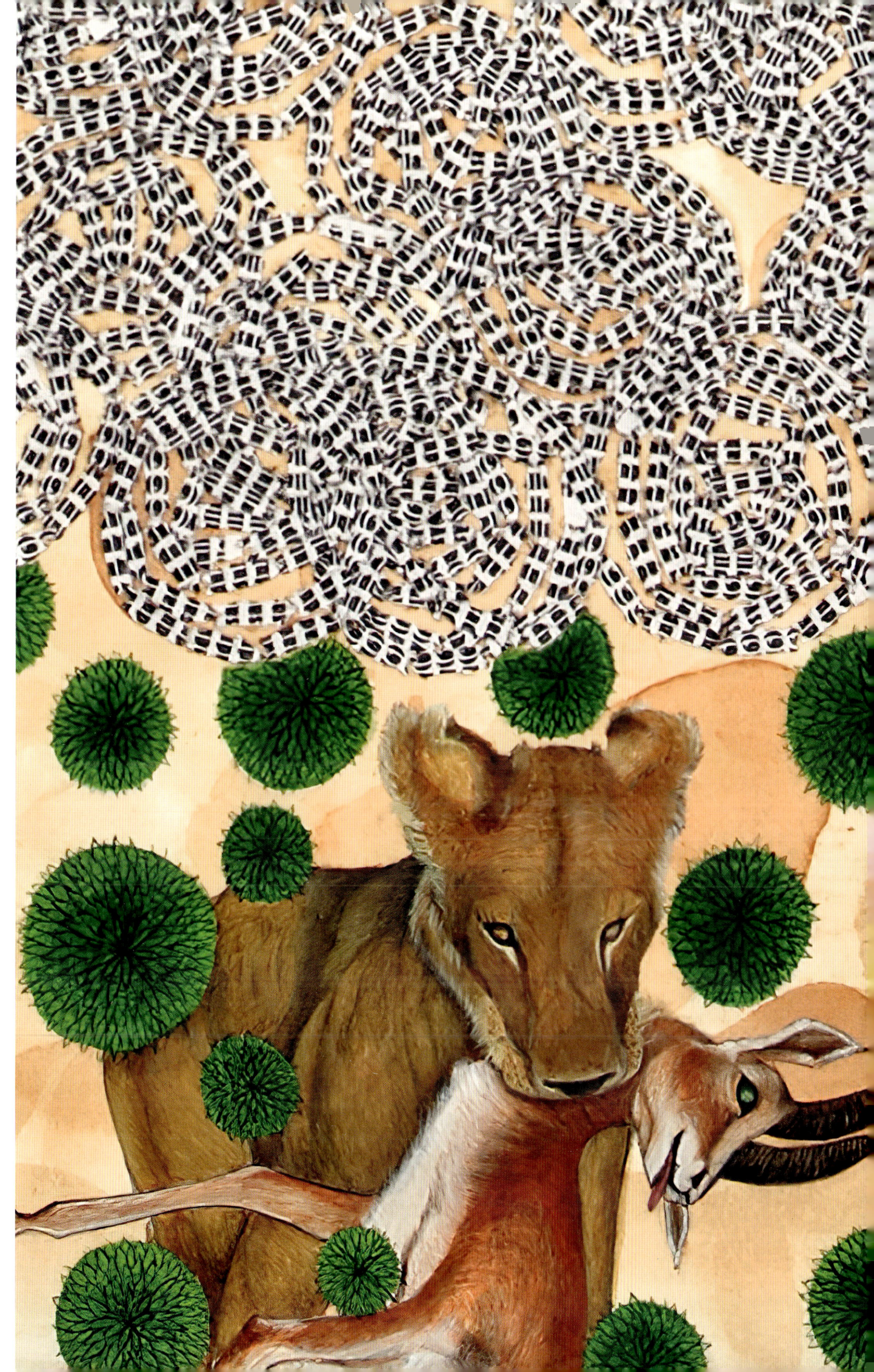

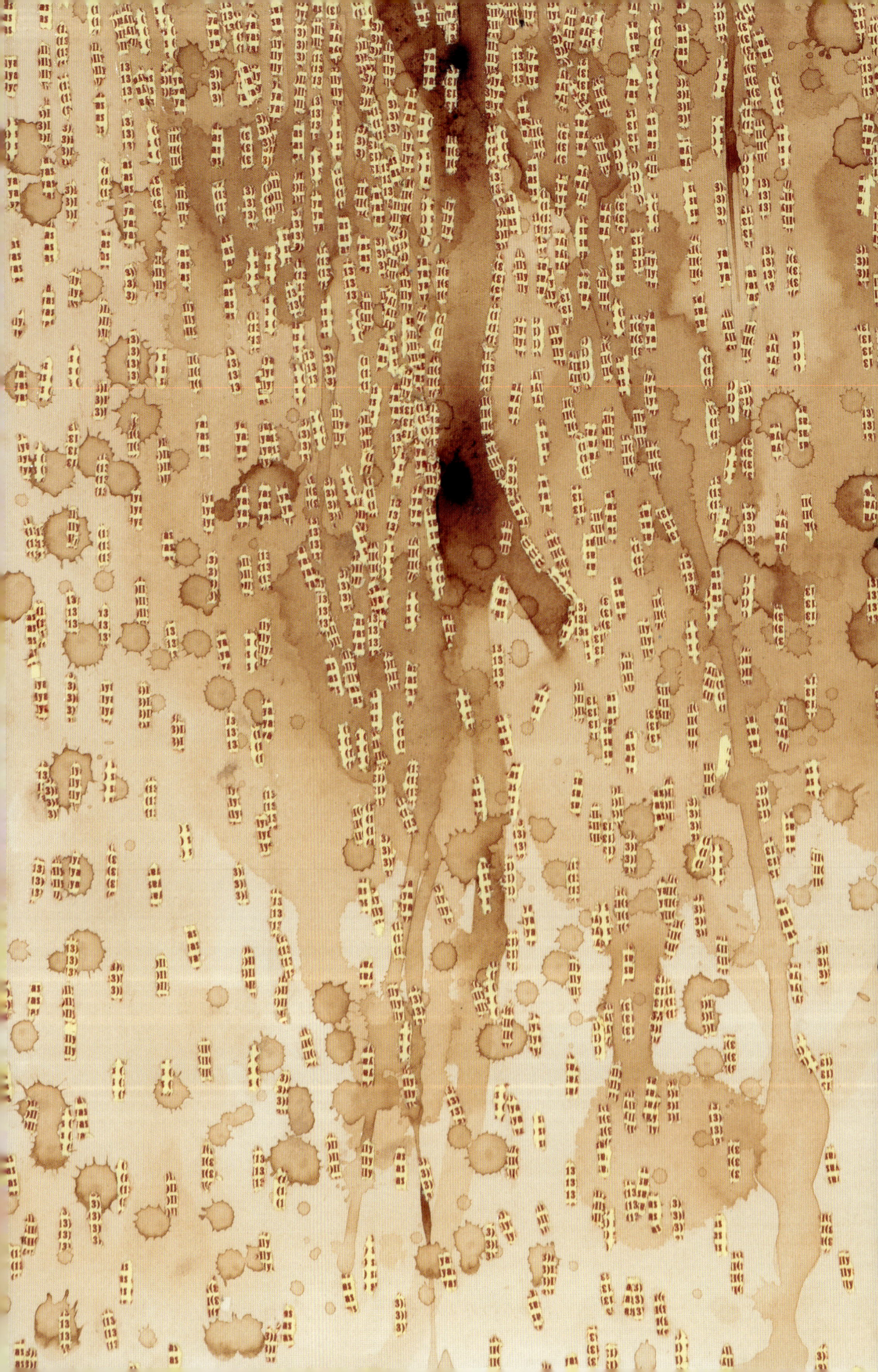

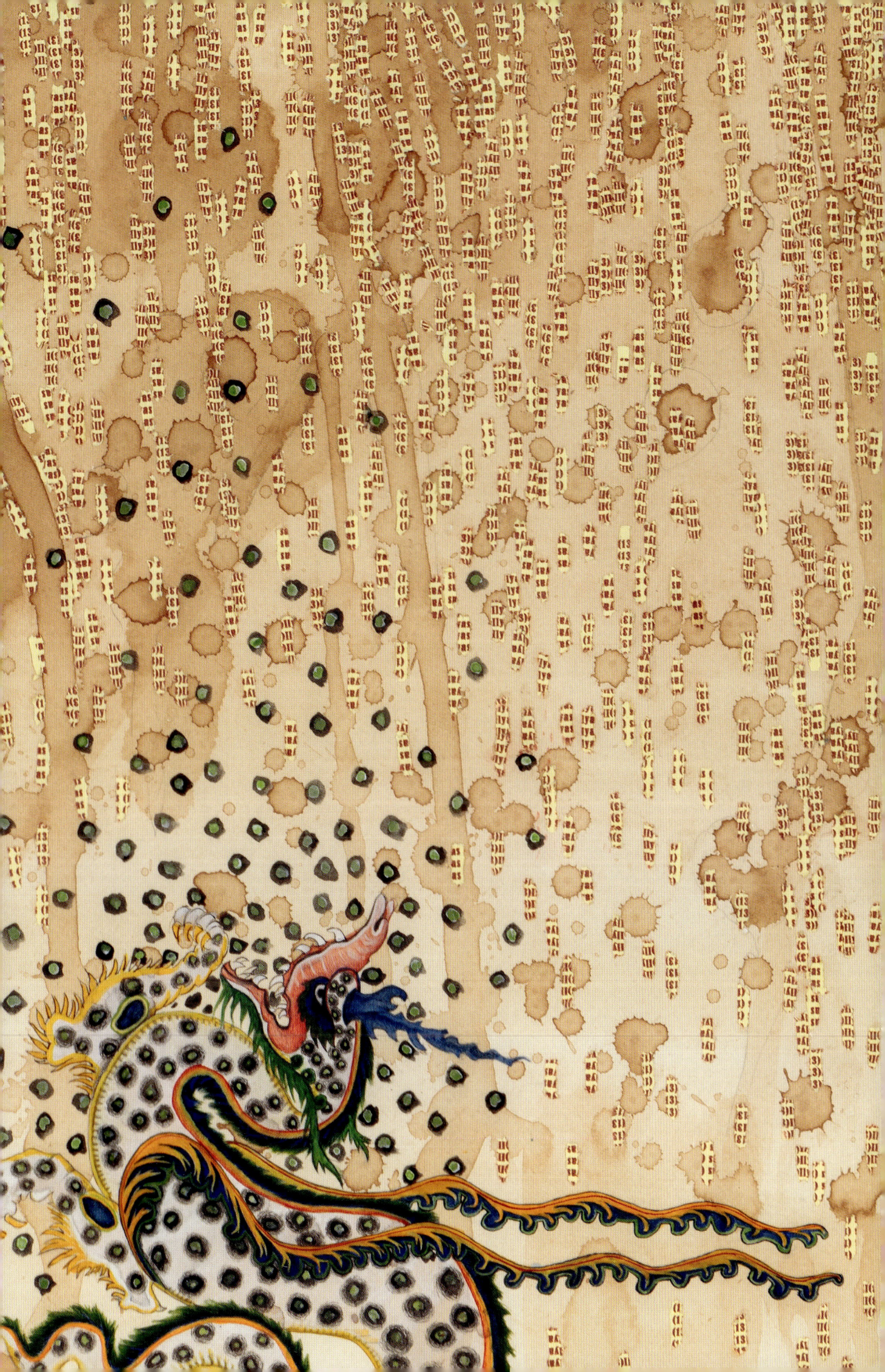

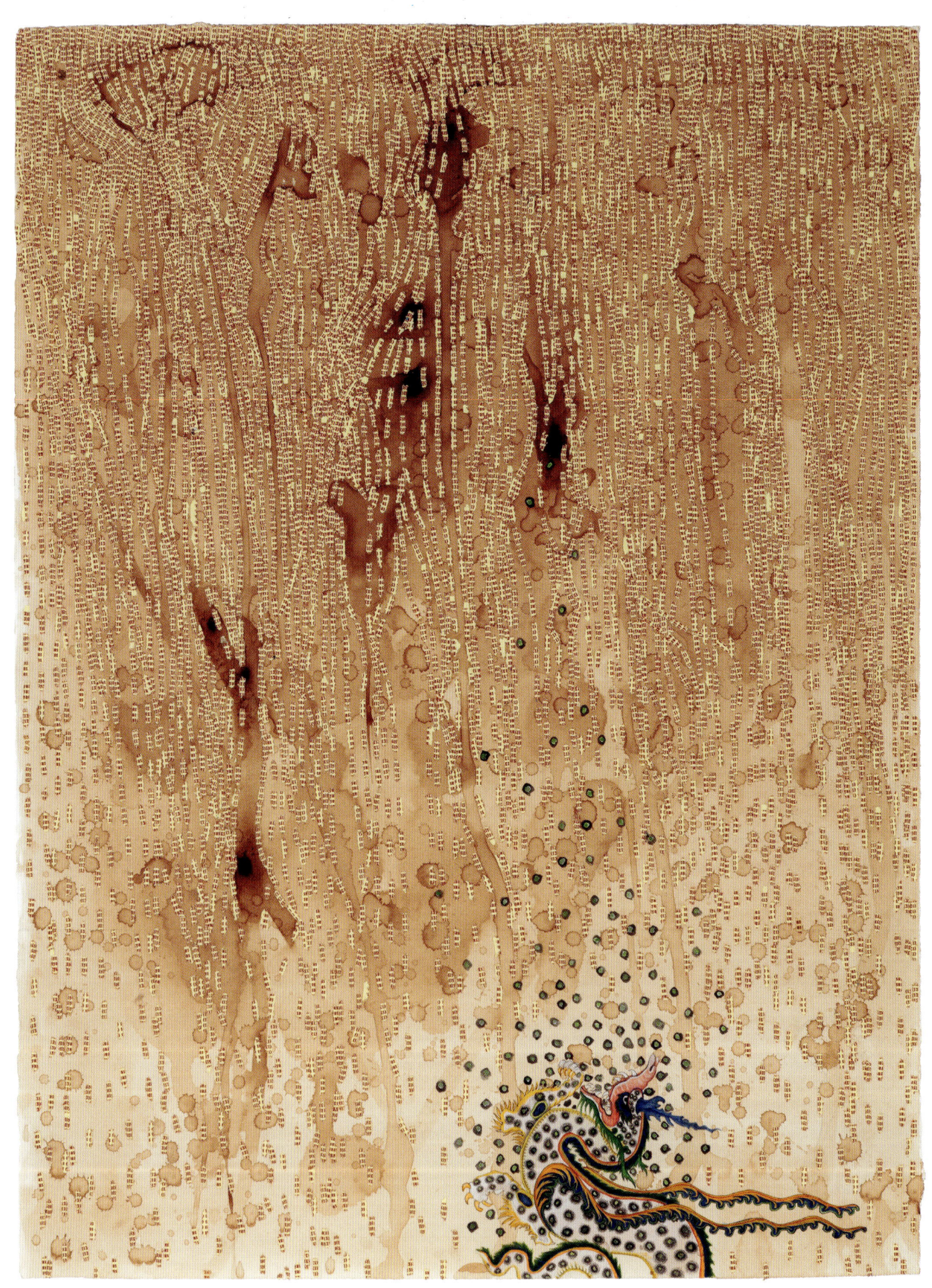

PREVIOUS PAGE (DETAIL)/ABOVE *Illyas (13)* 2018
FROM THE SERIES Say My Name
Watercolor with white gouache and collage of torn text
on tea-stained paper, 29 × 21 inches

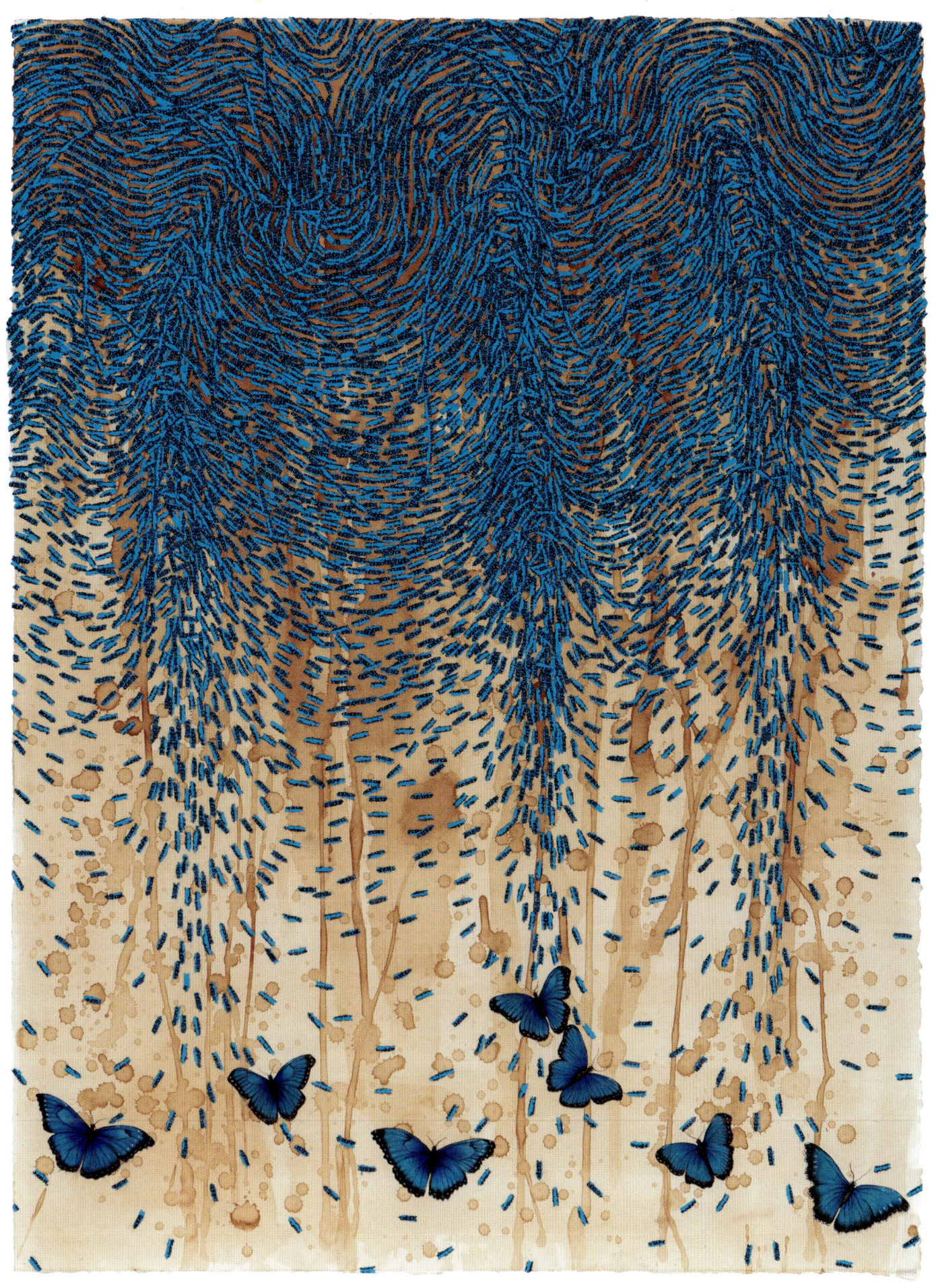

ABOVE/OVERLEAF (DETAIL) *Shoaib (8)* 2018
FROM THE SERIES Say My Name
Watercolor with white gouache and collage of torn text on
tea-stained paper, 29 × 21 inches

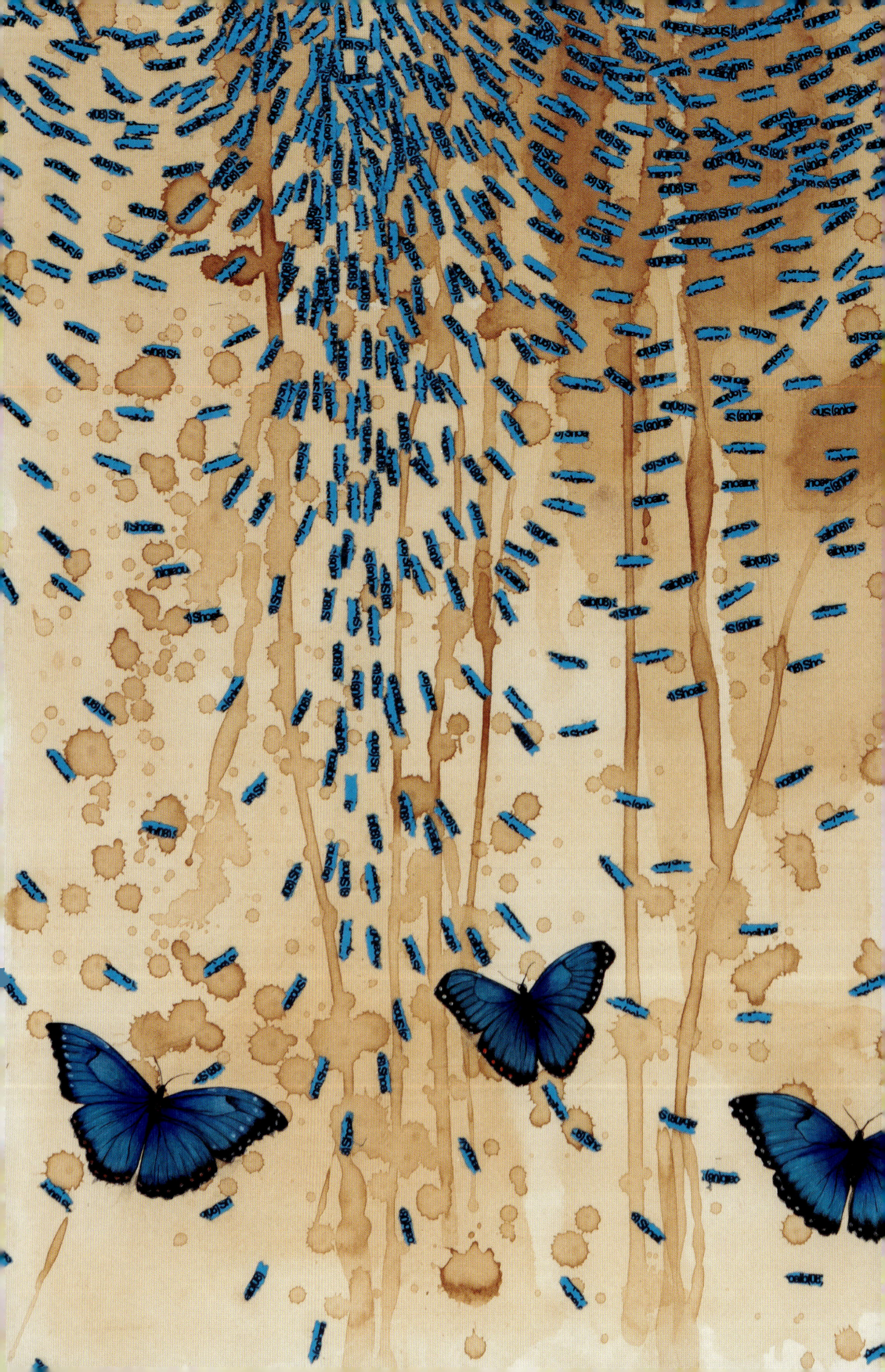

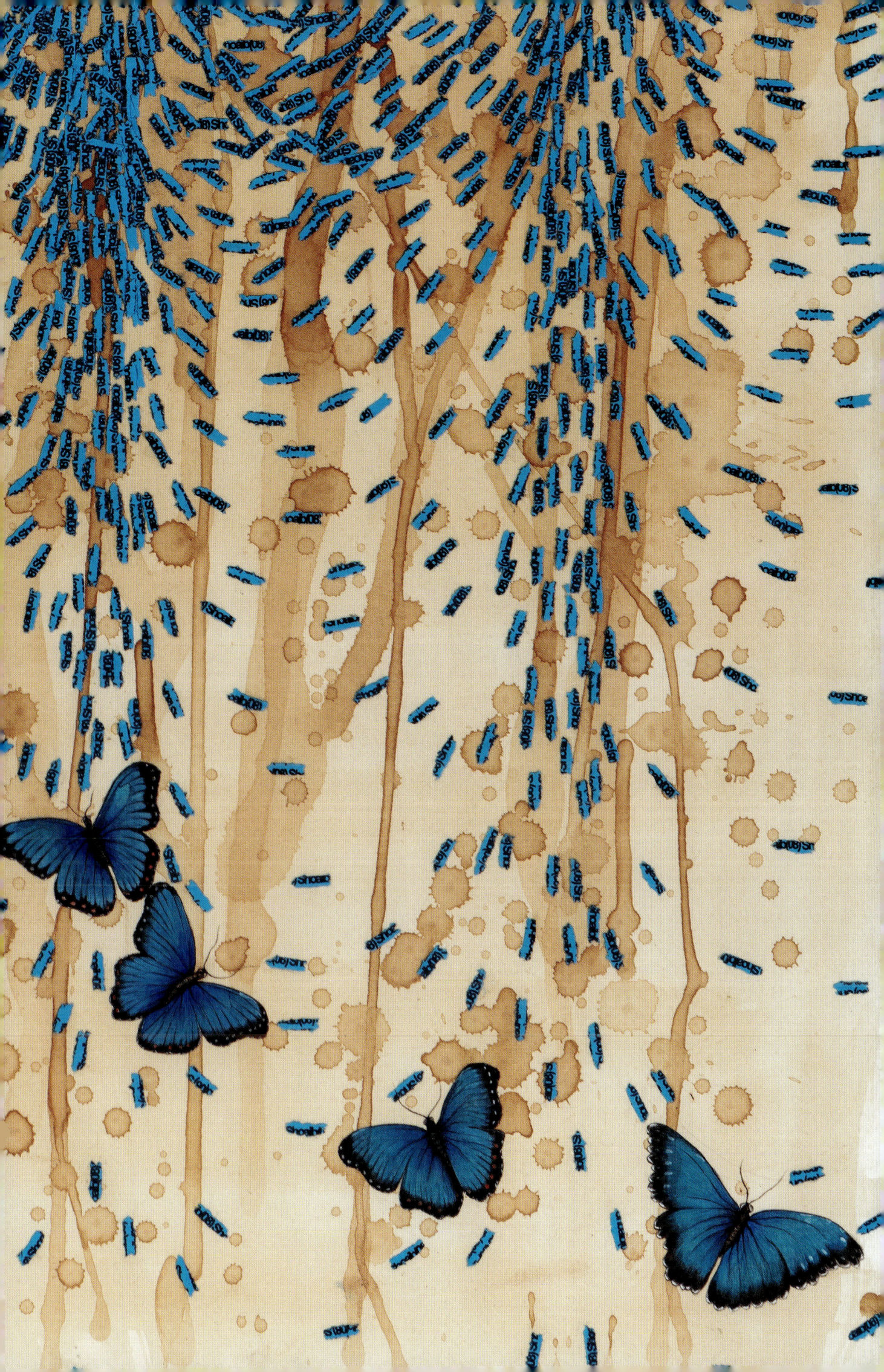

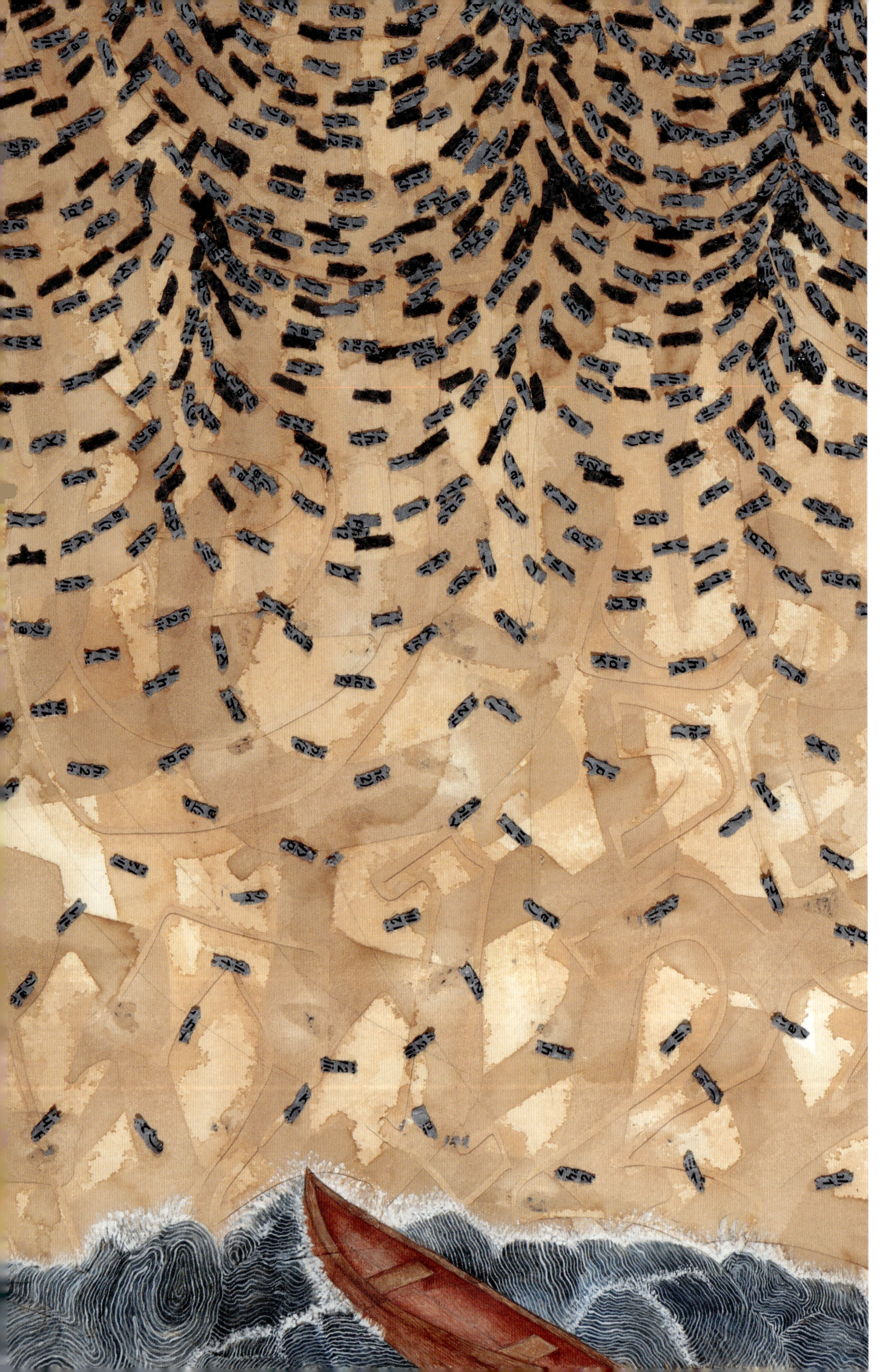

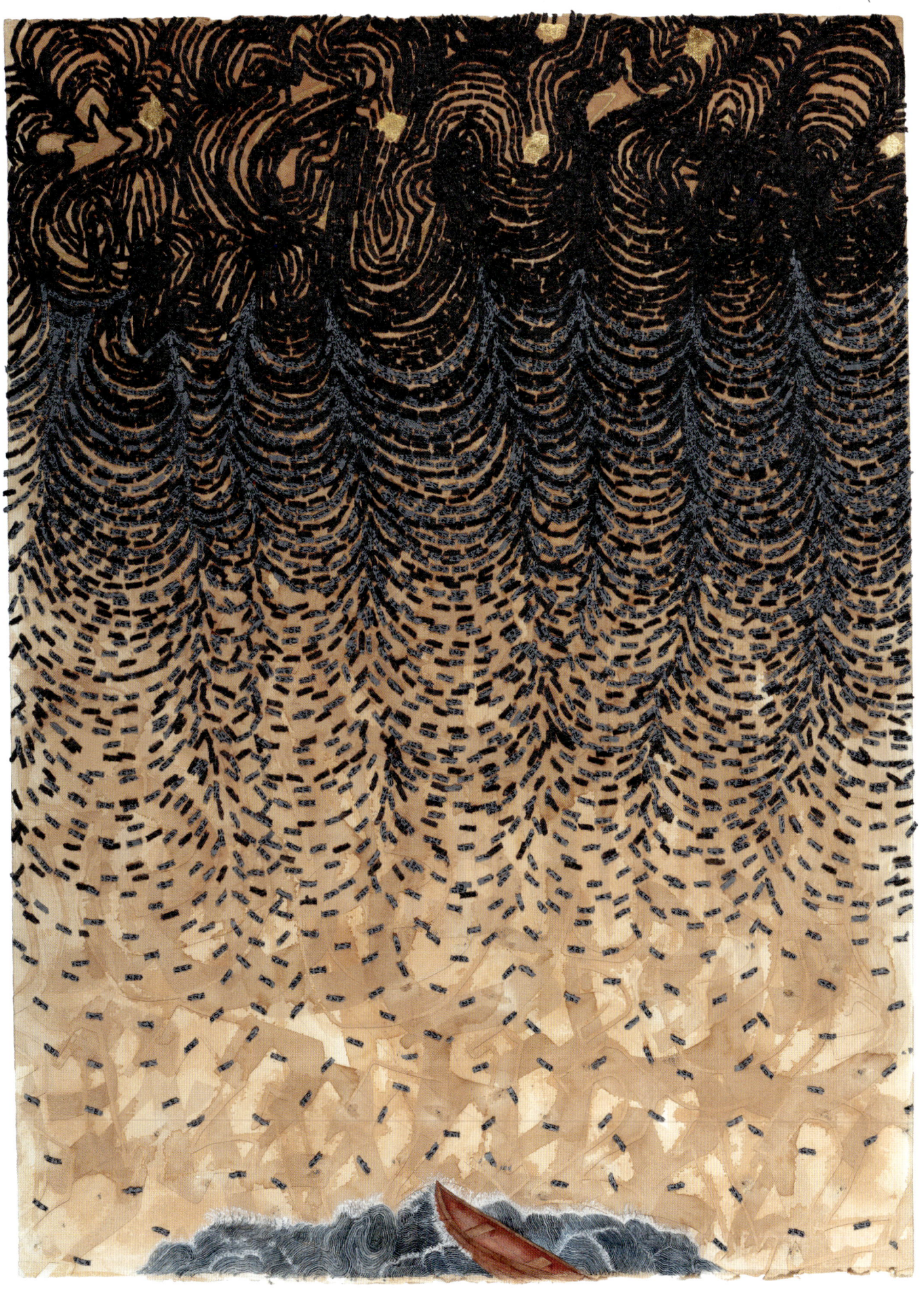

OPPOSITE (DETAIL)/ABOVE ***Khalid (12)*** 2020
FROM THE SERIES Say My Name
Collage of text, gold leaf, watercolor with white gouache and
laser engraving on tea-stained paper, 30 × 22 inches

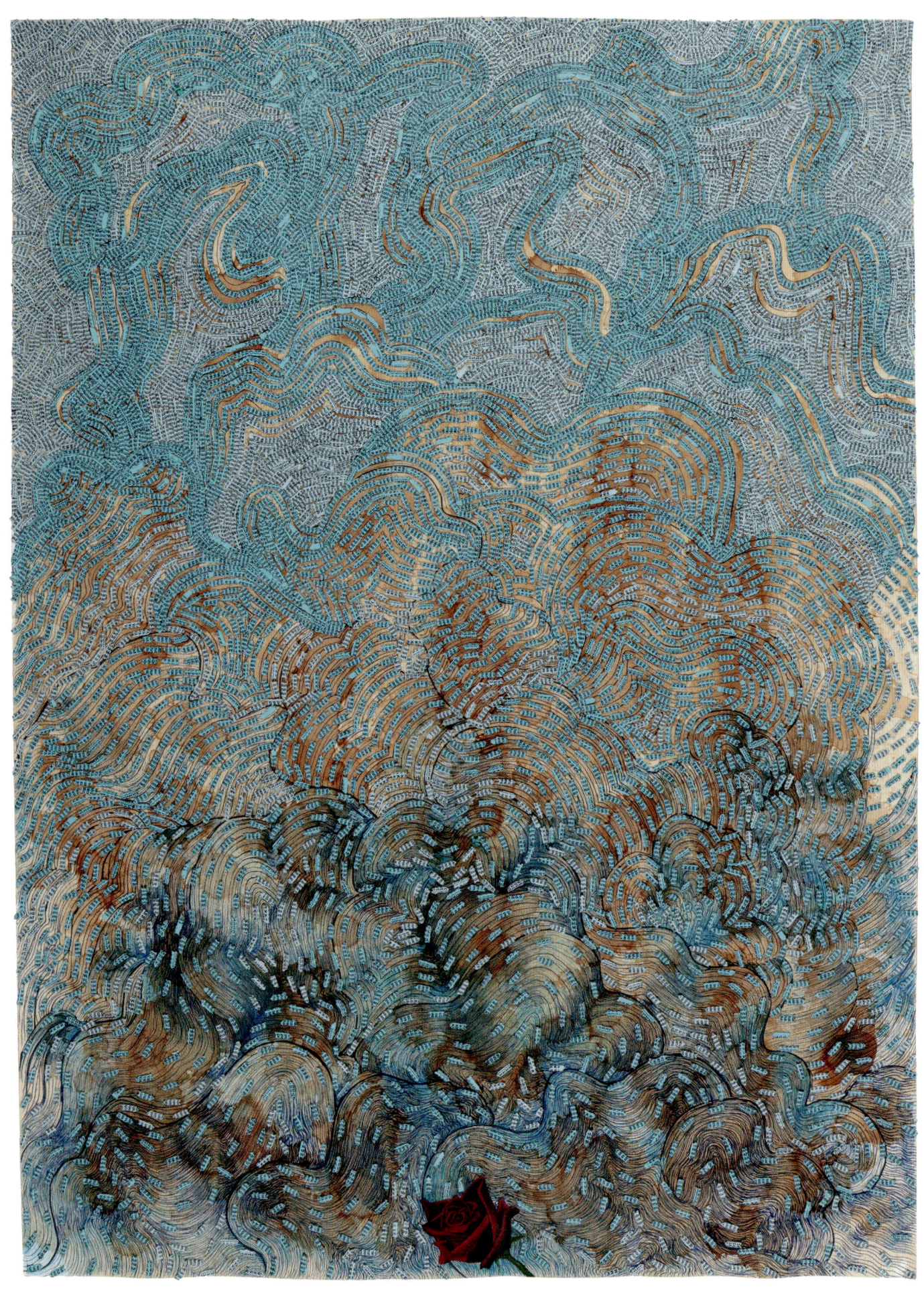

ABOVE/OPPOSITE (DETAIL) **Mohammad Yaas Khan (16)** 2020
FROM THE SERIES Say My Name
Collage of torn text, watercolor with white gouache and
pen on tea-stained paper, 30 × 22 inches

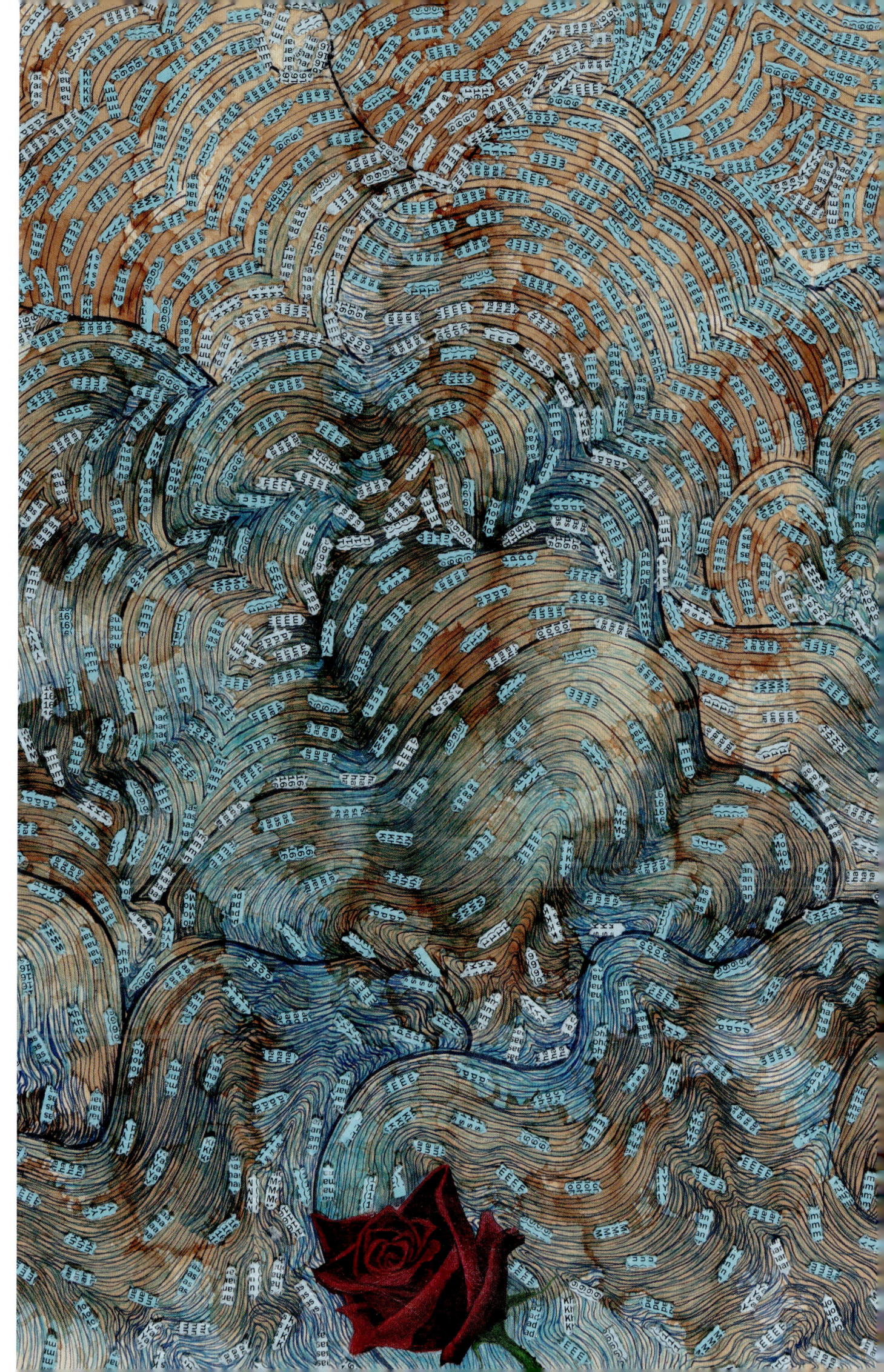

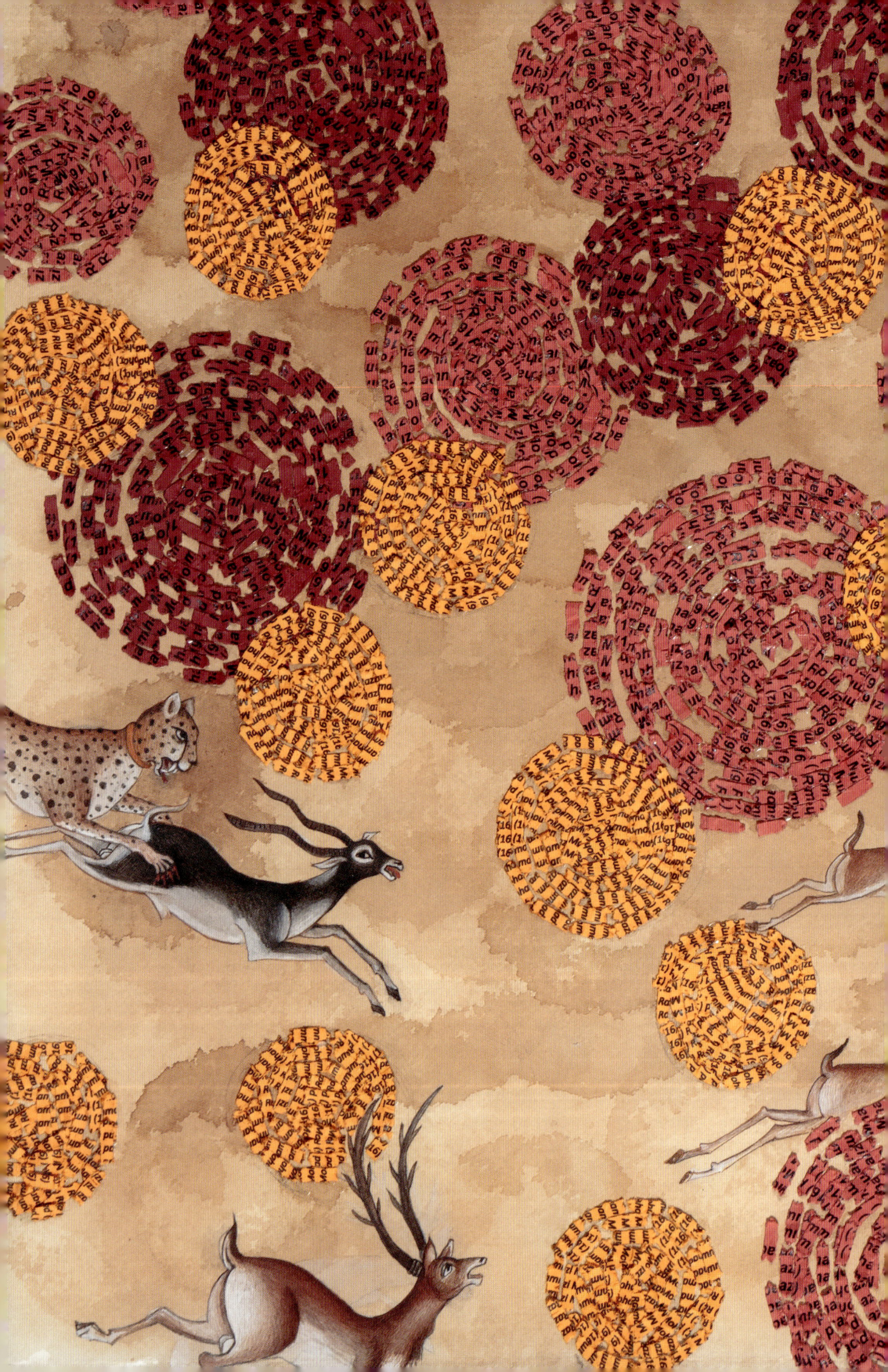

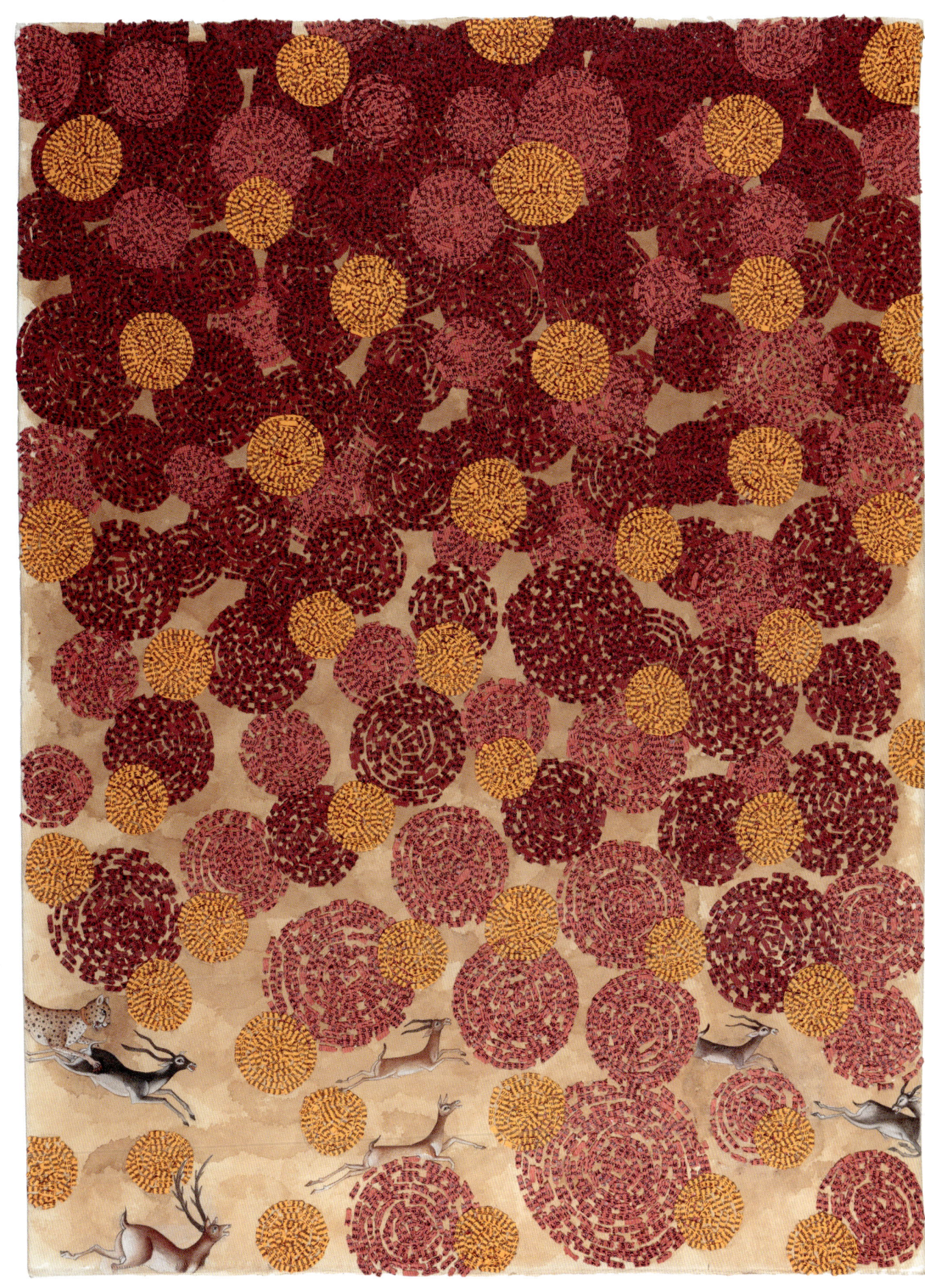

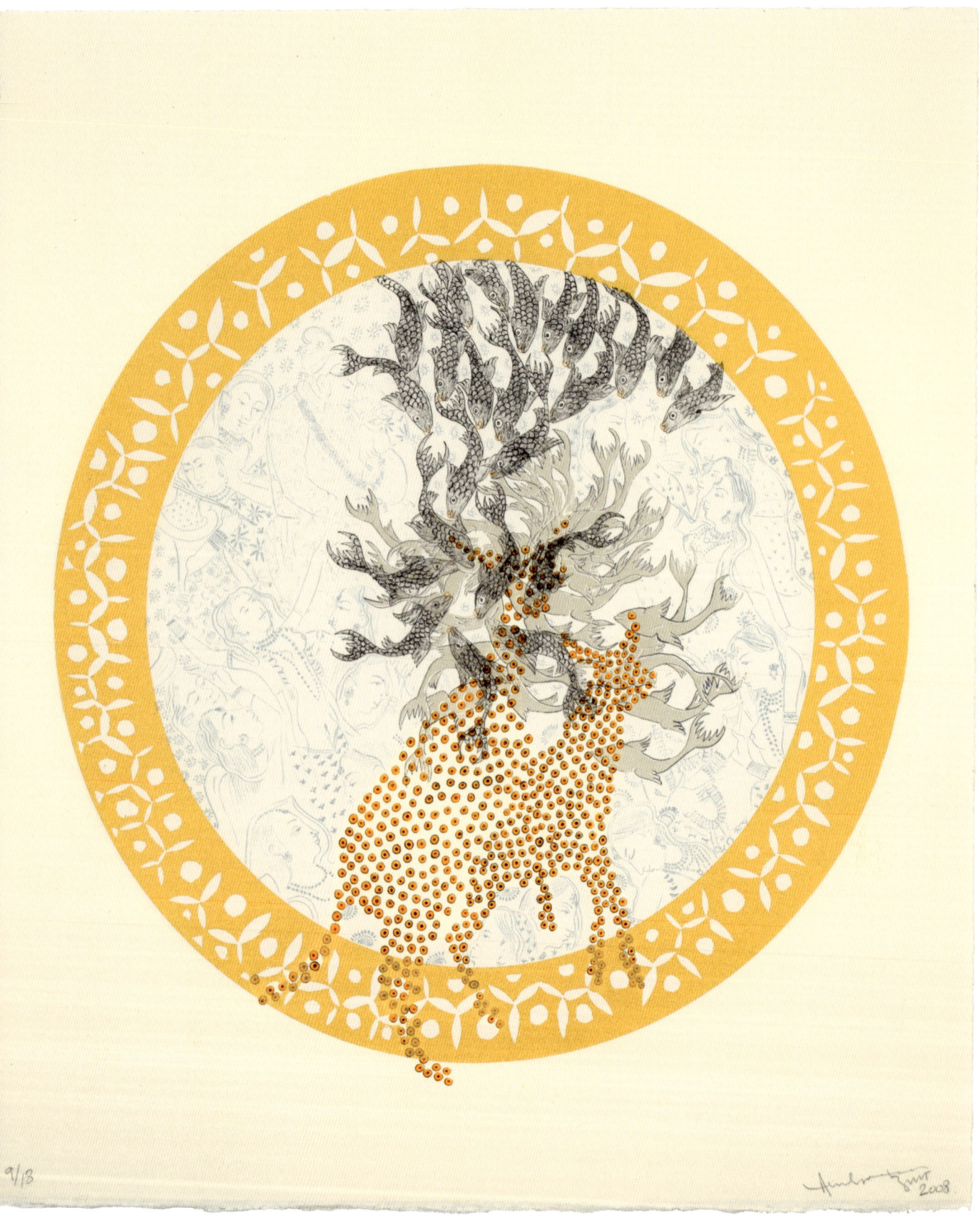

9/13

Untitled 2008
FROM THE SUITE Dirty Pretty
Lithograph and silkscreen printing on BFK Rives paper,
17½ × 14½ inches, edition of 23

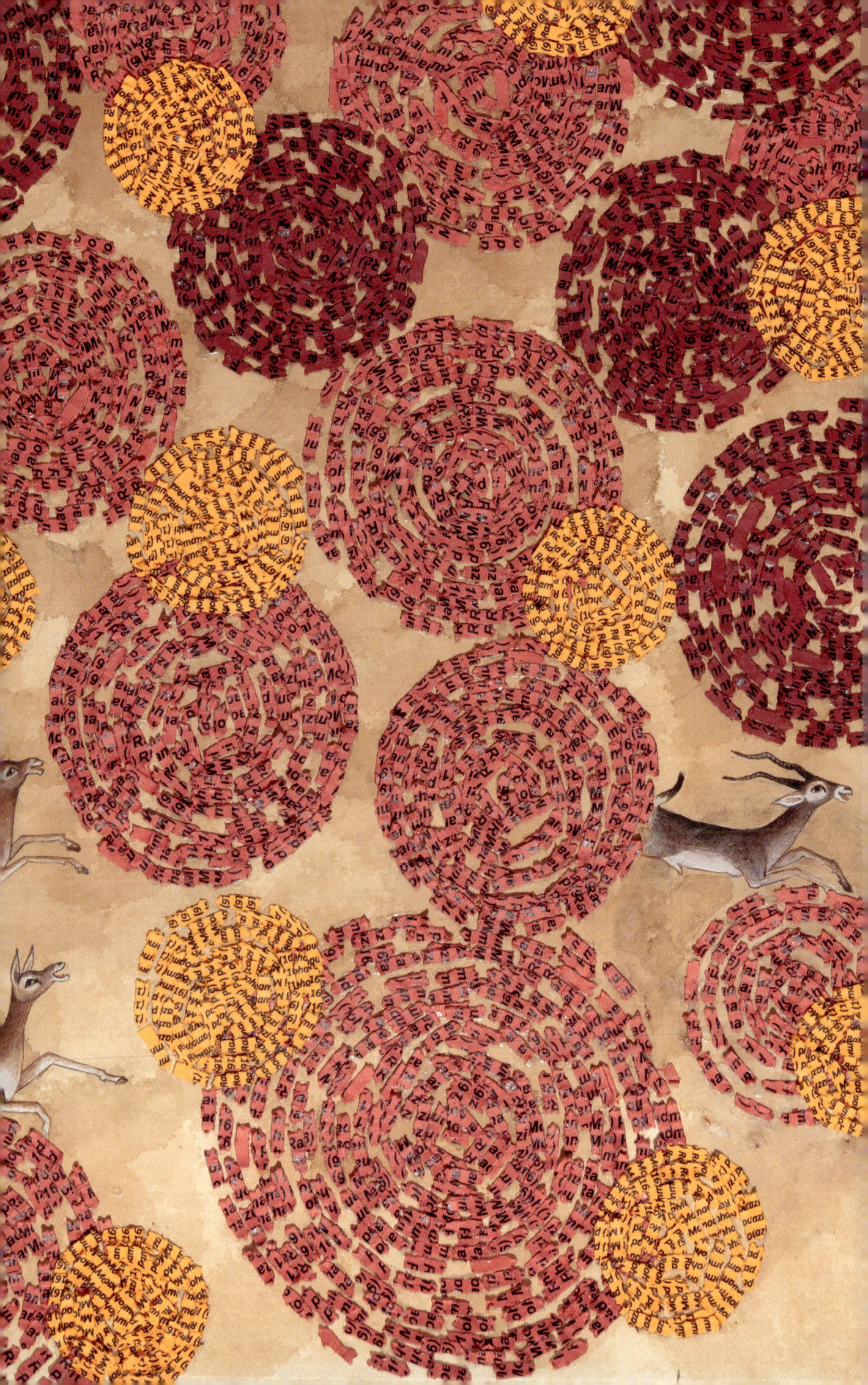

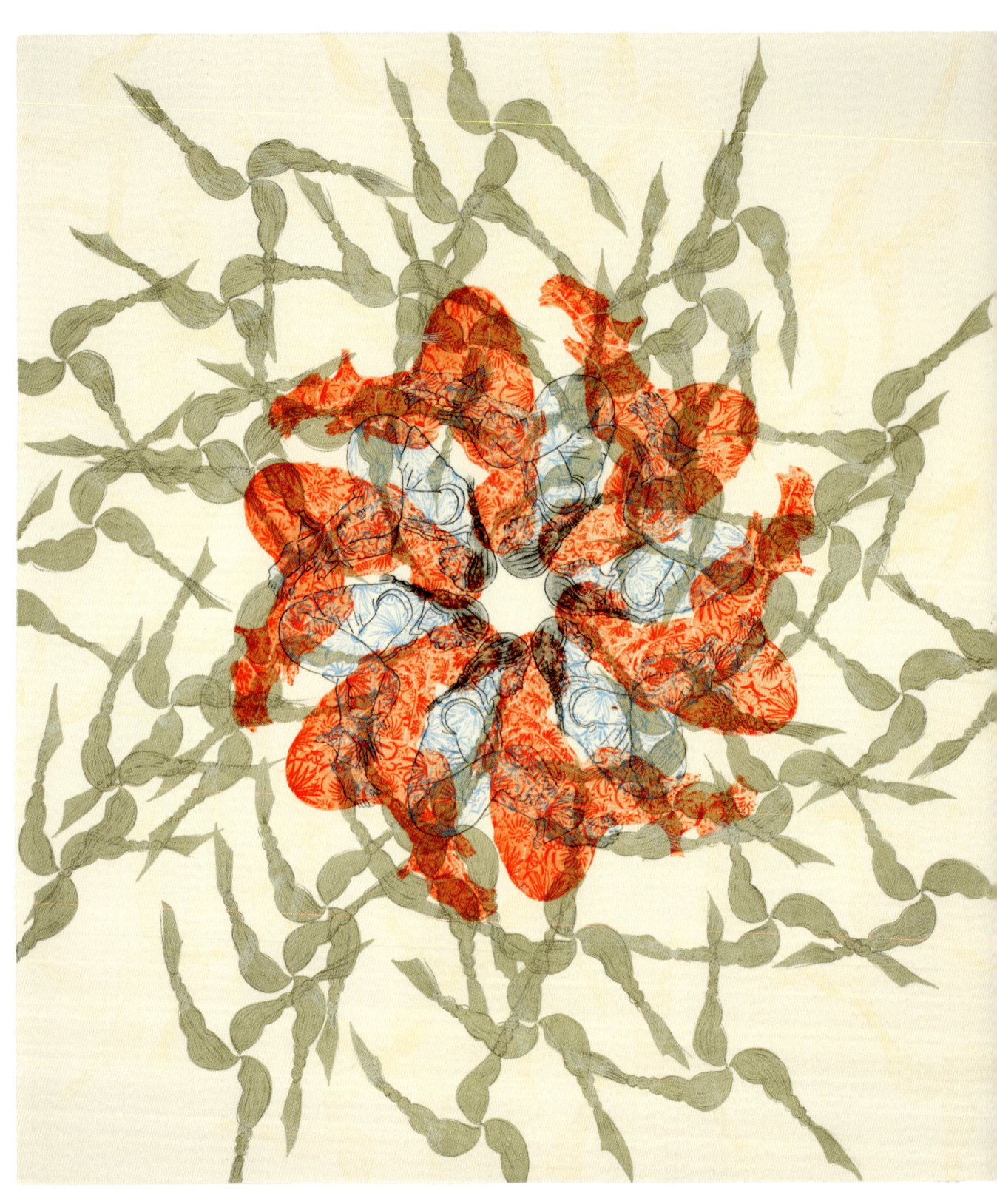

Untitled 2008
<small>FROM THE SUITE</small> Dirty Pretty
Lithograph, etching, and silkscreen printing on BFK Rives
paper, 15¾ × 14 inches, edition of 22

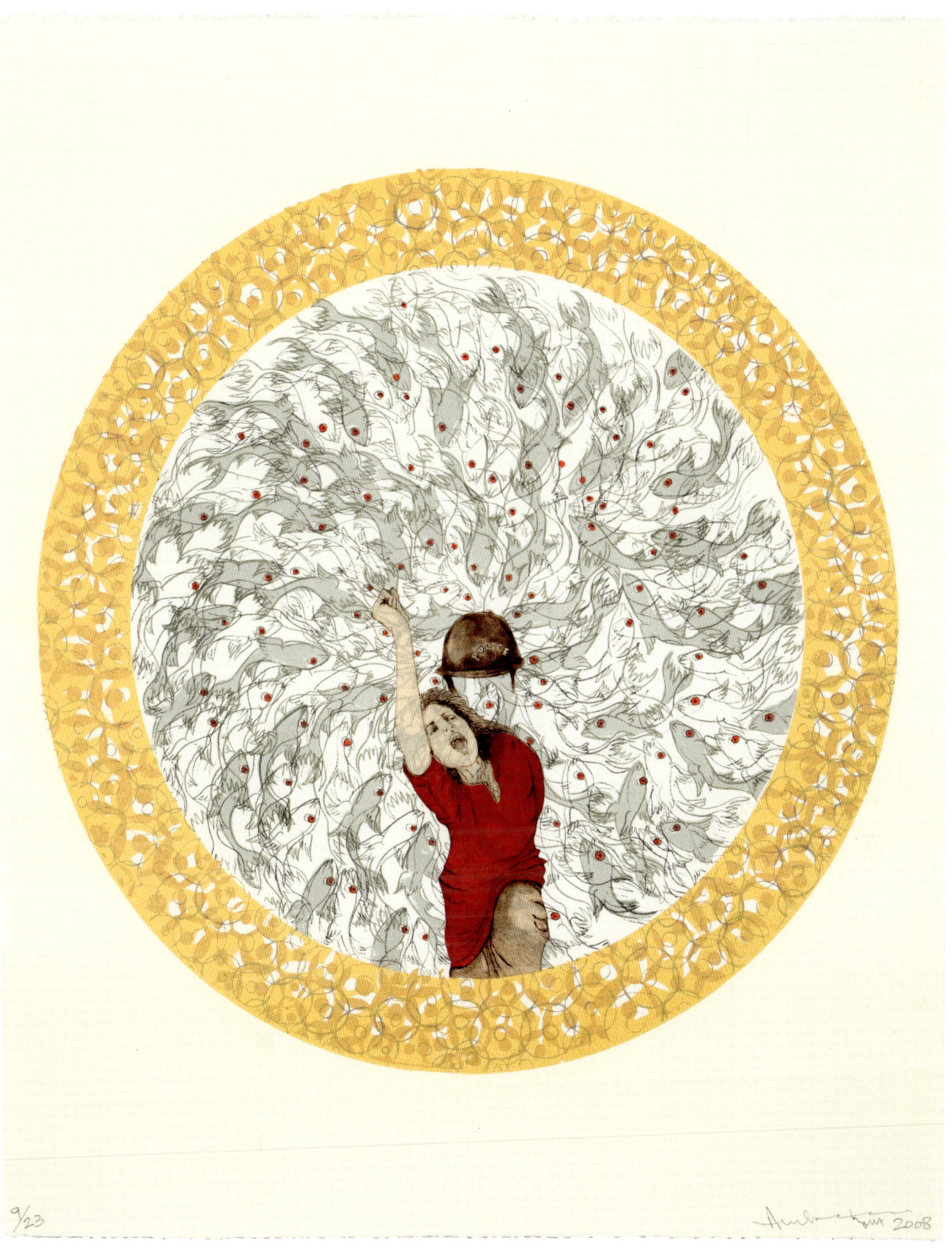

9/23

Untitled 2008

FROM THE SUITE Dirty Pretty
Lithograph, etching, silkscreen printing and chine collé
on BFK Rives paper, 17½×14½ inches, edition of 23

47

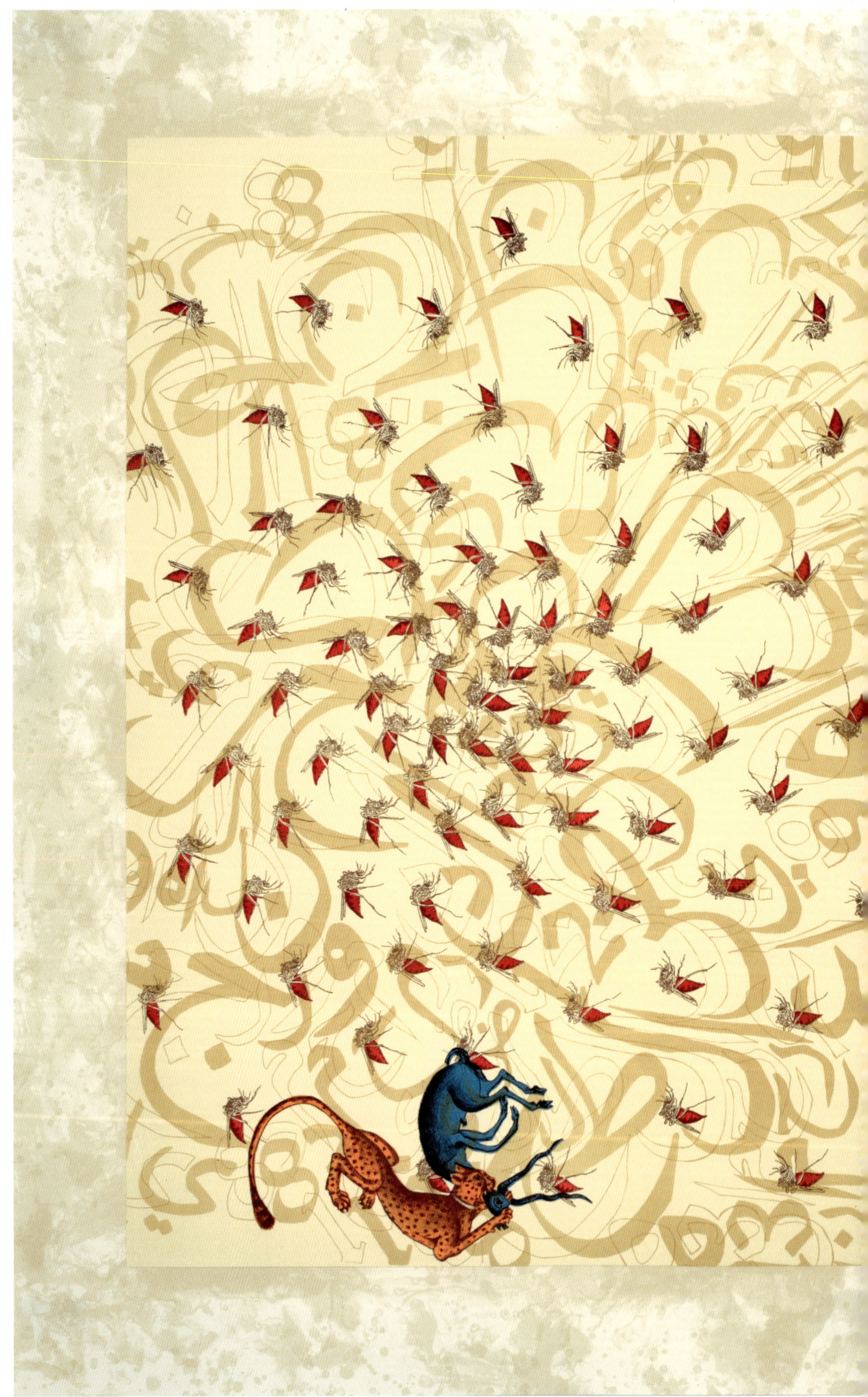

48

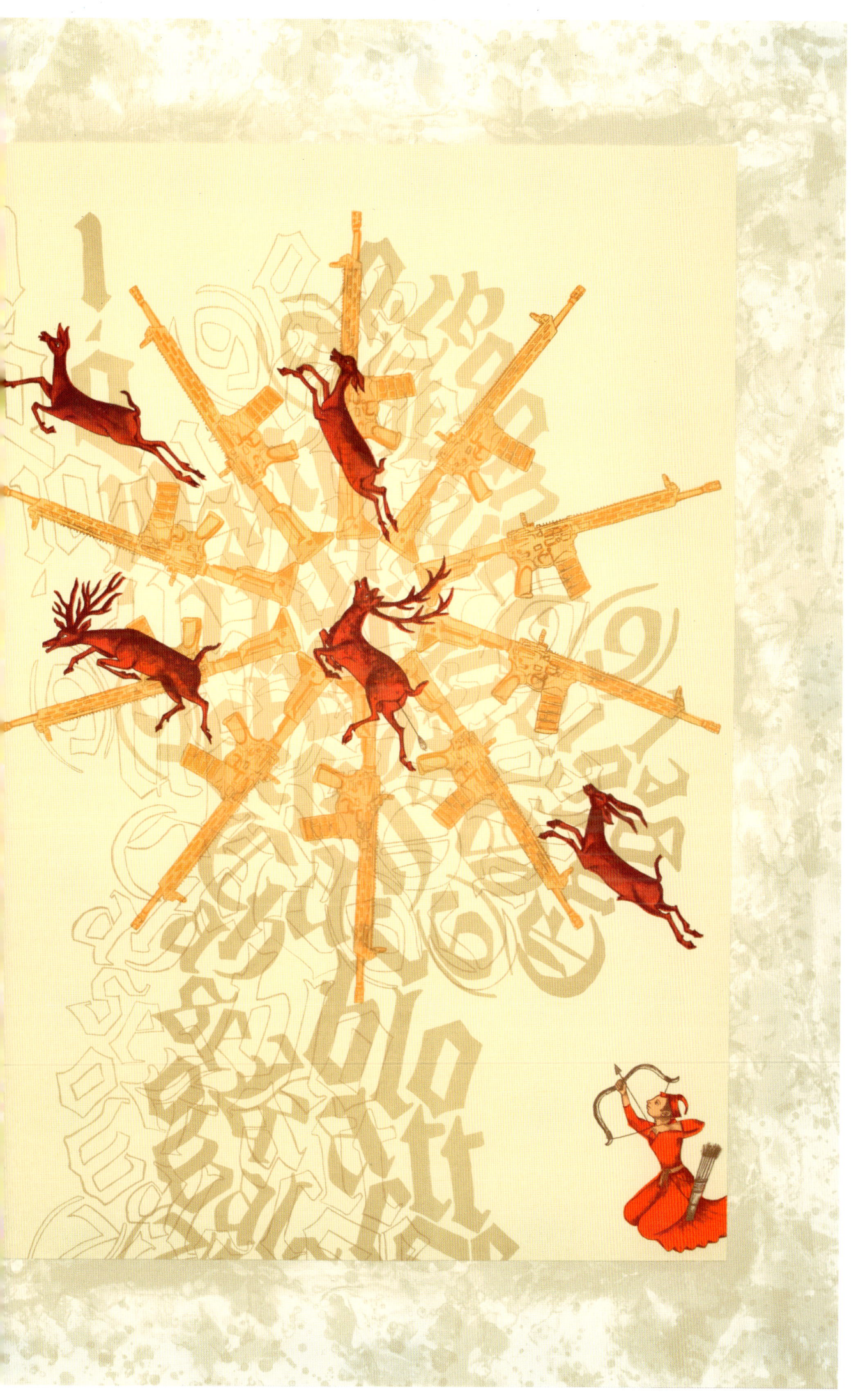

Say My Name 2018
Lithograph, each 36½×24½ inches, edition of 30

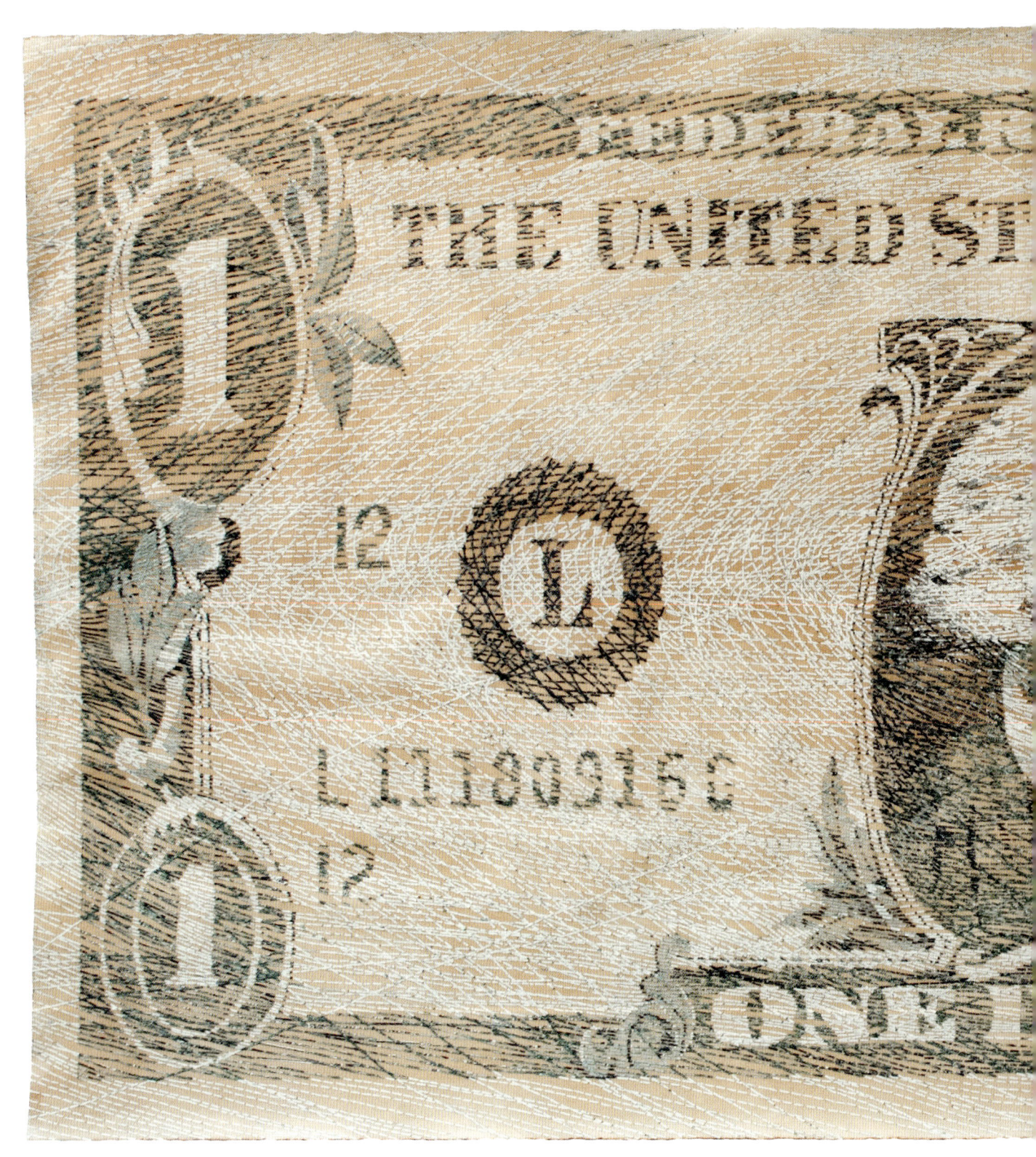

ABOVE/OVERLEAF (DETAIL) *Dollar 1* 2012
FROM THE SERIES In God We Trust
Shredded dollar bills on tea-stained paper,
approx. 90×44 inches

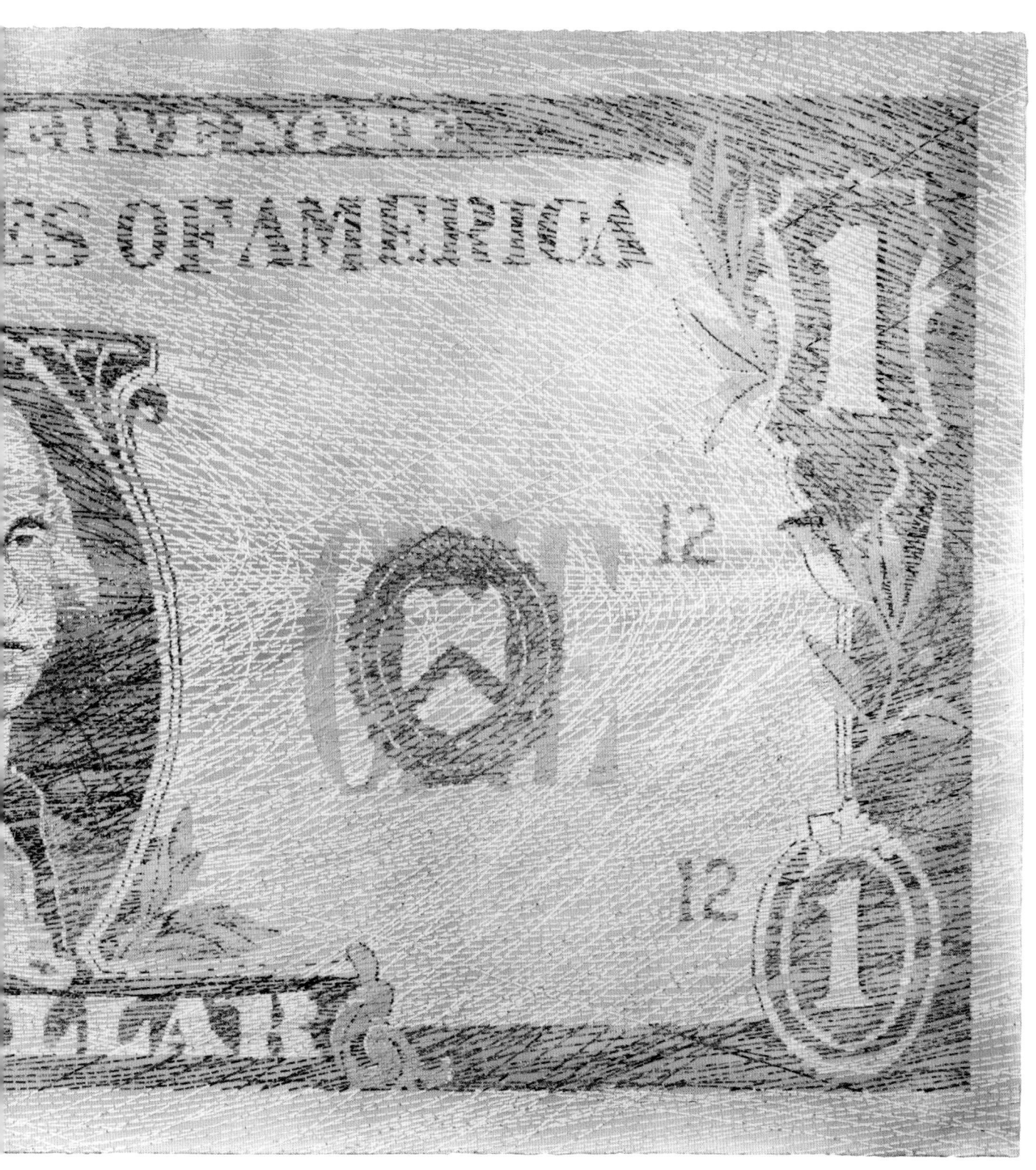

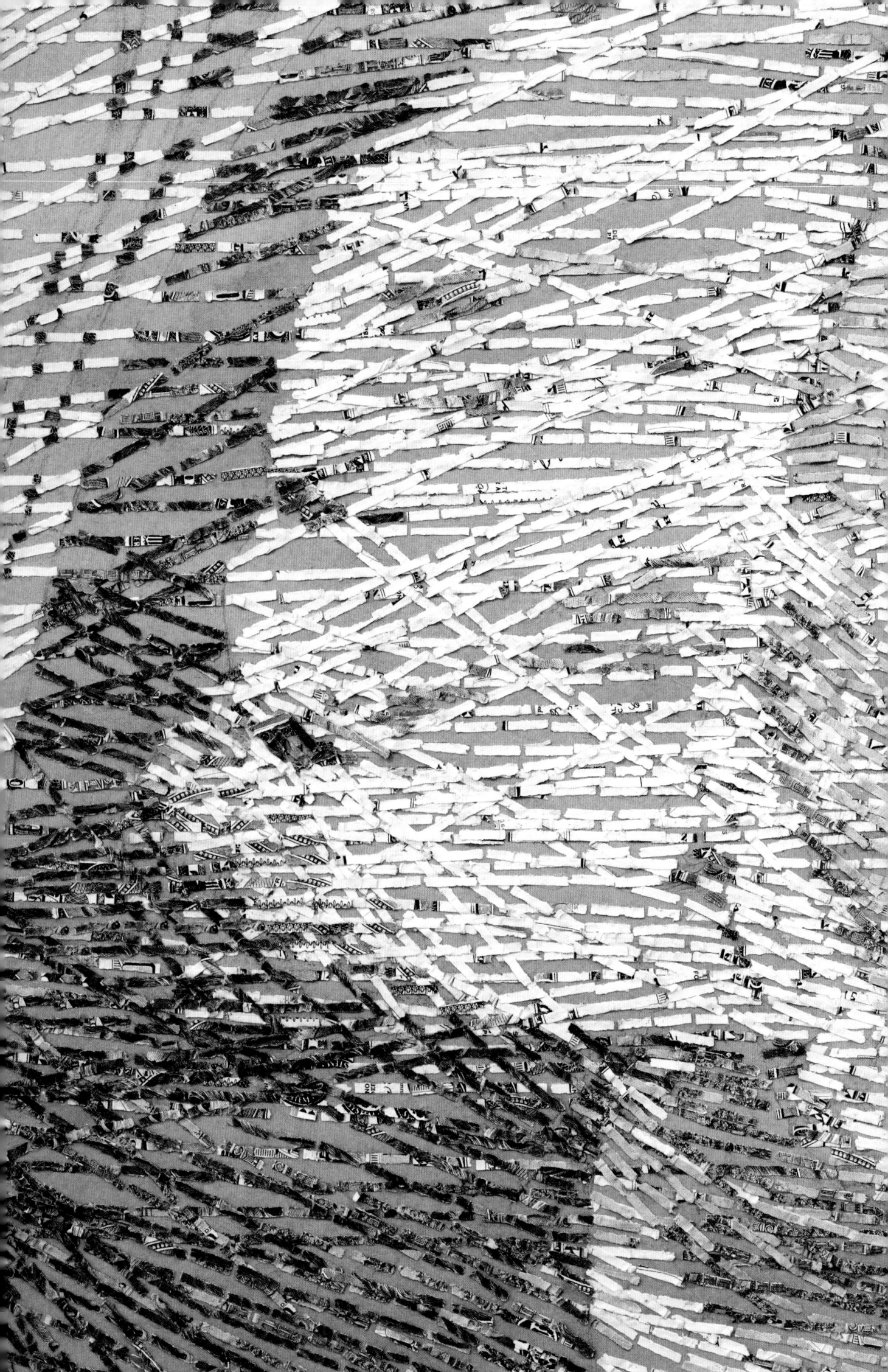

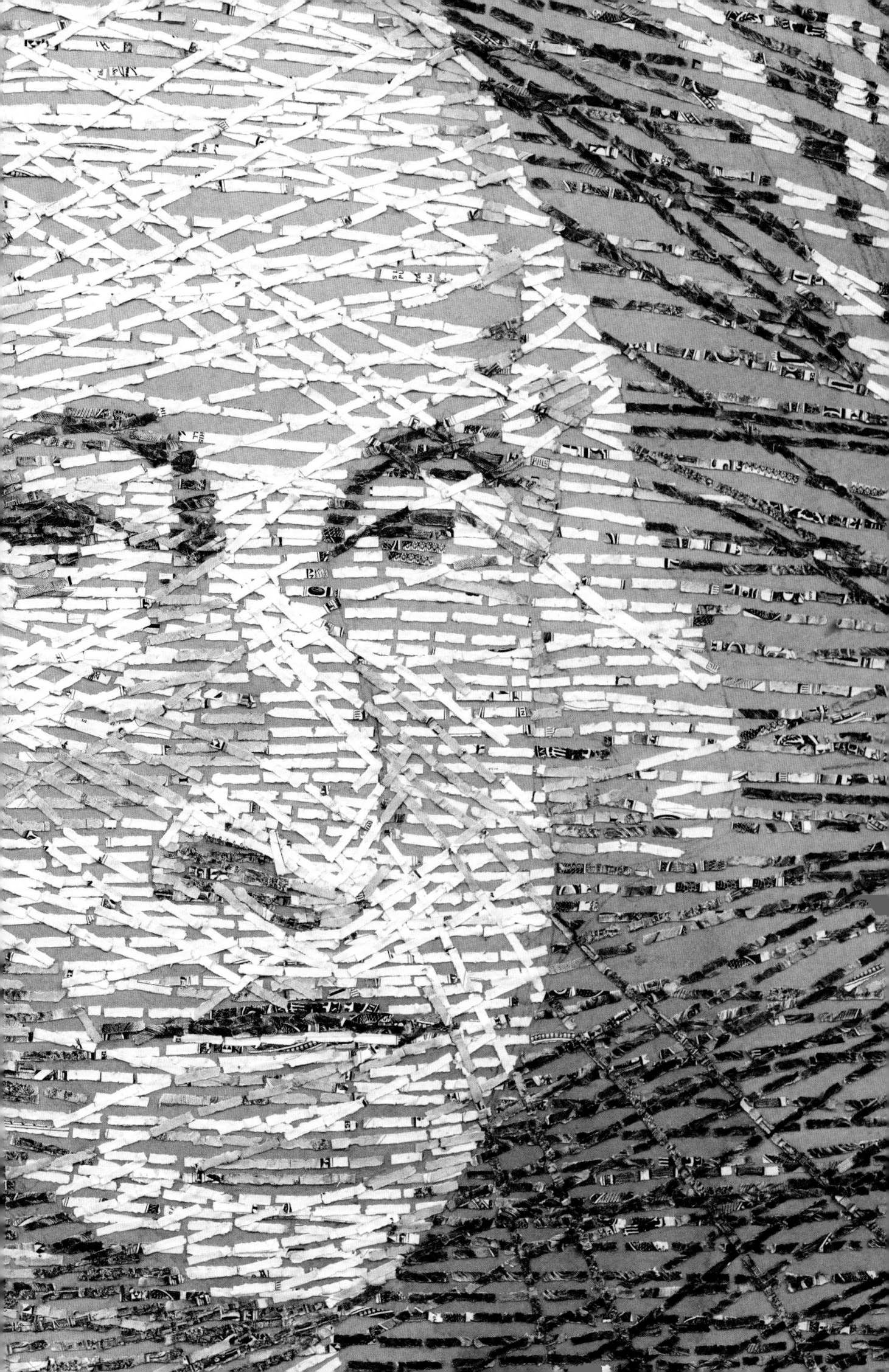

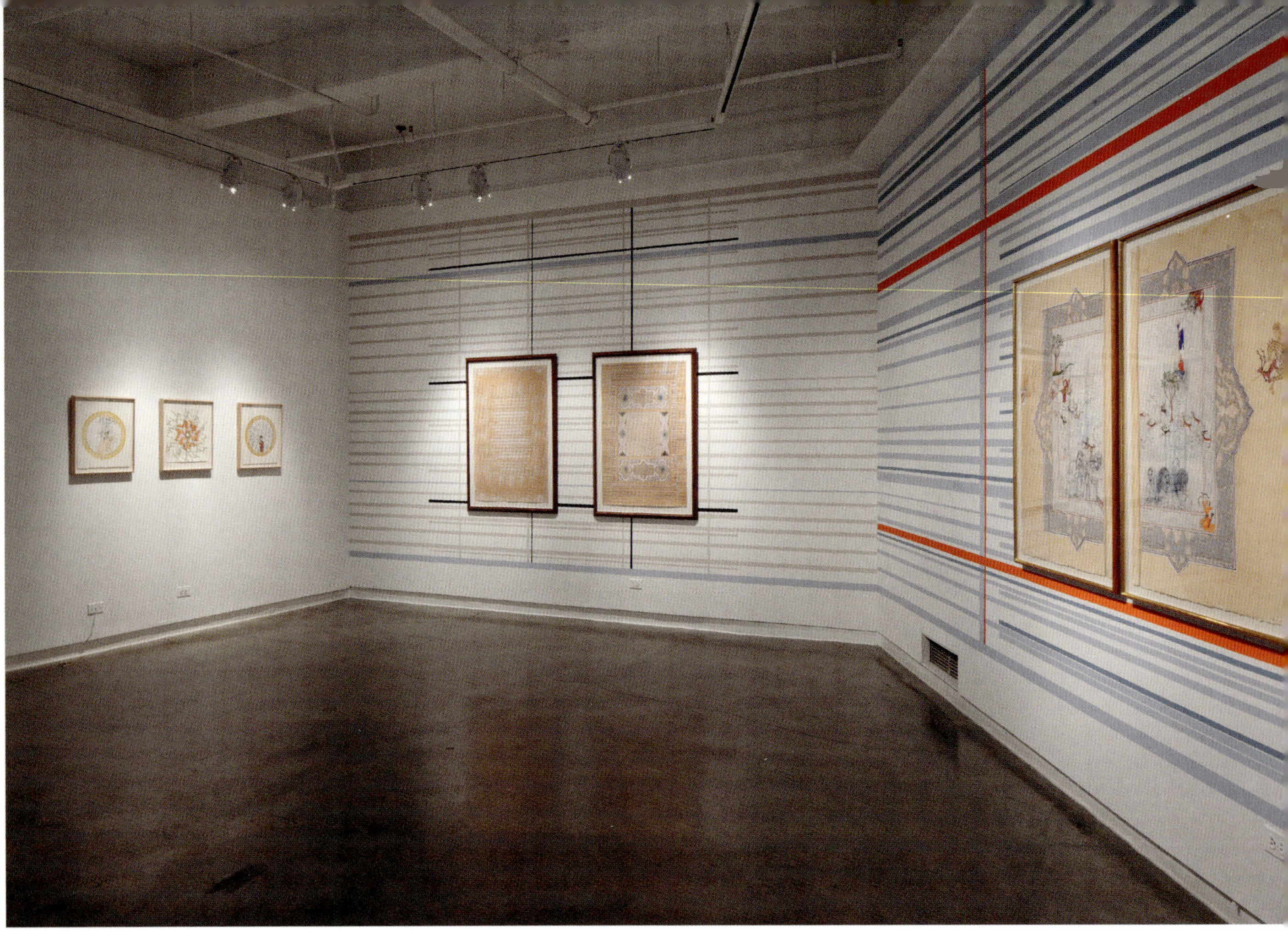

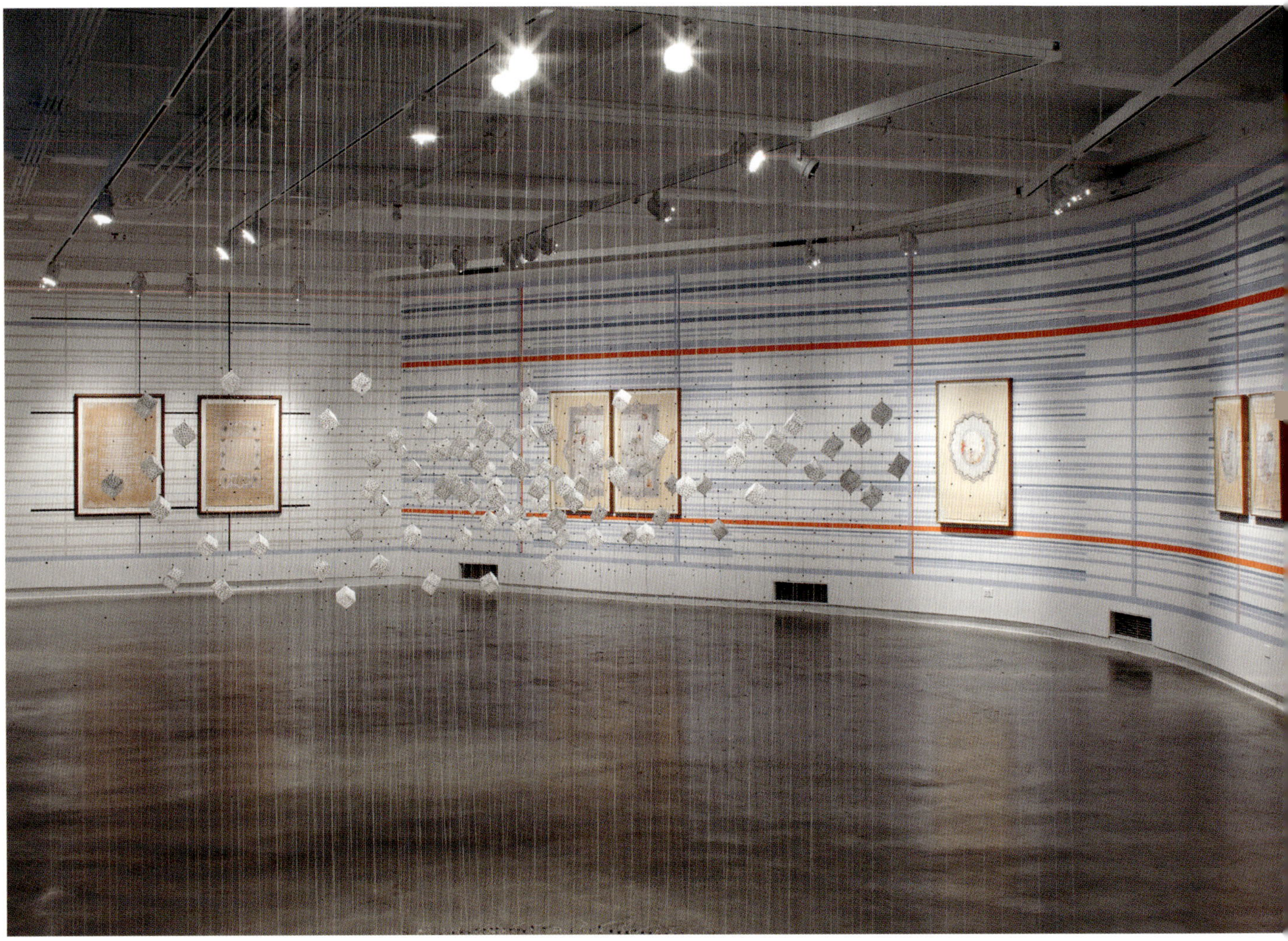

TOP AND BOTTOM/OPPOSITE "Dirty Pretty and Other Stories" 2010
Installation views, Jaffe-Friede Gallery, Dartmouth College,
Hanover, New Hampshire

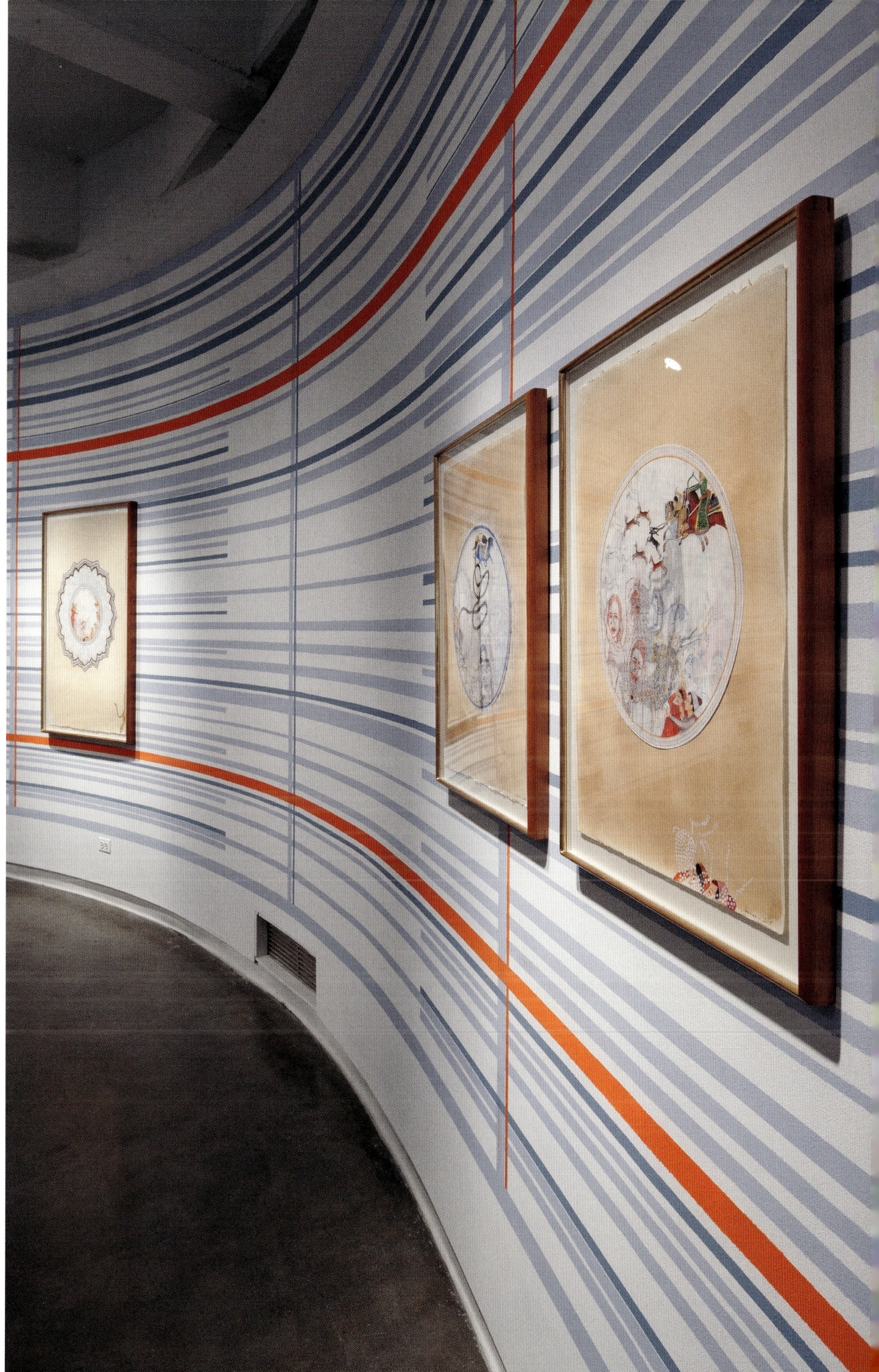

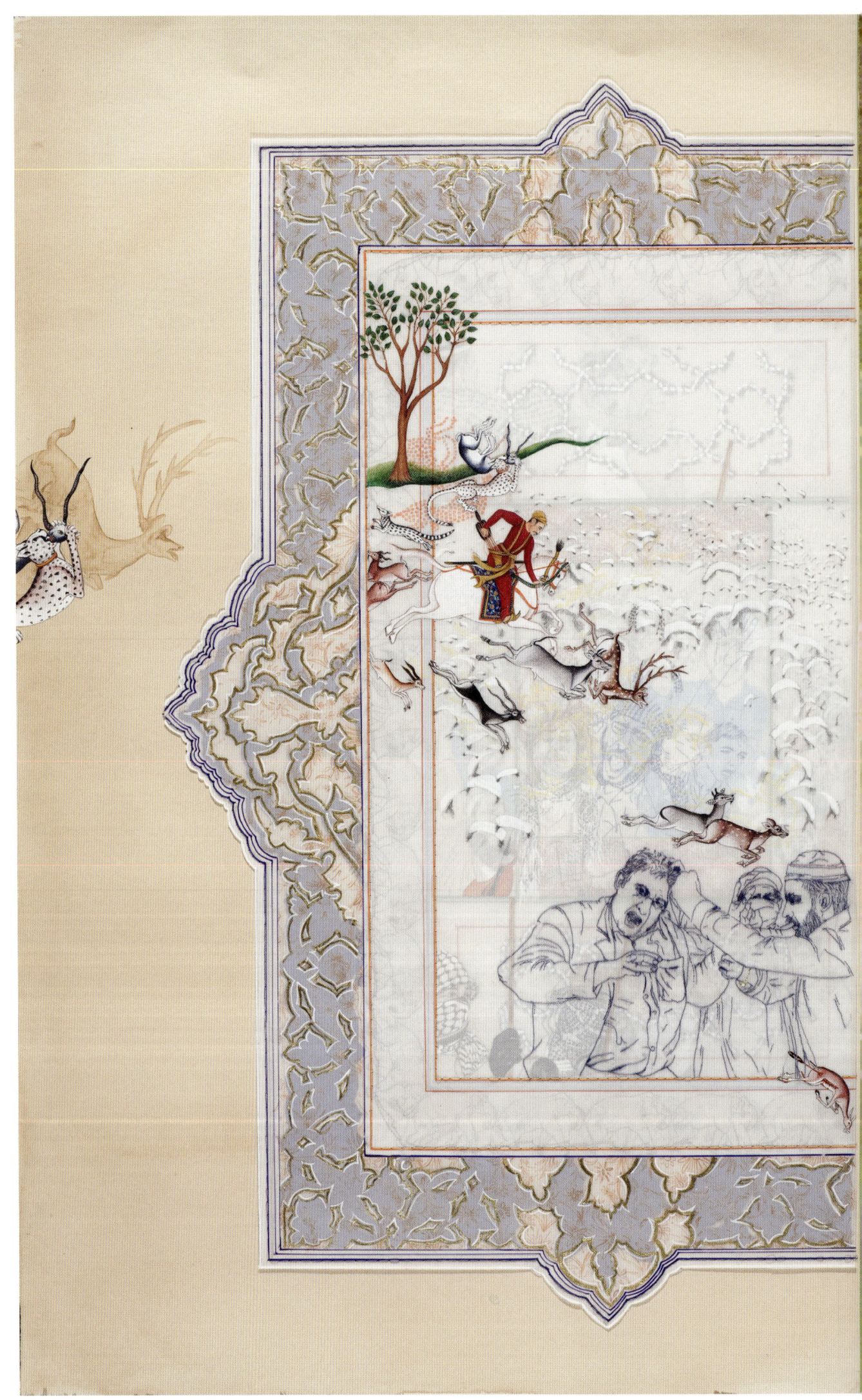

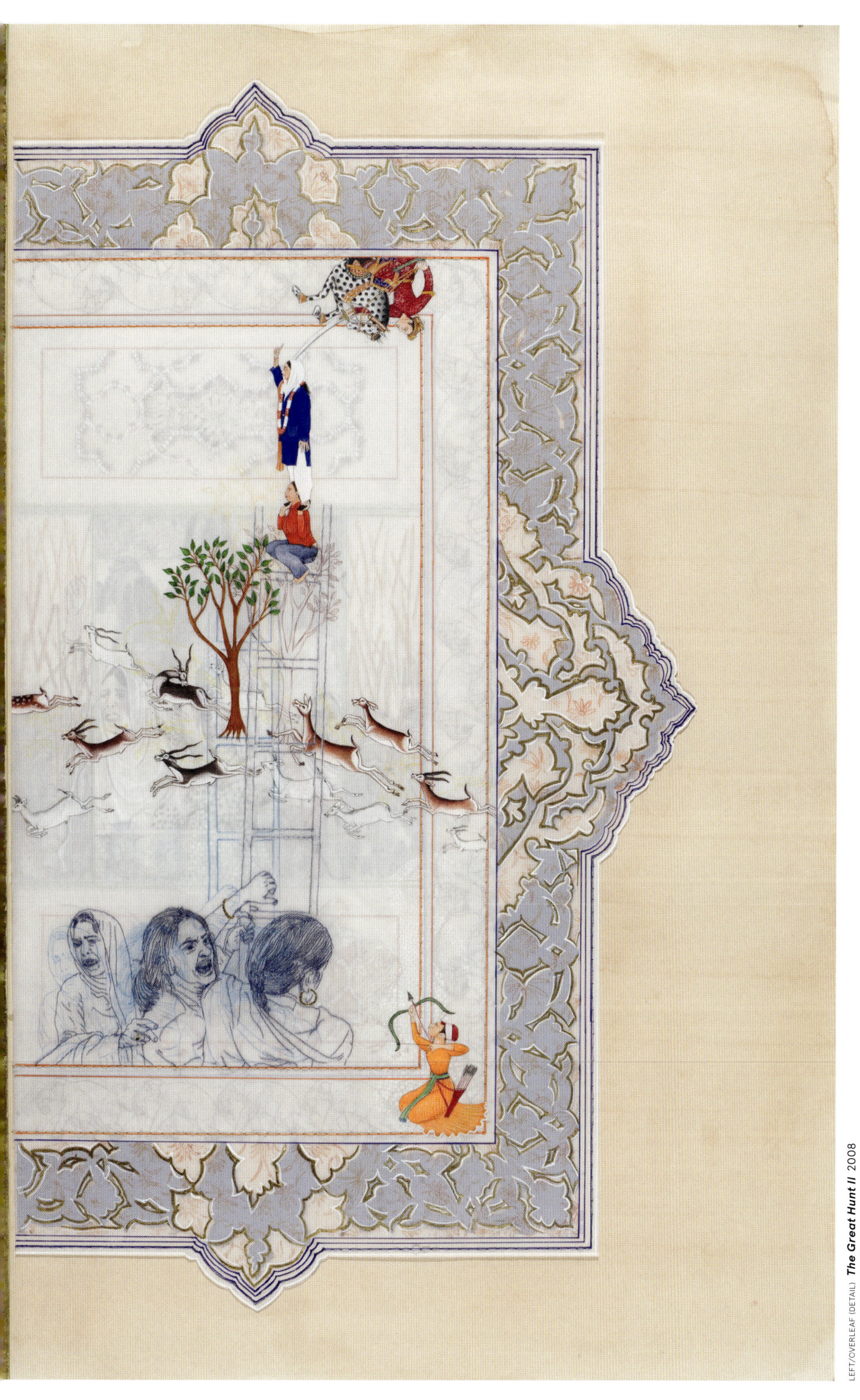

LEFT/OVERLEAF (DETAIL) *The Great Hunt II* 2008

FROM THE SERIES Dirty Pretty

Pigments, gouache, text, thread, and gold leaf on Mylar and tea-stained paper, 45×60 inches

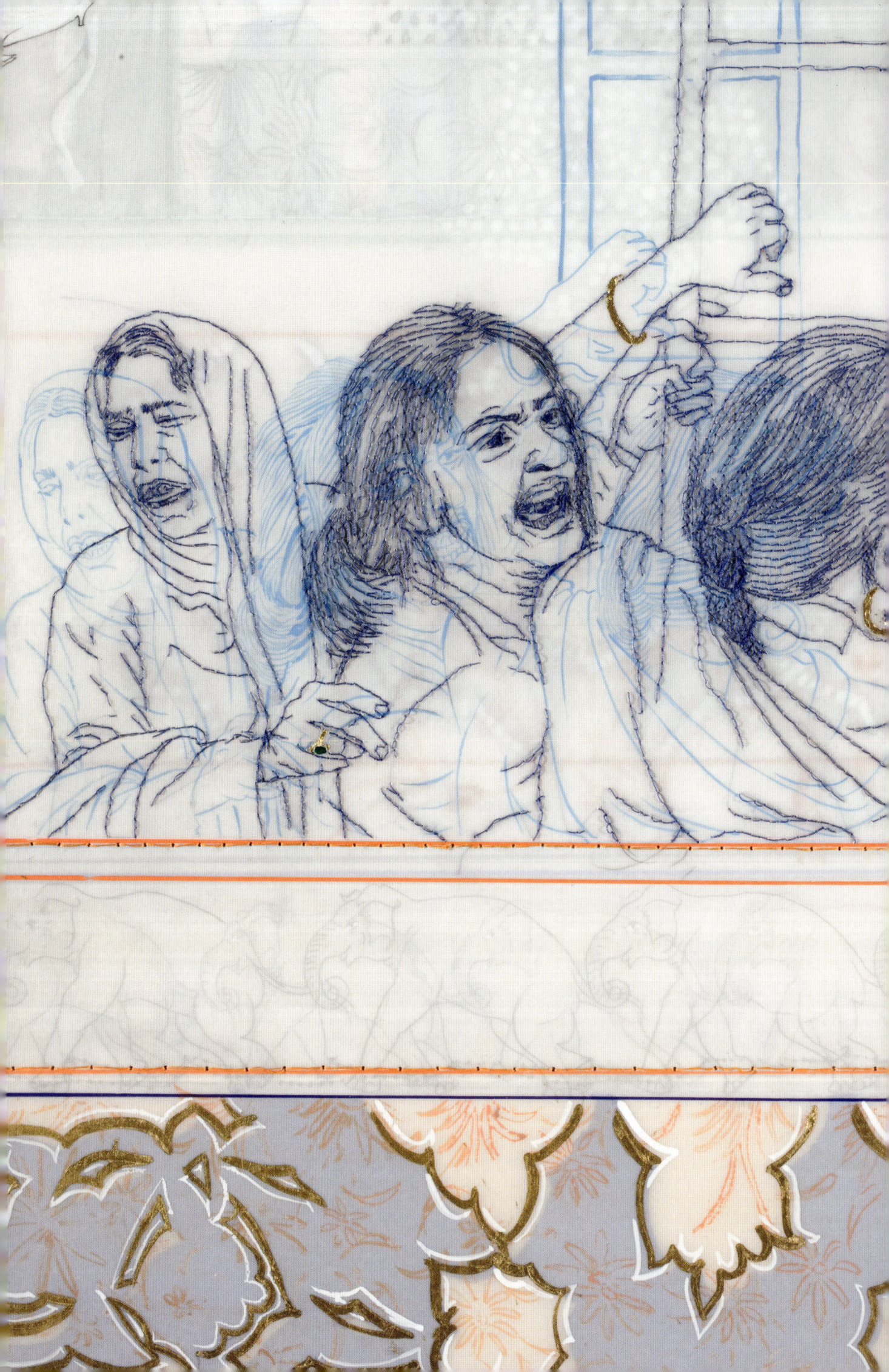

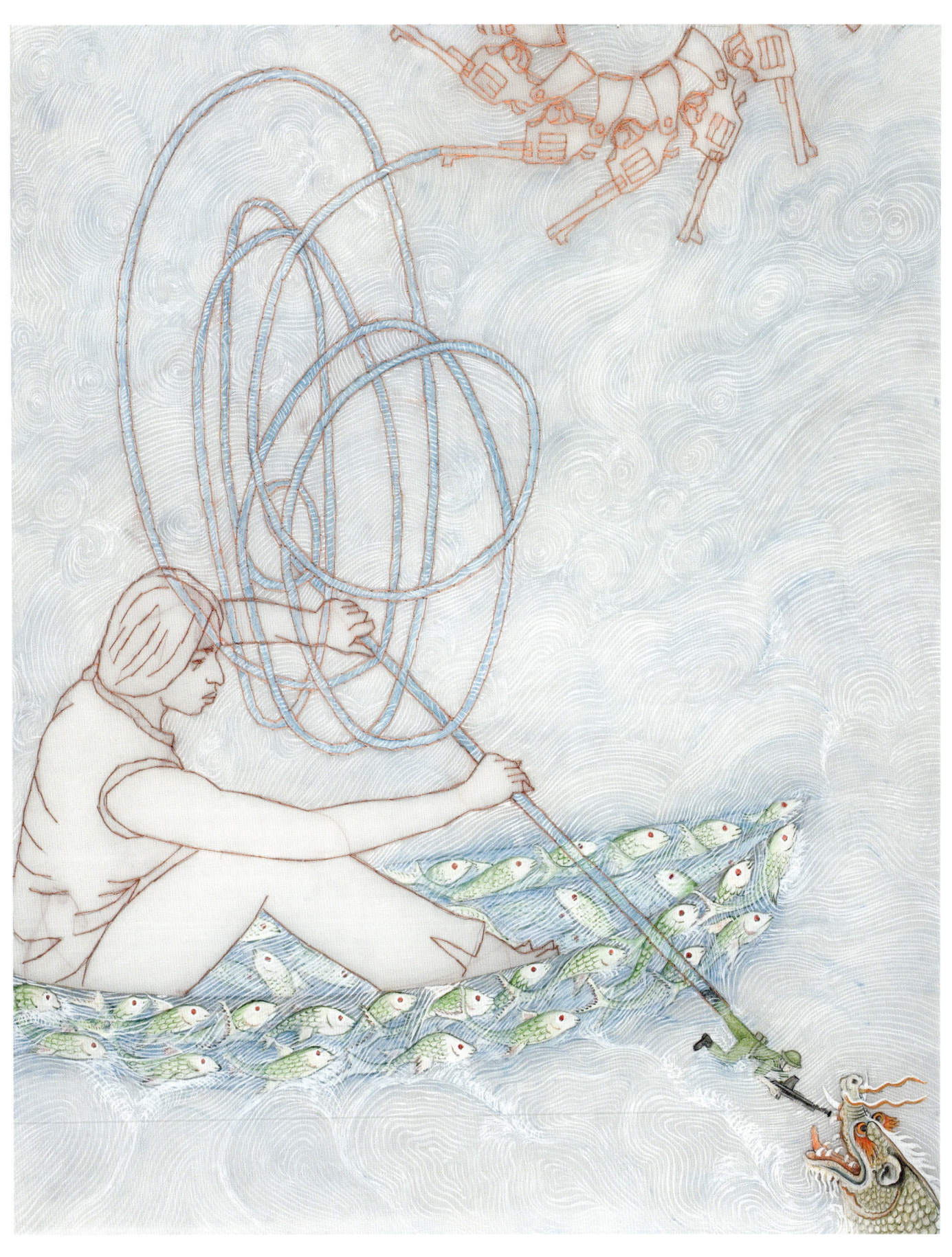

Untitled 2006
<small>FROM THE SERIES</small> Cirque Du Monde
Watercolor with white gouache and stitching on layers of
Mylar and handmade paper, 15 × 12 inches

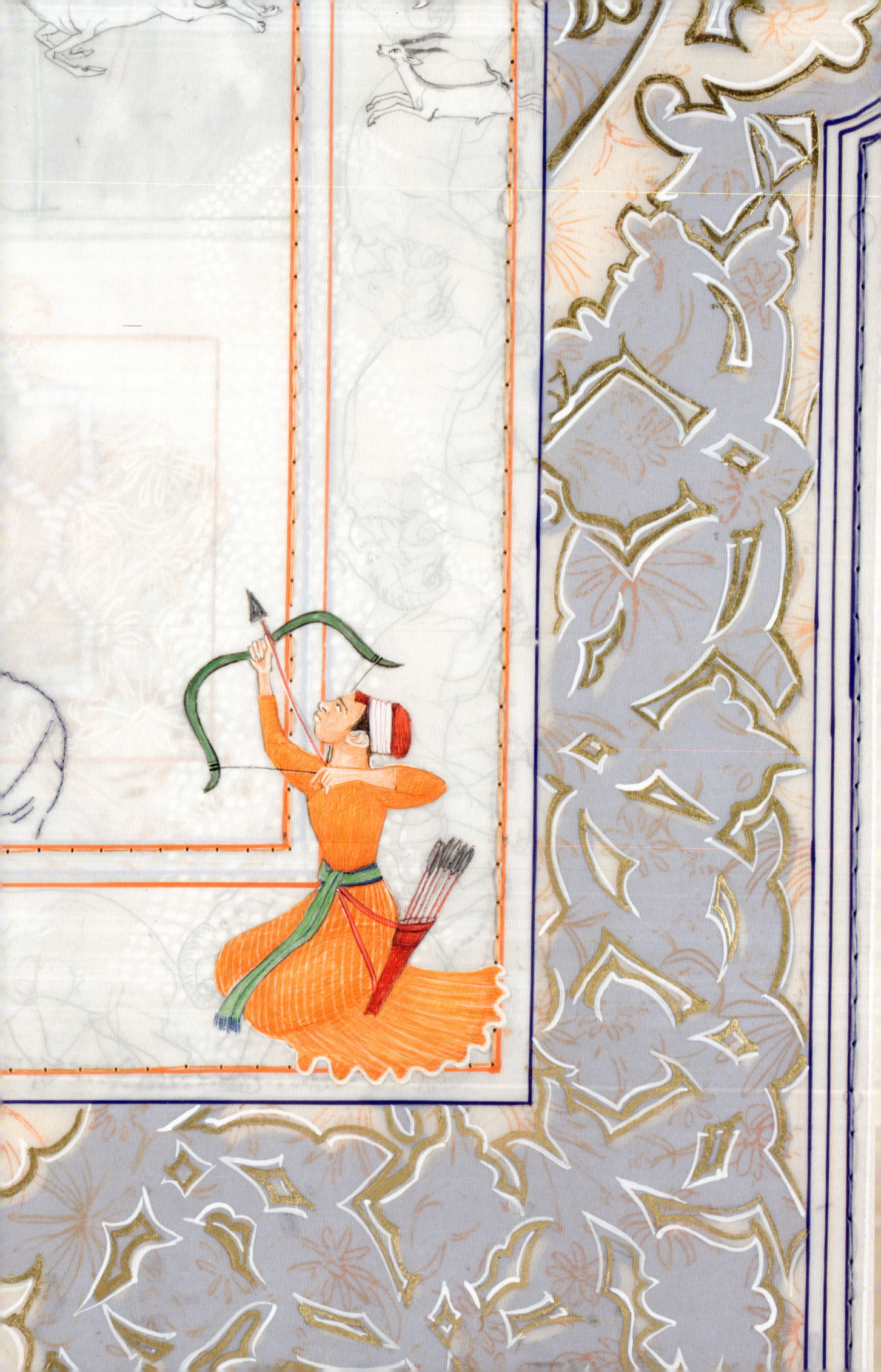

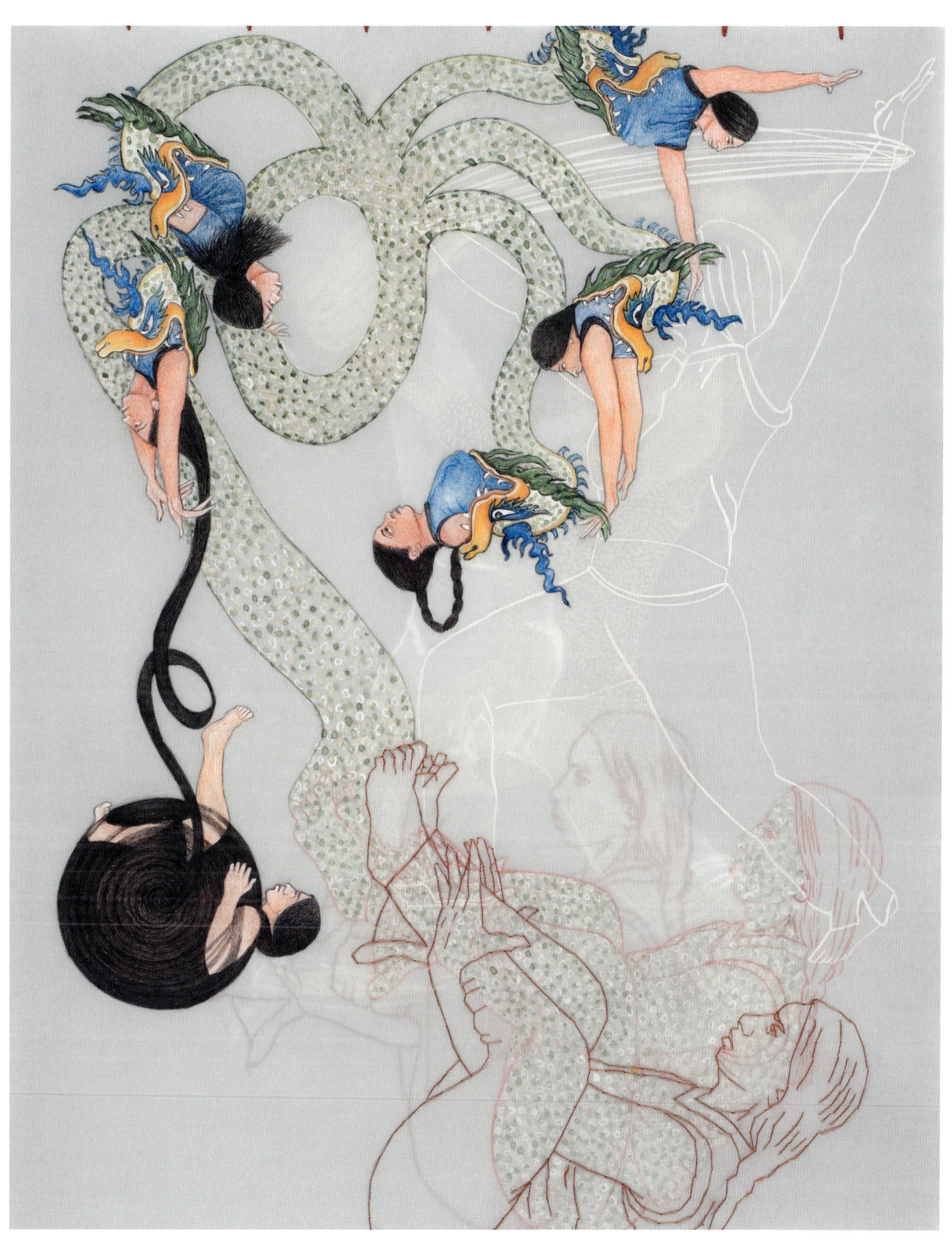

Multiplicité 2006
FROM THE SERIES Cirque Du Monde
Watercolor with white gouache and stitching on layers of
Mylar and handmade paper, 15×12 inches

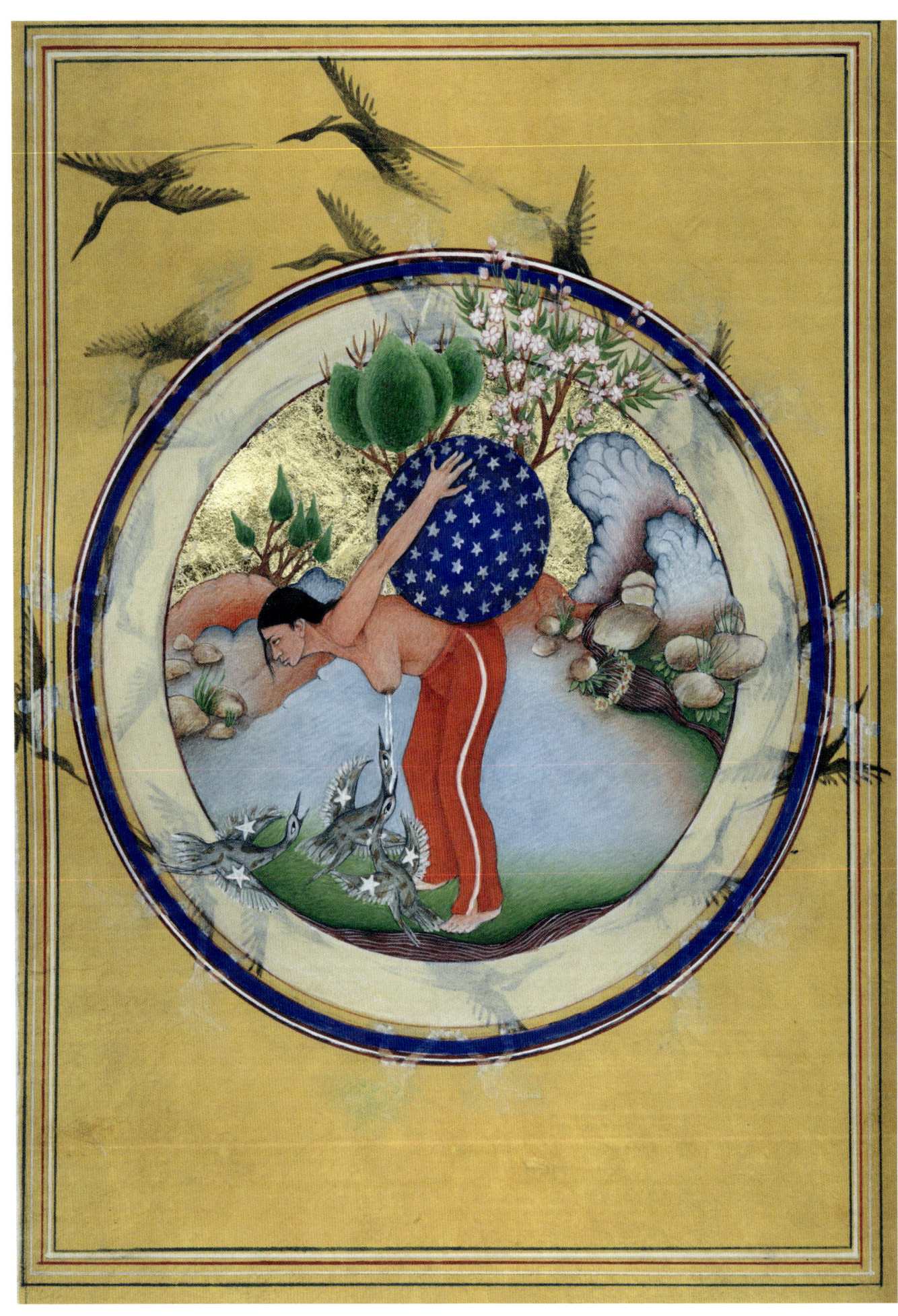

Untitled 2004
from the series I Must Utter What Comes To My Lips
Watercolor, white gouache and gold leaf on wasli paper,
11½ × 8¼ inches

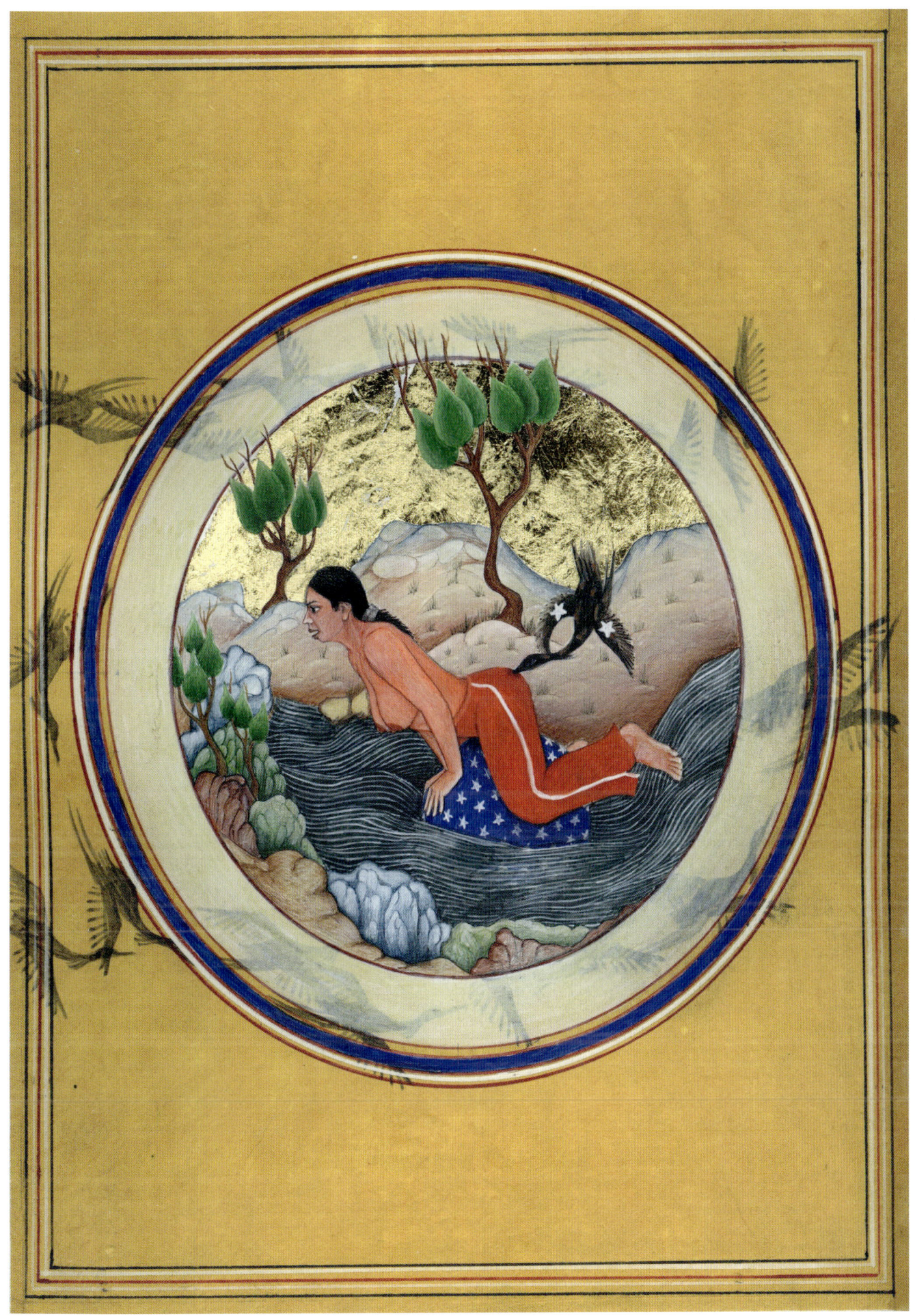

Untitled 2004

FROM THE SERIES **I Must Utter What Comes To My Lips**
Watercolor, white gouache, and gold leaf on wasli paper,
10⅞ × 8⅛ inches

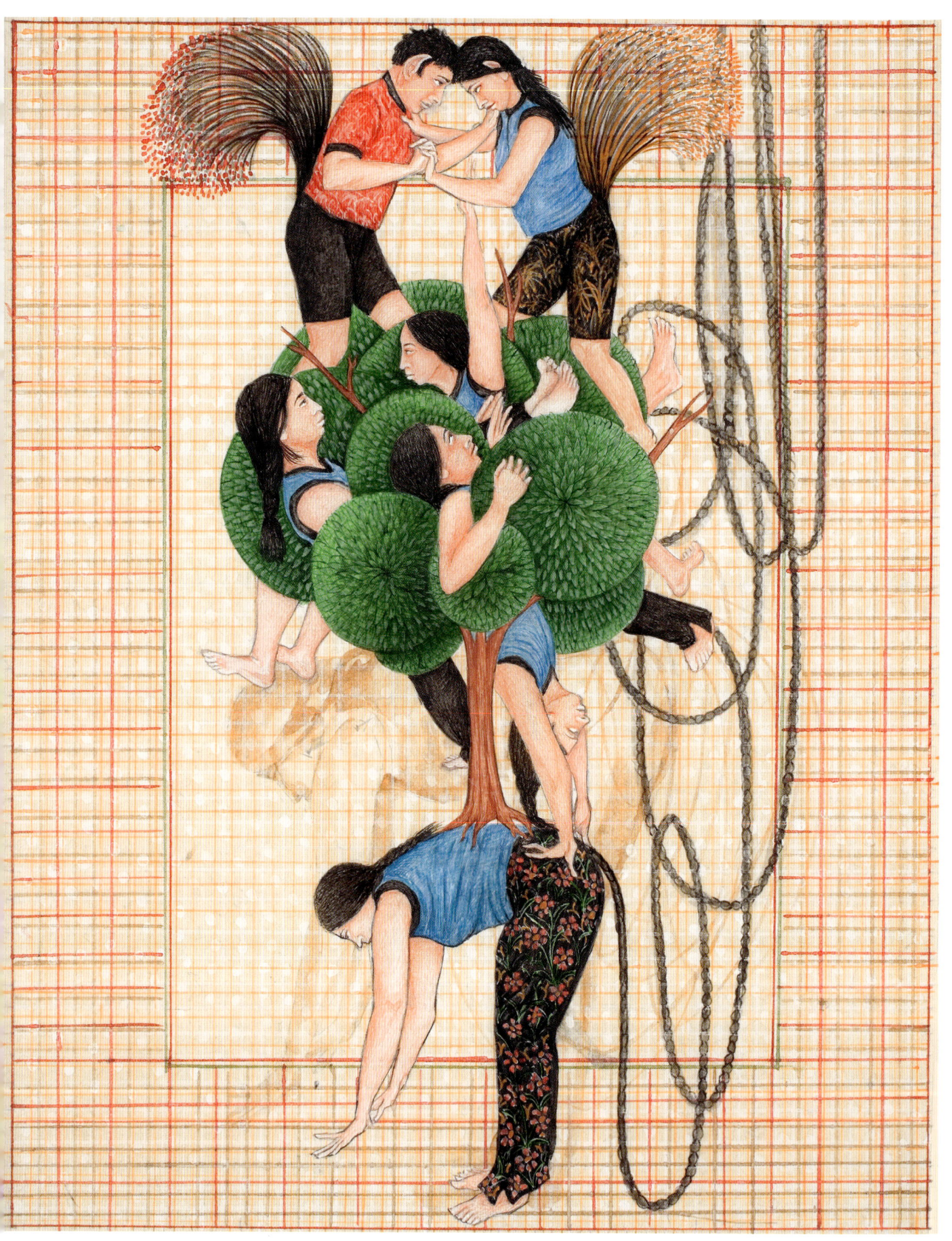

Untitled 2006

FROM THE SERIES Cirque Du Monde
Watercolor, white gouache and tea on handmade wasli
paper, 11×9 inches

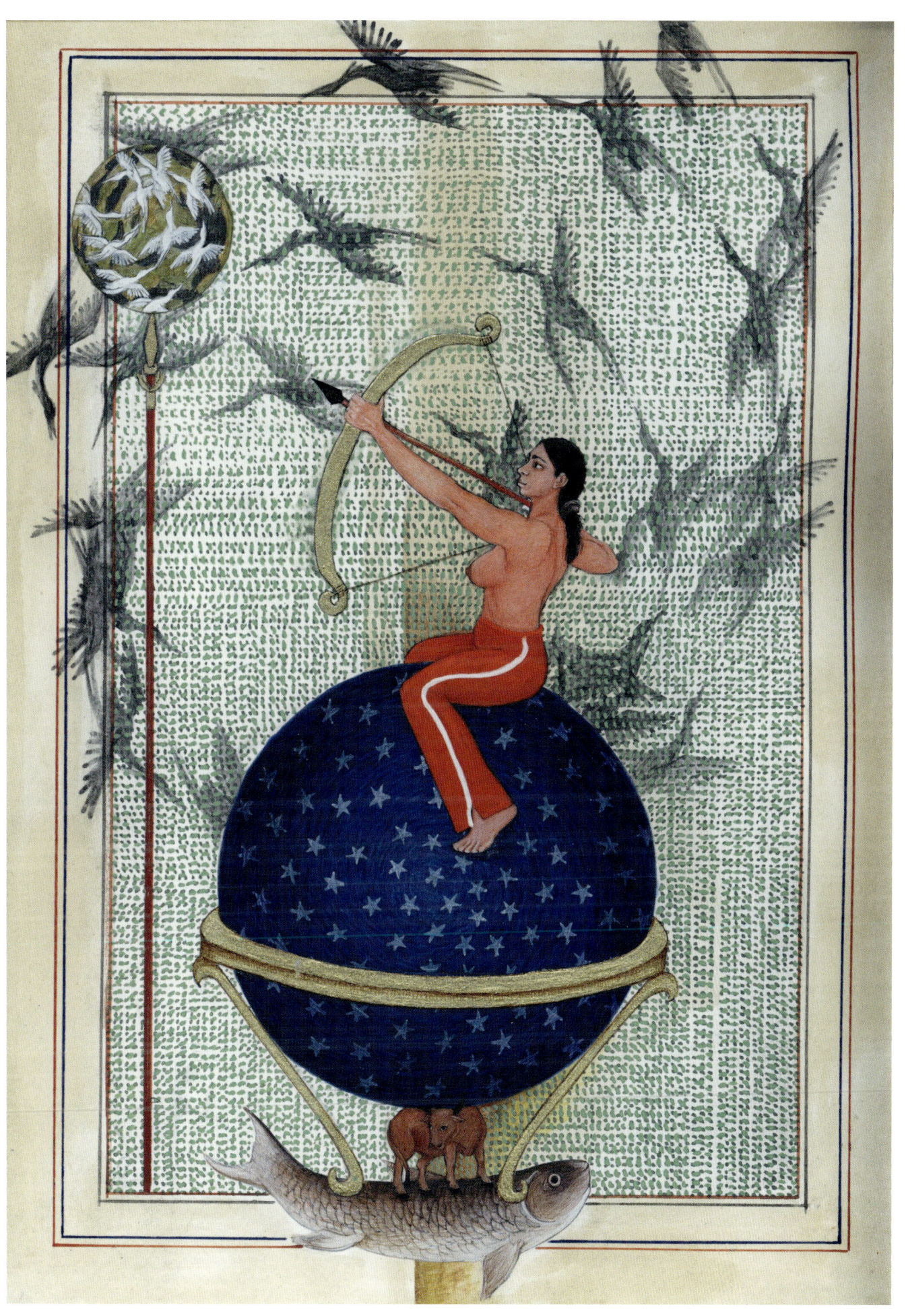

Untitled 2004
FROM THE SERIES **I Must Utter What Comes To My Lips**
Watercolor, white gouache, and gold leaf on wasli paper,
11½ × 8¼ inches

63–64

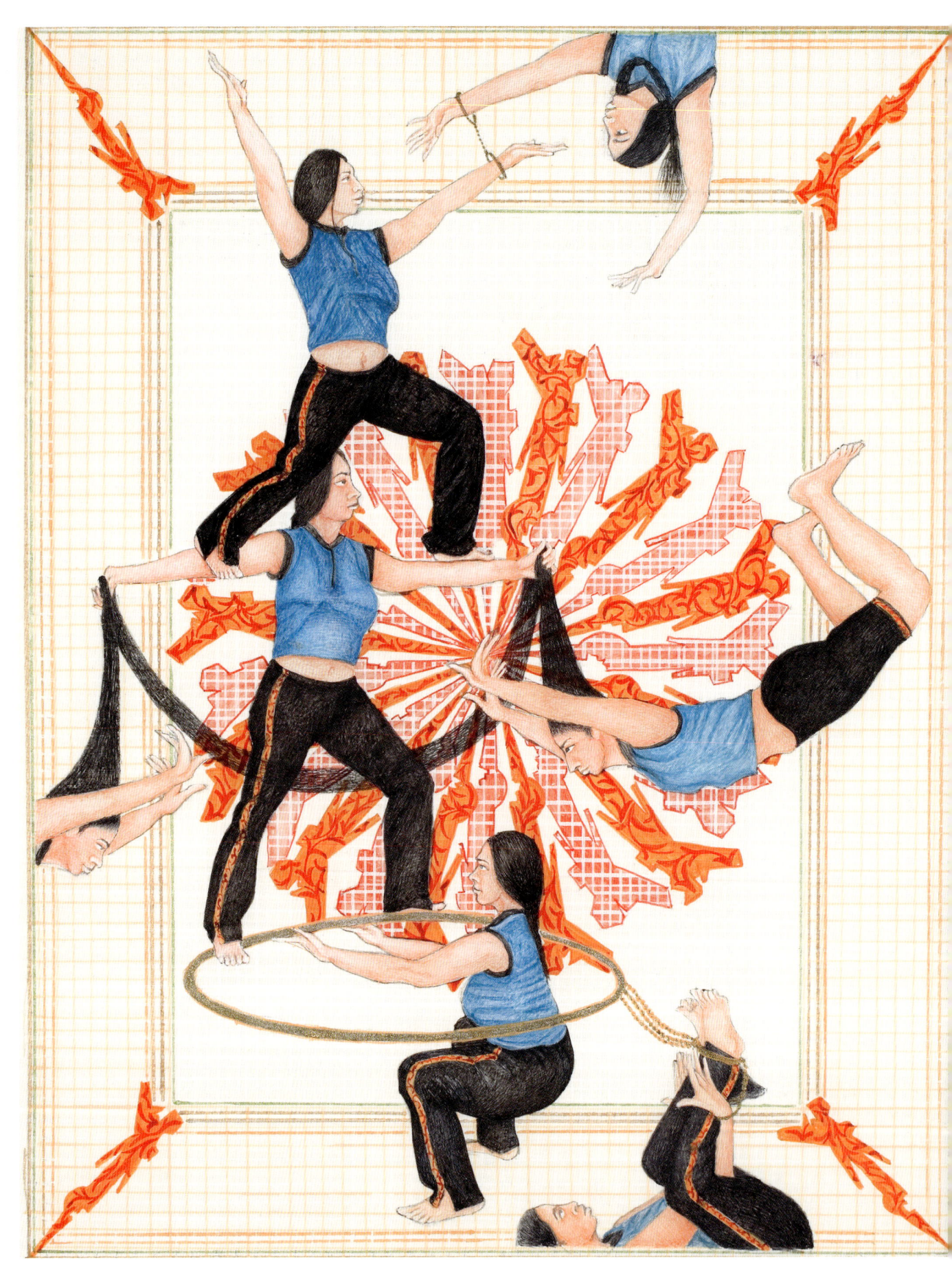

Untitled 2006
FROM THE SERIES Cirque Du Monde
Watercolor, white gouache and tea on handmade wasli
paper, 12½ × 9½ inches

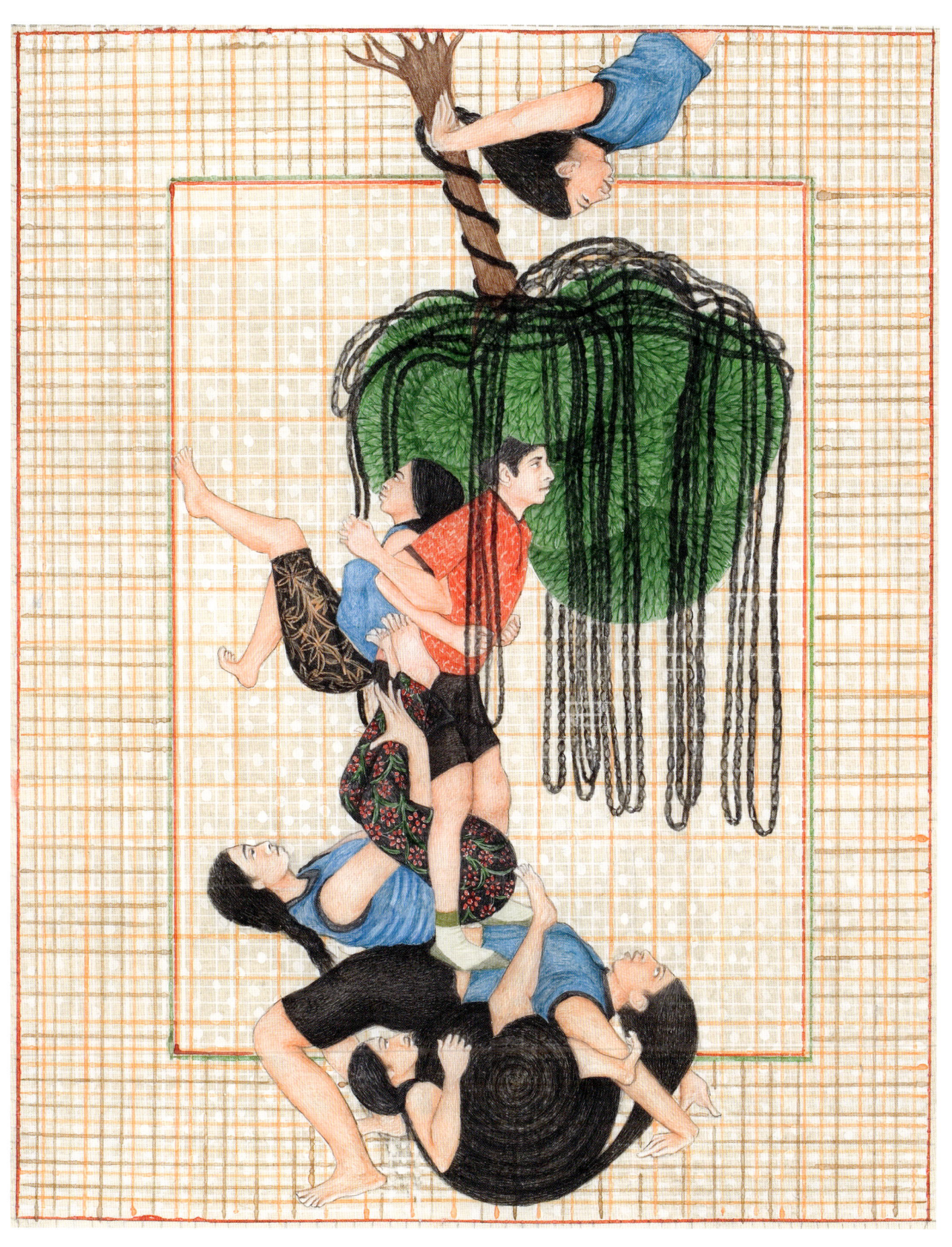

Untitled 2006
<small>FROM THE SERIES</small> Cirque Du Monde
Watercolor, white gouache and tea on handmade wasli
paper, 11×9 inches

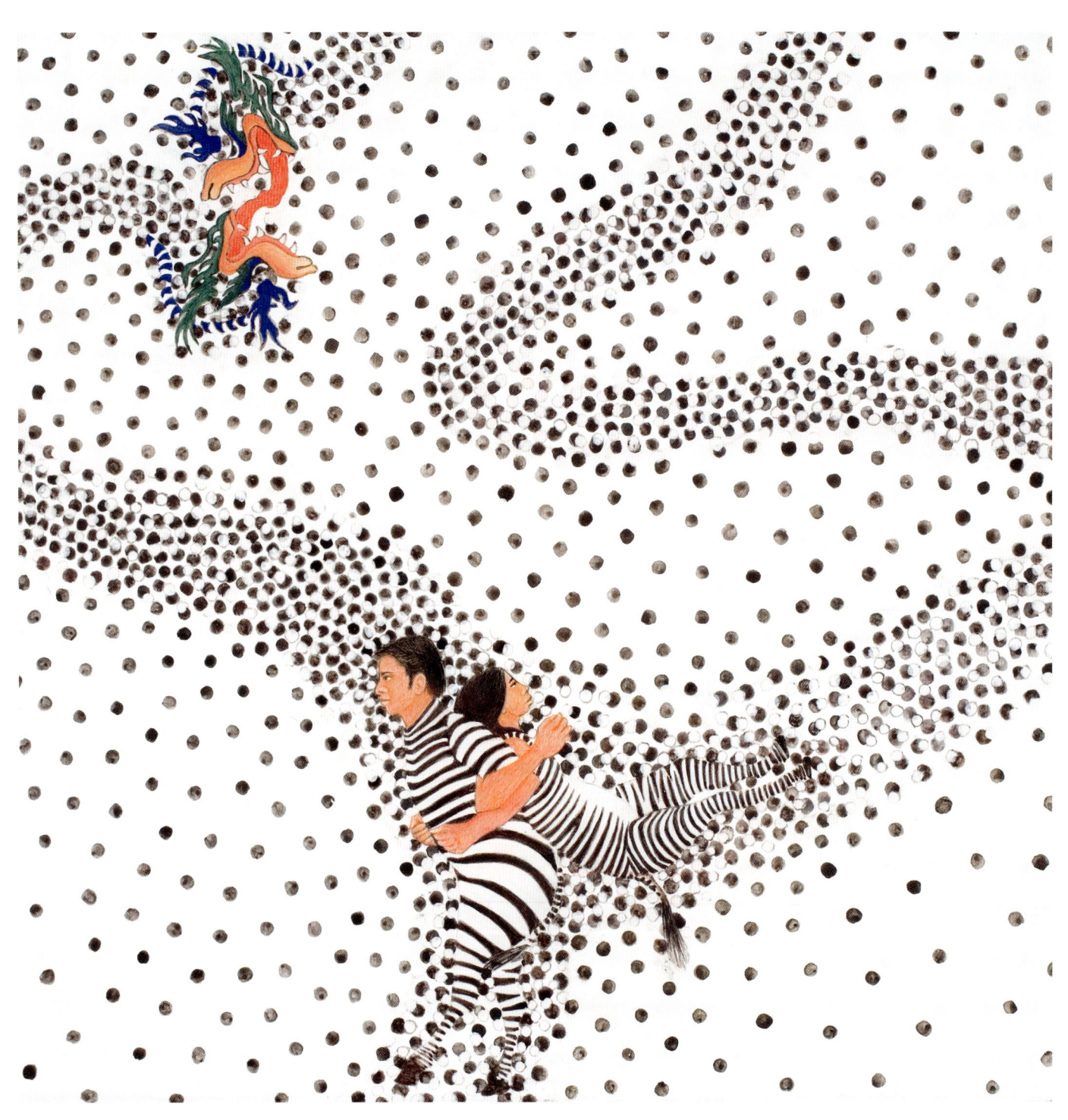

Untitled 2007
FROM THE SERIES Cirque Du Monde
Egg tempera on canvas over panel, 12 × 12 inches

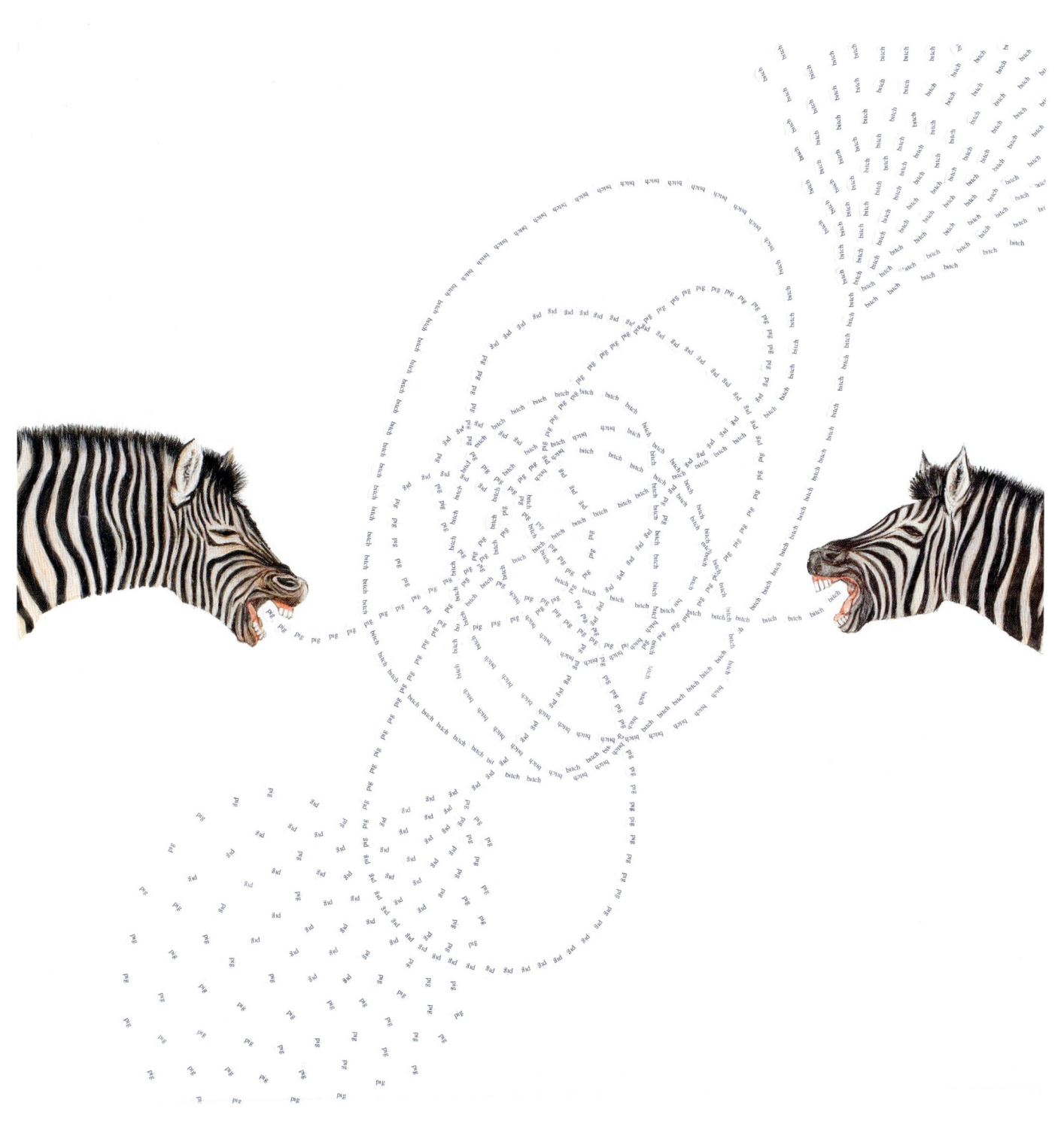

Untitled 2007
FROM THE SERIES Cirque Du Monde
Egg tempera and collage of text on canvas over panel,
12×12 inches

69

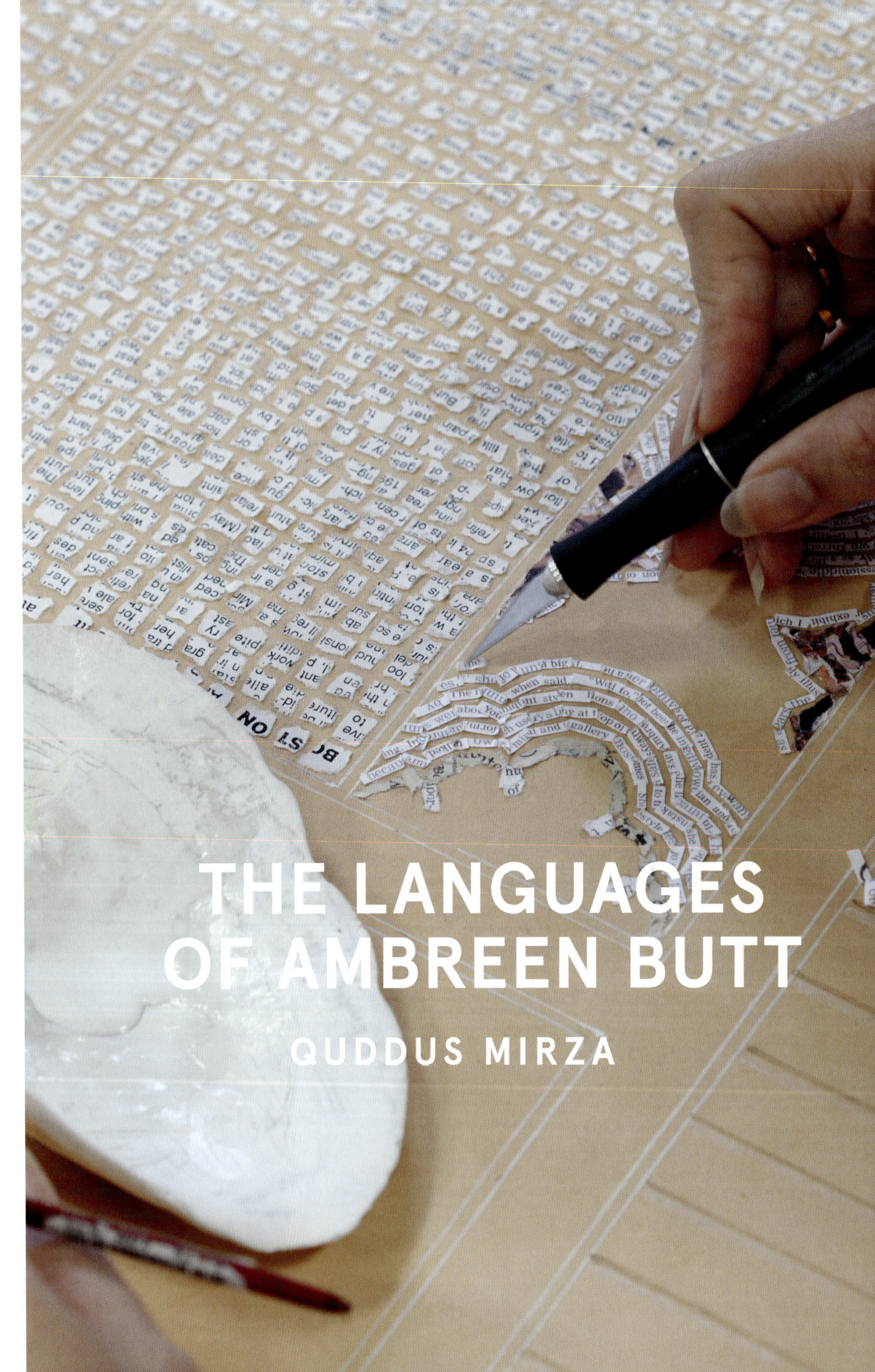

THE LANGUAGES
OF AMBREEN BUTT

QUDDUS MIRZA

In a book of his interviews, the great Israeli novelist Amos Oz reflects upon the creative process thus: "Take an apple. What makes an apple? Water, earth, sun, an apple tree, and a bit of fertilizer. But it doesn't look like any of those things. It's made of them but it is not like them. That's how a story is."[1] This explanation is as true for visual arts as it is for literature. Memory, experience, observation, influences, and process all contribute in the creation of an artwork—one that, in the end, may not look like any of these or even remotely close.

The survival of an artwork is dependent upon independence from its origins; it also depends on its existence, relevance, acceptance, and comprehension over a period of time. The art of Ambreen Butt unfolds a new set of meanings each time one looks at it and tries to locate its context. There are references in the past to the tradition of Mughal miniature, to the more recent ideas of the Clash of Civilizations, the War on Terror, death and destruction caused by militants, political struggle for human rights and democracy, and the presence of women in public space.

From her formative years while studying the art of miniature at the National College of Arts Lahore from 1989 to 1993, to her later works on paper, mixed media, and installations, her feminist position is all too evident. She looks at the world through the lens of gender; especially the way the question of gender is connected with physical, societal, cultural, psychological, and religious backdrops.

Linda Nochlin, in her seminal text *Why Have There Been No Great Women Artists,* recognizes that "like any revolution, the feminist one ultimately must come to grips with the intellectual and ideological basis of the various intellectual or scholarly disciplines—history, philosophy, sociology, psychology, etcetera—in the same way that it questions the ideologies of present social institutions."[2] Judging it against Nochlin's statement, Butt's work transcends a narrow and confined definition and categorization. In its essence, it deals with the personality of the artist, the history of being a woman, and her gender in a male-dominated society like Pakistan. But it also addresses political suppression, the burden of heritage, the hegemony of world powers, voices of the marginalized, and ideological violence. The latter influences, like rain, do not distinguish between genders while drenching people across boundaries.

In *One Thousand and One Nights*, there is a story about a man who, on the threshold of sleep and wakefulness, feels as if a jinnee is transporting him to an unknown destination.[3] Upon arriving at another place, he starts his life, begins a business, gets married, has children, grows old. Lying one night in his room, he senses he has been lifted by the same jinnee, and on opening his eyes, finds himself on the same old bed, forsaken years ago—but it seemed that he had not left for a second.

The fable is a perfect analogy for two phenomena: migration on a massive scale in the 20th century, and the act and outcome of artmaking. In both instances, a person leaves their place, either physically or virtually, but in a sense or in essence is never away from it. One resides in multiple times.

Actually, the matter of time is more urgent for expatriates who are always caught between two time zones. In the newly adopted country, they look at the clock but each time it reminds them of what time it must be in the abandoned homeland. They start seeing their present self in a mirror that holds their culture, history, and land as background. The creative practice of artists and writers who leave their land of origin becomes one such mirror; it becomes their identity.

In the case of Butt, the connection with her roots first emerged around 1999 when the artist began portraying herself in the midst of a whirl or web of hair. These strands, which you can just get cropped at a neighborhood salon, have a serious connotation for South Asian societies. Women, especially from conventional Muslim backgrounds, are not supposed to cut their locks because not only would this be an act against their womanhood—specifically, their beauty —it would be seen as a challenge to norms (or God's gift).

To an extent, for Butt, hair serves as a metaphor for connecting with the abandoned homeland, women's freedom, and an individual's choice in how they want to appear. The association with the homeland is tied to a feminist position because cutting hair can be an act of liberation and emancipation from a culture or homeland for women. These layers of hair are apparent in the mind of Butt when she draws herself with a long, winding mane, encircling the body like an expanding serpent. She snips this whirl of hair, thus releasing herself from several demands. Clipping of hair is a meaningful gesture because it demonstrates the artist's moving beyond conventions of all sorts: identity issues, cultural baggage, artistic heritage, training in a traditional discipline.

Yet hair remains present—as a line and as a lineage. The parallel between hair and line is not uncommon. The line continues in multiple forms and guises throughout Butt's oeuvre. It exists in her series Dirty Pretty, 2008, where images of women and men protesting against the subjugation of the judiciary by Pakistan's then military dictator are drawn with threads. Women lawyers shouting, being dragged into police vans and scuffled by female constables, along with male agitators, are rendered in embroidery on a translucent Mylar sheet.

In these works, the artist keeps coming back to structures, characters, formats, and techniques of miniature painting, which was originally an art of documentation created because "imperial patrons wanted visual records of their deeds as hunters and conquerors."[4] In Dirty Pretty, multiple eras breathe in the same atmosphere. Visuals of female lawyers, captured from news footage, accompany the figures of Mughal royalty engaged in hunting with their bows drawn, arrows aimed, animals targeted. Her compositions denote the story of another hunt, another suppression, another killing—of women, of resistance, of local dissidents such as Dulla Bhatti, Guru Teg Bahadur, or Chhatrapati Sambhaji by the mighty Mughals.

Today, miniature painters are proud to be the heirs of a tradition making elaborate, intricate, and exquisite

[1] Oz, Amos and Shira, Hadad, *What Makes an Apple?,* Princeton: Princeton University Press, 2022, p 3.
[2] Nochlin, Linda, *Women, Art, and Power and Other Essays*, London: Thames and Hudson, 1989, p 145.
[3] Dawood, N. J., ed. *Tales from the Thousand and One Nights*, Baltimore: Penguin Books, 1973.
[4] Danto, Arthur C., *The Madonna of the Future*, Berkeley: University of the California Press, 2001, p 288.

artworks, a legacy of the courts of Mughal emperors in India. What they ignore perhaps is that the history of Mughal India is a cruel chronicle, written with alphabets of war, blood, occupation, exploitation, and deception. Mughal rulers trained cheetahs for their hunts, and took hundreds of them to their expeditions; these beasts attacked deer and other animals for their masters. When Ambreen Butt juxtaposes this visual or historical reference on the page, composing it as a traditional manuscript along with images of ordinary citizens being beaten, manhandled and captured by the police constables, she creates a composite picture of oppressors, collaborators, and victims. Also, in some frames, a ruler and his partner are enjoying the entire hunting spectacle—not unlike our present-day viewers of television and users of social media, exposed to footages of killings, disasters, bombardments, accidents, explosions, all while safely situated in their living rooms, or sipping their drinks at a café.

Sometimes, a medium is not just the message, but a means to dissect ideas, histories, political situations, and existential scenarios. Butt's preference for layers of transparent surfaces is not merely a formal choice; it entails a content beyond the mere depiction of police force and protestors, or a Mughal ruler at his hunting enterprises. The translucent layers of paper, and hence imagery, confirm that what takes place in front of our eyes or on our TV screens—an atrocity, a crime, an act of vanquishing opponents by the rulers—is not a unique phenomenon. It has lingered on in history only with a change of characters, settings, and goals.

This body of work also informs how an act of cruelty can have aesthetic value. People visit museums around the world with collections of Indian miniature paintings, and look admiringly at images of carnage, killing, bloodshed, decapitating opponents, skinning of enemies, or the slaying of animals, because of the usage of chromatic order, mastery in portraying faces, figures, landscape, and extraordinary composition. This is just like the contemporary public experiencing the reportage of war in Ukraine, conflict in the Middle East, or uprising in Sri Lanka. One wonders if the reporter or cameraman are concerned more about the misery that surrounds them or the quality of pictures, all too aware of the power of presentation.

Butt's rendering of imagery in embroidery since 2008 is a major decision in terms of an artist's position and includes another kind of combat, another coat of resistance, another form of feminism—this time through material.

Art materials, even though they might appear meek, neutral and apolitical, have myriad political subtexts. Historically, oil painting has been associated with European men (although now a long list of important women painters has become available from Renaissance to later periods, including Caterina van Hemessen, Sofonisba Anguissola, Artemisia Gentileschi, Judith Leyster, Angelica Kauffman, Anna Seymour Damer, Élisabeth Louise Vigée Le Brun and many more). Butt deconstructs this myth, first by preferring the water-based media used in miniature painting (a non-European mode of image-making), but

more by incorporating embroidery as a medium. Women protesting and assaulted men are drawn in thread.

There is a local lineage too. For many women in traditional societies such as Pakistan, needle and thread are the primary means of image-making. Stylized flowers, geometric patterns, and decorative borders are stitched, crocheted, or appliquéd by women of all ages, regions, classes, and exposures. A number of female artists today, such as Faith Ringgold, have acknowledged this practice as a kosher form of artmaking.

When it comes to art, material is merely a crust to cover the complex system of power. Even gouache on paper in Mughal India was a domain of male painters and patrons. Butt employs the same medium to imagine episodes of a woman's world. Using her own body in her series of paintings titled Cirque Du Monde, 2007, she illustrates herself performing incredible tasks which remind one of a performance in a circus, though her movements signify a greater content. The female protagonist is engaged in impossible acrobatics, and her companions are none other than herself, proving that women can act and accomplish without a male accomplice. Intriguingly, the background of these various impossible acts is reminiscent of the format of traditional miniature painting—especially of those with images enclosed in a decorative border, often having motifs of flowers or animals. In Butt's works these borders include beasts, looking like dragons or have skins which recall the layout and details of the American flag on their coat. The circus of this world is not devoid of violence, with a circular sun of guns or the rotating formation of fighter planes as a backdrop pattern. The same character, a young girl, confronts other demons— creatures which are either domesticated birds, or dragons sprouting from her mouth—like tongues, like language.

These paintings allude to a new world order, one in which the U.S. trained militants against the Russian-supported but local Afghan government and later had to suffer when the "monster" returned for vengeance on 9/11. The girl's tracksuit, as well as the burden on her bare back, suggest the stripes and stars from the American flag. Perhaps, the girl is the great American soul—yet we know she is from the subcontinent (if not specifically resembling the artist). So the natural question is: who is the fighter and who's the victim? Who is the demon and who is the target? The situation becomes further entangled as the demon emerges from her mouth, big, unbearable, unmanageable, and threatening—like words.

Demons are not those made with intricate layers of paint; they are real and can be sighted in different disguises—preying on the dispossessed, de-situated, and marginalized. They can be an imperial power or a home-grown species, like the Taliban in the present day Afghanistan and in the recent past of Pakistan. Pakistan, the country of Butt's origin, suffered carnage, bomb blasts, target killings, and terrorist attacks by the militants bent on imposing their version of Sharia. In the first decade after 9/11, there were explosions, targeting innocent lives at urban sites, including busy markets for

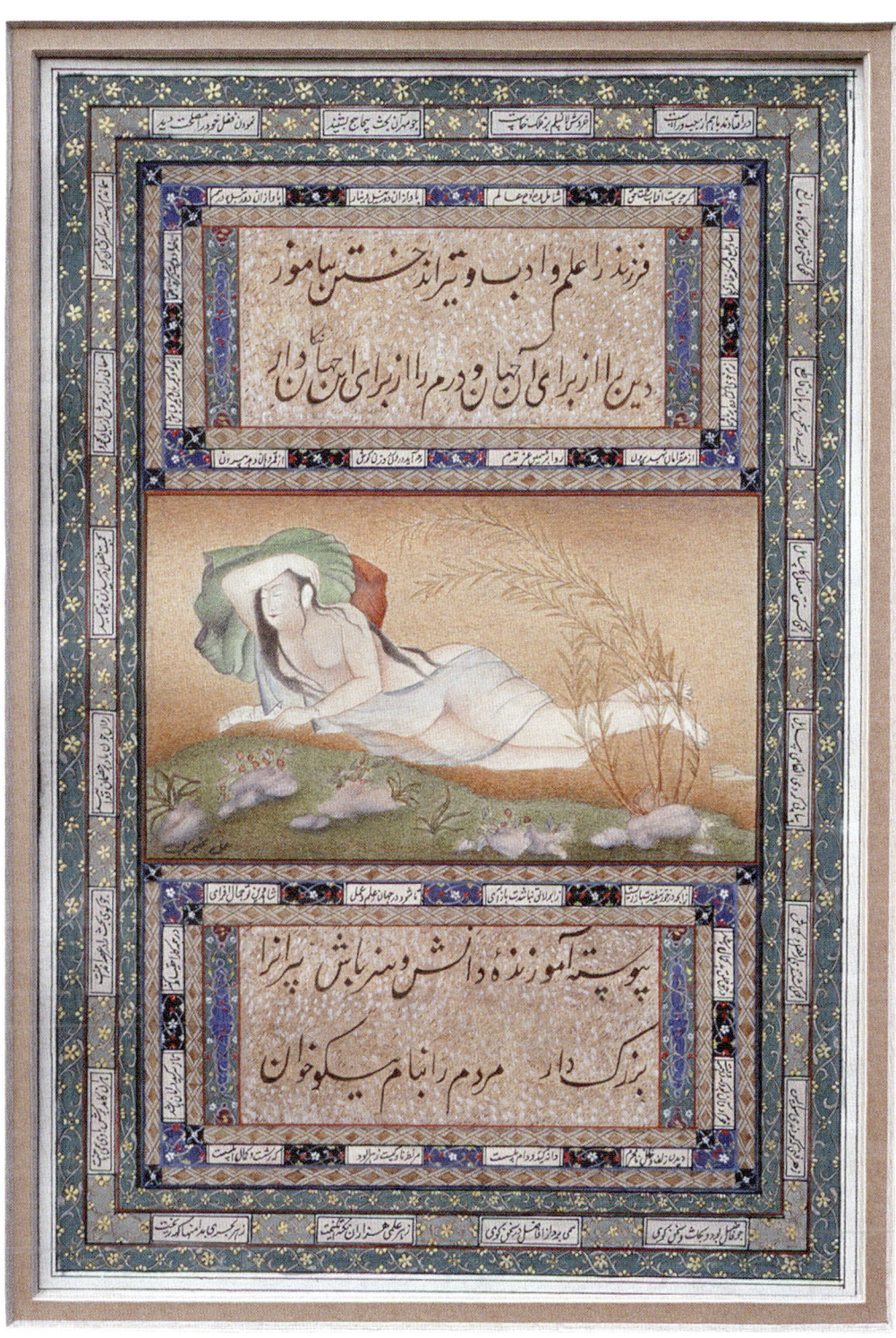

Reclining woman from a study for Persian miniature
painting techniques 1993
Watercolor with white gouache and tea on handmade
wasli paper

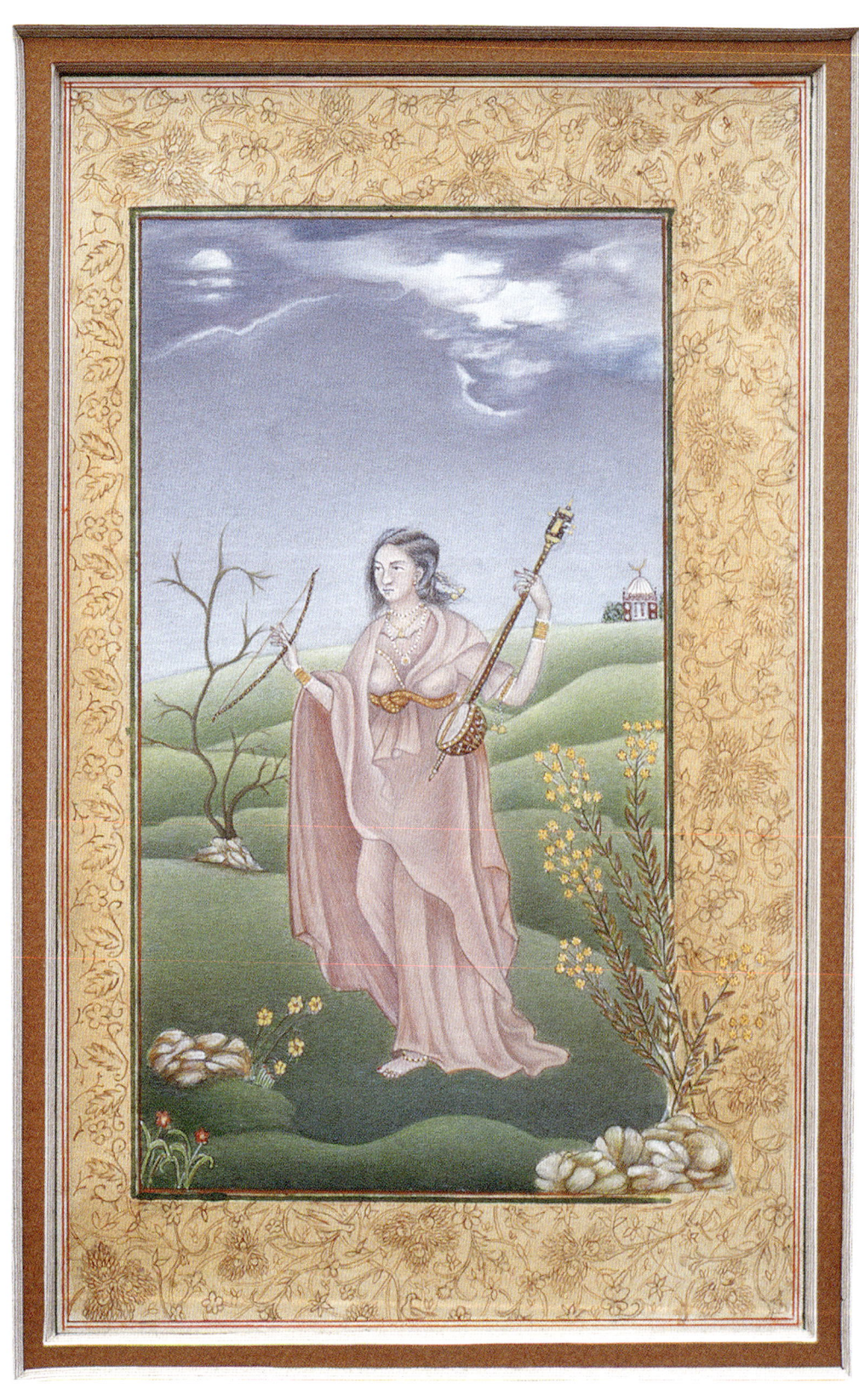

A lady with Ektara from a study for mughal miniature
painting techniques 1993
Watercolor with white gouache and tea on wasli paper

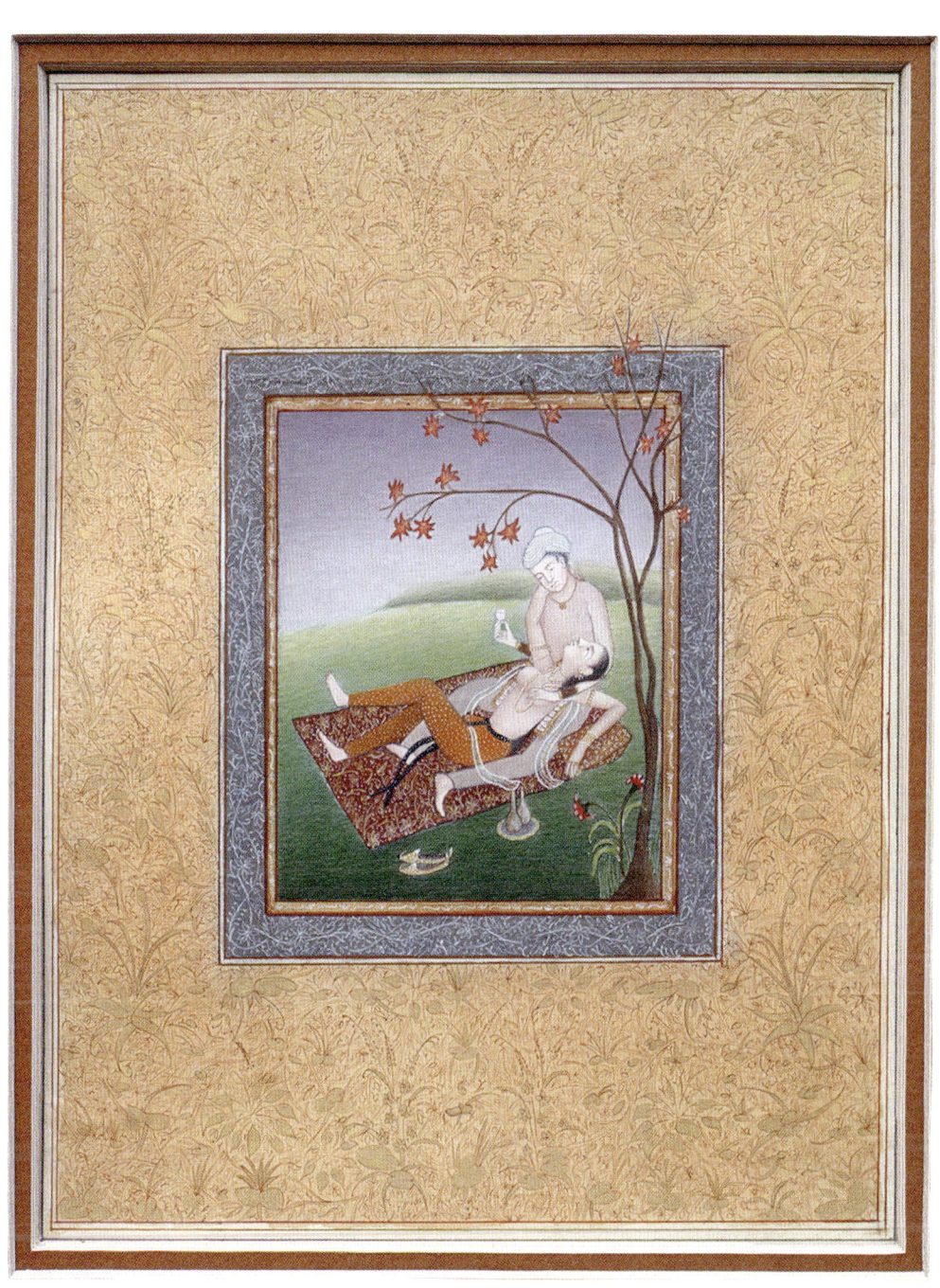

A couple from a study for mughal miniature painting
techniques 1993
Watercolor with white gouache, tea, and gold leaf
on wasli paper

working-class people, mosques during Friday prayers, parks on public holidays, bus terminals, train stations, courts, schools. No place was safe; even funerals and graveyards were targeted. Butt's installation *I Am My Lost Diamond,* 2011–12, refers to one such incident—in fact a close call—in which one of Butt's friends changed her plans to go to a popular shopping area at the last minute and in so doing avoided a bomb blast that claimed many lives.

Language is so deceptive that it immediately reduces living bodies to names, numbers, addresses after they are hit by a terrorist attack. I have never been to an actual site of a terrorist attack, but looking at the footage I realize that thoughts, desires, longings, aspirations, failures, frustrations, memories, and future strategies all end up as scattered parts of the body. Unnameable, unapproachable, untouchable, unrecognizable.

In *I Am My Lost Diamond,* Butt recalls that phase in which life was a lease from chance. The artist once lost one of her toenails and learned how traumatic it was to part even with one such insignificant segment. Losing a toenail is like losing a precious object, a diamond. But life is much more than a precious crystal, or a toenail. When it is lost, like the ground of an air crash or the site of a terrorist attack, it offers bits and pieces to construct the whole. In Butt's installation, there are casts of toes and fingers, either on the wall as an eruption, or on the floor like a prayer rug—both formations deeply rooted in the practices of present-day Islam. In a sense, these replicas comment on voyeuristic consumption, no different from watching the news footage of dismembered bodies at the location of the latest terrorist attack.

Alongside the reportage of these attacks, society's turn towards religious cleansing has led to episodes of mob killing of those accused of blasphemy in Pakistan. The devotees do not want to see any document, proof, truth, or hear the accused's version, but prefer to act as complainant, prosecutor, judge, and executor in the span of a few hours. This has happened to several families belonging to minority faiths, individual Muslims and even to Salman Taseer, the Governor of Punjab, Pakistan's largest province. In January 2011, he was gunned down by one of his own security staff, Mumtaz Qadri, because he had questioned the man-made law of blasphemy that had landed a poor Christian woman in jail. (This is a crime that reminds of another Salman—Salman Rushdie, of course—whose book was publicly burnt in 1989. This violence reaffirmed Heinrich Heine's line from his 1821 play *Almansor:* "Where they burn books, they ultimately burn people".)

An artist is not a holder of truth but its maker. In her work *Out Beyond The Ideas Of Rightness & Wrongness, There Is A Place, I'll Meet You There,* 2012, Butt produces a transition between the killer and the deceased. A finely drawn portrait of Mumtaz Qadri swiftly merges and ends up as the picture of Salman Taseer, asserting that there is hardly a difference between the sufferer and the aggressor. In a postcolonial society, one comes across colonized people behaving as their white masters. Both

Qadri, the killer, and Taseer, the martyr, are two sides of a coin that is slowly turning into a one dimensional entity, dissolving into one another.

For many makers of literature, like J. M. Coetzee (as in his novel *Disgrace*), it is impossible to distinguish between the accused and the procurator. In a world after 9/11, it is increasingly difficult to discern between the responses of various participants in a spectacle. As Arthur C. Danto notes, "The composer Karlheinz Stockhausen proclaimed as 'the greatest work of art ever' the terrorist attack on the World Trade Center in New York on September 11, 2001".[5] This observation is not different from the sentiments of millions of moviegoers—perfectly peaceful and law-abiding citizens otherwise—for whom the villain, a character who indulges in manslaughter, stabbing, robbery, and arson, could be adorable (as happens in Quentin Tarantino's movies).

Actually this split between good and evil, right and wrong, or charity and crime, is an individual's private problem. In Islam, sin and virtue are documented by two separate angels perched on each shoulder of every human being. It is also a society's dilemma when a populace finds it hard to choose or even differentiate between the two sides. When it comes to perpetrators of terrorism in Pakistan, many have supported their deeds as truly following the diktats of Islam. One such sympathizer led a mosque and seminary in the capital city of Pakistan. In 2007, a majority of the female students at this seminary, clad in black burqas and carrying sticks in hand, tried to force their orthodox doctrine onto their neighborhood. This militancy had to be controlled by the Pakistani armed forces.

The dichotomy which attracts Butt to produce her etchings *Daughters Of The East,* 2008—a mob of burqa-clad women brandishing their batons in a sky populated with ladybugs—is a crucial point for the artist, especially one who happens to be female and diasporic. It's a difficult position, because those young women asserting their physical and religious power were in a way empowering women in a male-dominated society. A debate was extended by several theorists including Saba Mahmood[6], but it created doubts in the minds of many who viewed these liberated fanatics as a threat to the freedom of one's own beliefs, practices, and preferences.

In a sense, the confusion in the realm of politics, religion, and gender is not too distinct from the doubt of a creative person. You know that the text is perfect, the picture is complete, the sculpture is finished, the video installation is ready, yet you are not confident about the truth of what you have created in the solitude of your studio. You survive in speculations, like a community which has to cope with the "truth." But whose truth? In Butt's *Pages Of Deception,* 2011–12, statements both defending and persecuting a young American of Arab origin, charged with terrorist links to the Middle East, are placed side by side in a format reminiscent of court decrees, or official manuscripts of Mughal India, or even the opened pages of holy books (as well as Butt's circular paintings with the artist's figure amid a spin of hair from 1999). Presenting opposite

[5] Danto, Arthur C., *The Abuse of Beauty*, Chicago and Illinois: Open Court, 2005, p 18.
[6] Mahmood, Saba, *Politics of Piety: The Islamic Revival and the Feminist Subject*, Princeton: Princeton University Press, 2012.

accounts, both of the accused and the accuser, is a way of seeking the final truth, because both versions, no matter how conflicting, may allude to a uniform fact.

This is not political hegemony nor religious fervor but the power of words—how language becomes a tool as well as a trap in our circumstances. Words explain, yet also confine or restrict, because as soon as I utter the word "stone," I eliminate "pebble," "rock," "boulder," and "gravel" from my discourse. In a sense, speaking is censoring. By choosing one idea, one expression, one phrase, a person discards other possibilities.

Although Butt has collected transcripts of defense and persecution, she rips them. She shreds them to become circular and identical patterns of linear and lettered marks in *Call Me a Blasphemy*, 2011. She has dismembered something else also: the blasphemy law in present-day Pakistan. It is a document which is almost untouchable today (Salman Taseer was assassinated for questioning the rationale behind this local parliamentarians' amendment), but which regularly targets innocent lives in a religion-infested environment. Butt transforms this text along with arguments for plea or documents to keep the accused behind bars for indefinite years into small pieces of paper which are joined to make circular shapes. Eternal rounds of blasphemy become a pastiche on paper in the end—like the testimony of someone condemning another for sacrilegious acts.

Political, religious, and cultural connotation of spoken or written words (testimonies, statements, legal documents, detail of decrees) when touched by the hand of an artist, become questionable. Records of legal proceedings, or a recently added section of law, accusations of political or international crimes, and proclamation of innocence all end up as stripes of phrases, broken, and rearranged, not in a logical order. This somehow echoes Dayanita Singh's photographs of records, documents and folders of legal cases kept in government offices, immense accumulation, which with "the passage of time makes everything meaningless."[7]

In Butt's work, it is the language which is scattered, shattered, split, strayed, and stayed to create other contents. Language seems to be the real concern for her because, as a person trained in Mughal miniature painting, the narrative aspect of images was evident and intriguing. In her later art pieces, language may have waited in the wings, but works with shredded parts of court proceedings, crucial code of Pakistani law, as well as pieces of her journals, are about body, truth, and the supremacy of language.

Whether organizing text as a pictorial arrangement, or approaching visuals as codes, language becomes an important and open-ended tool for Butt, not unlike the Romanian peasant who, on a query by the Croatian author Dubravka Ugrešić about what he prays, replied that every morning he uttered the entire alphabets, and now it was up to the Lord what prayers He liked to make out of these 26 letters.

[7] Pamuk, Orhan. *Images you can Smell*. (UK: *Guardian*, 21 June 2022) https://www.theguardian.com/artanddesign/2022/jun/20/novelist-orhan-pamuk-dayanita-singhs-mesmerising-photos-indias-disintegrating-archives.

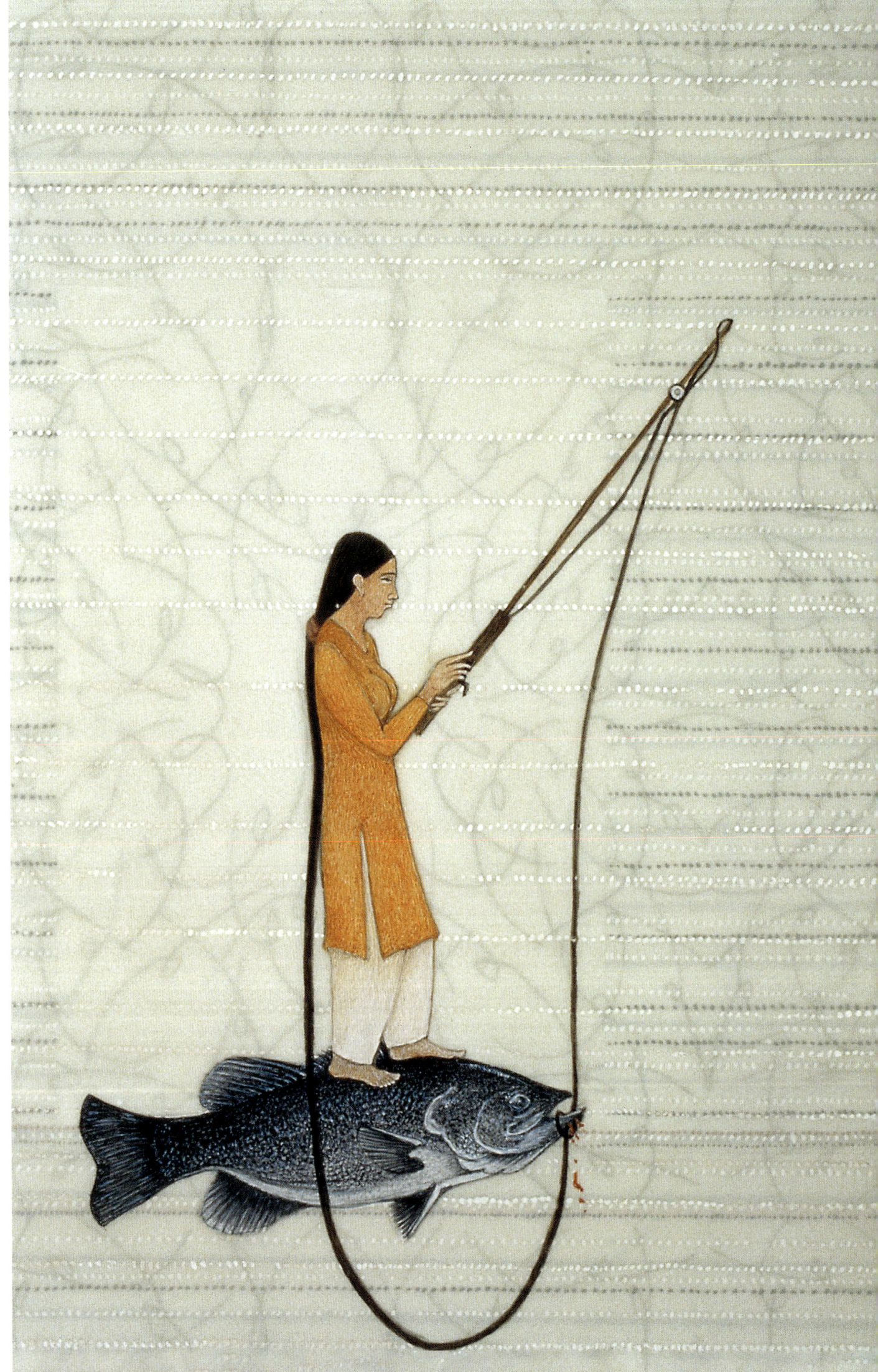

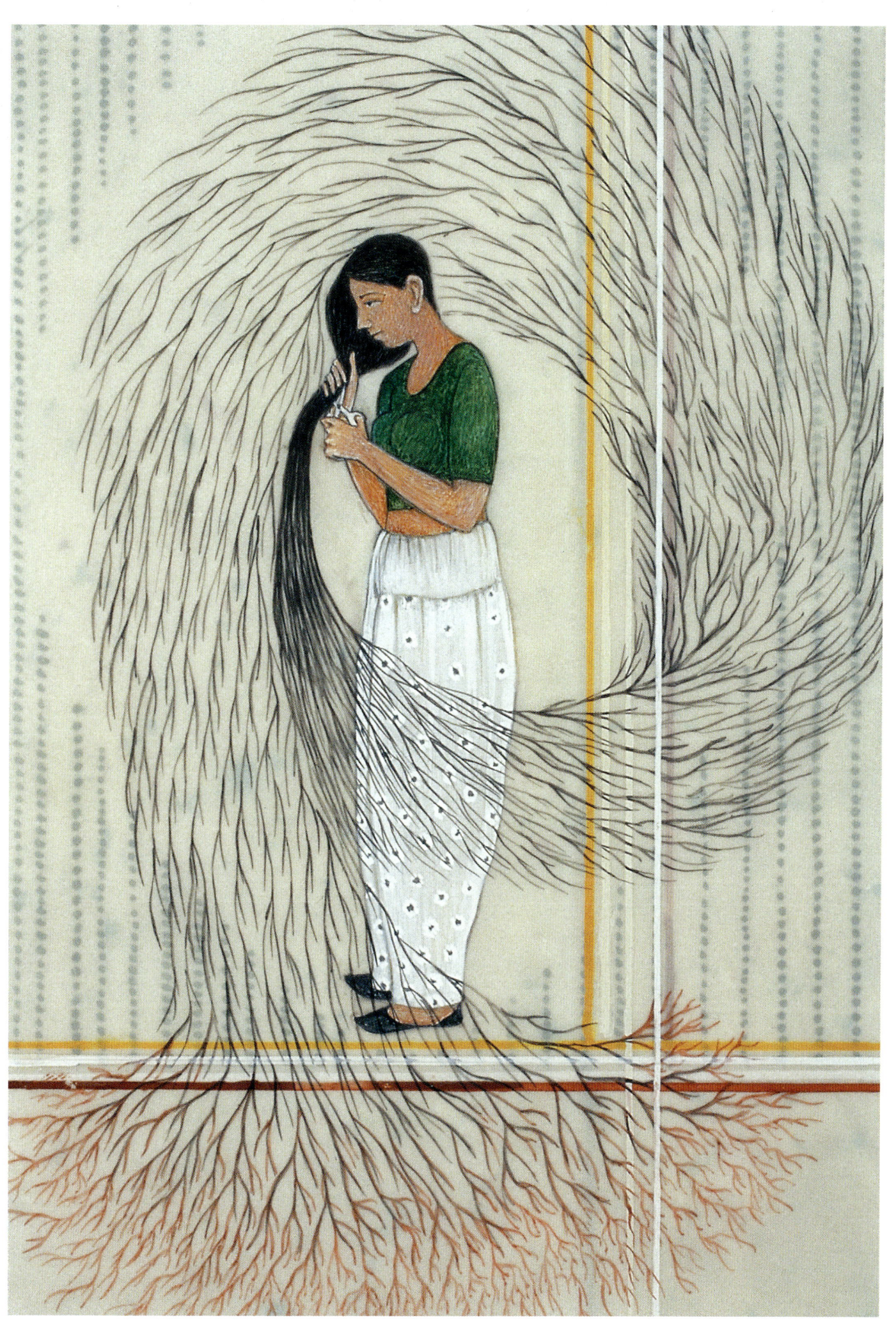

OPPOSITE AND ABOVE (DETAILS) *Untitled* 1999
FROM THE SERIES Bed Of My Own Making
Watercolor with white gouache and stitching on layers of
Mylar, 18 × 15 inches

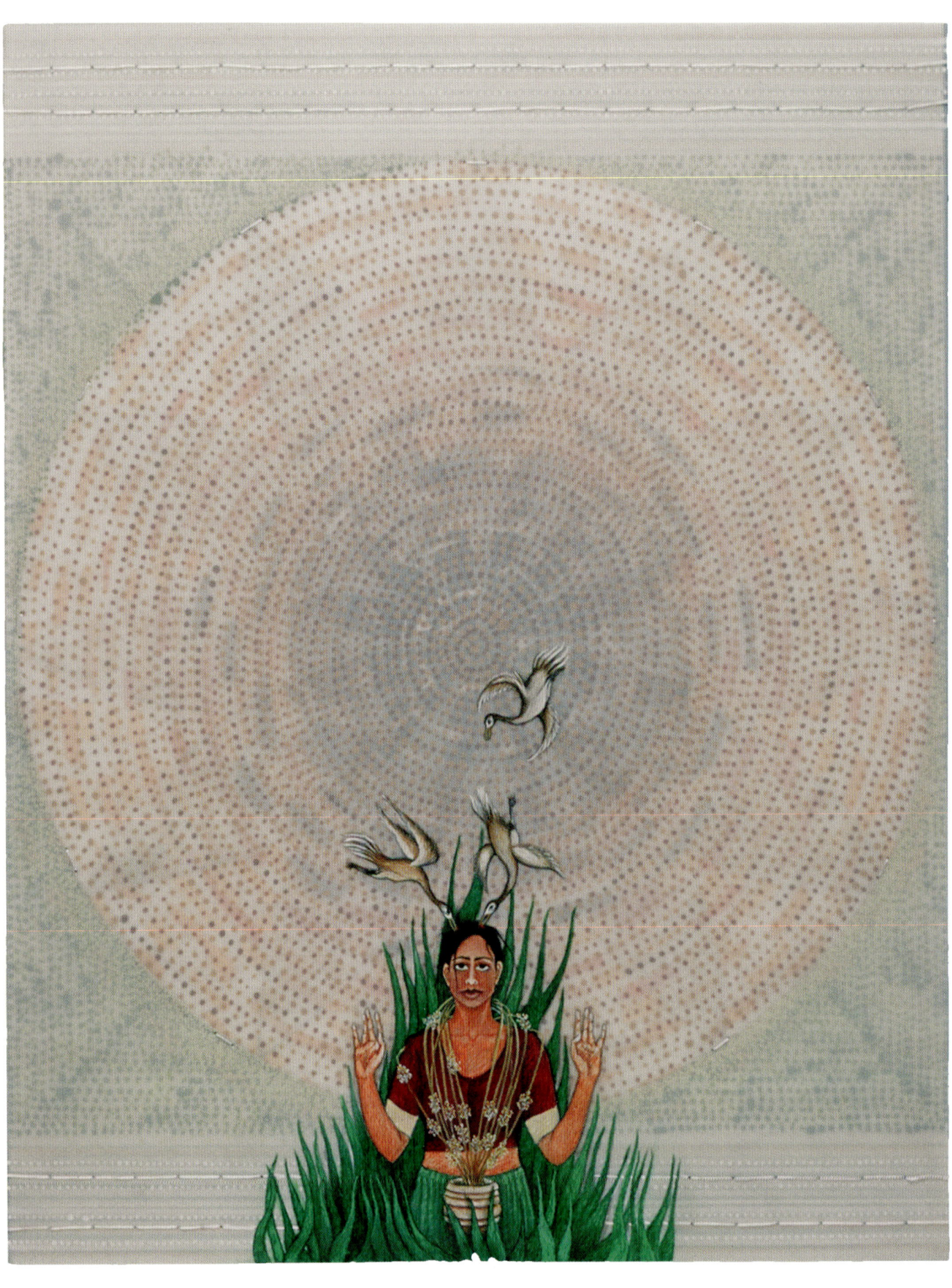

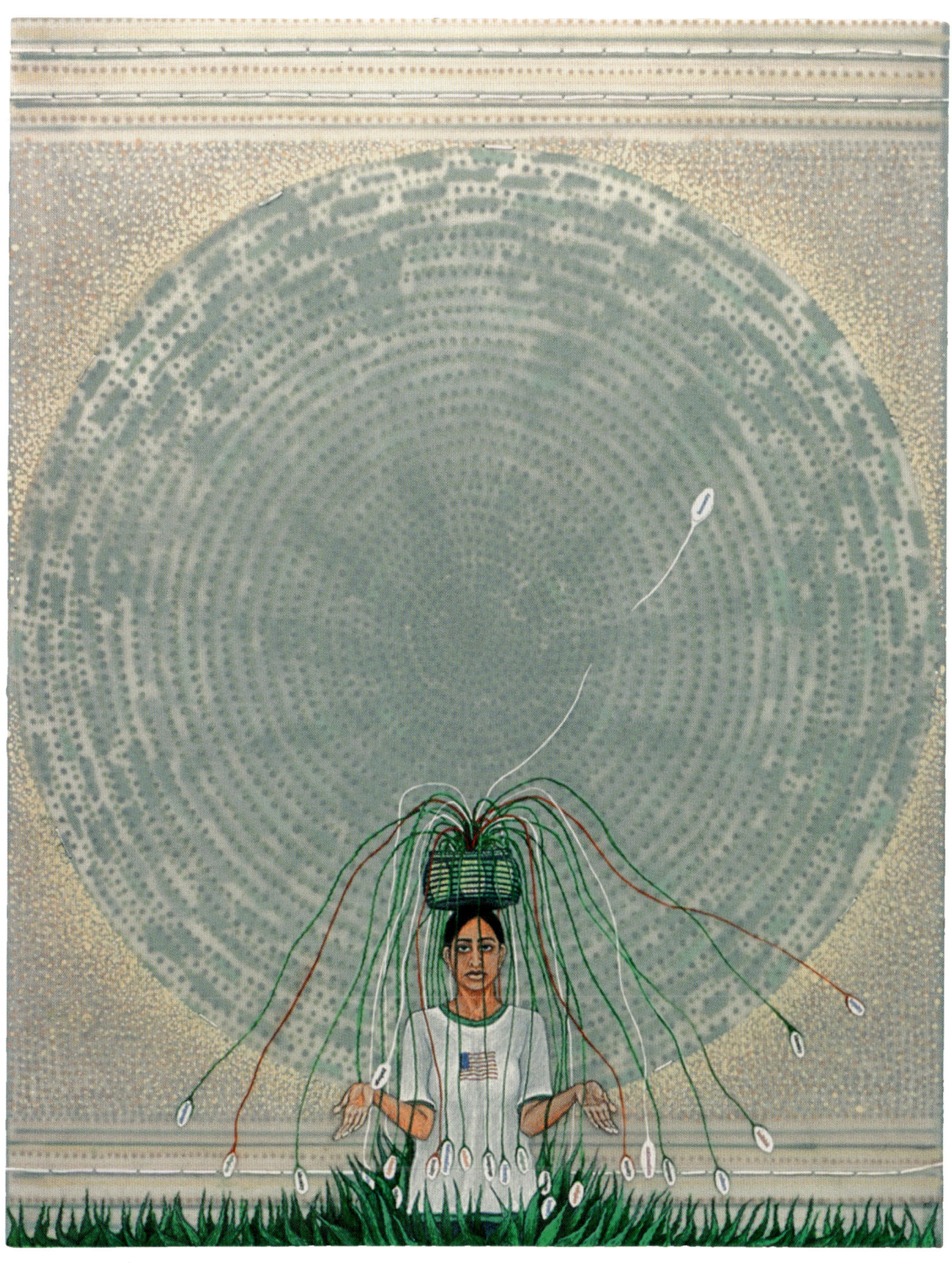

OPPOSITE/ABOVE **Untitled** 2001
FROM THE SERIES Home And The World
Watercolor, white gouache, collage and stitching on layers of
Mylar, 14 × 11 inches

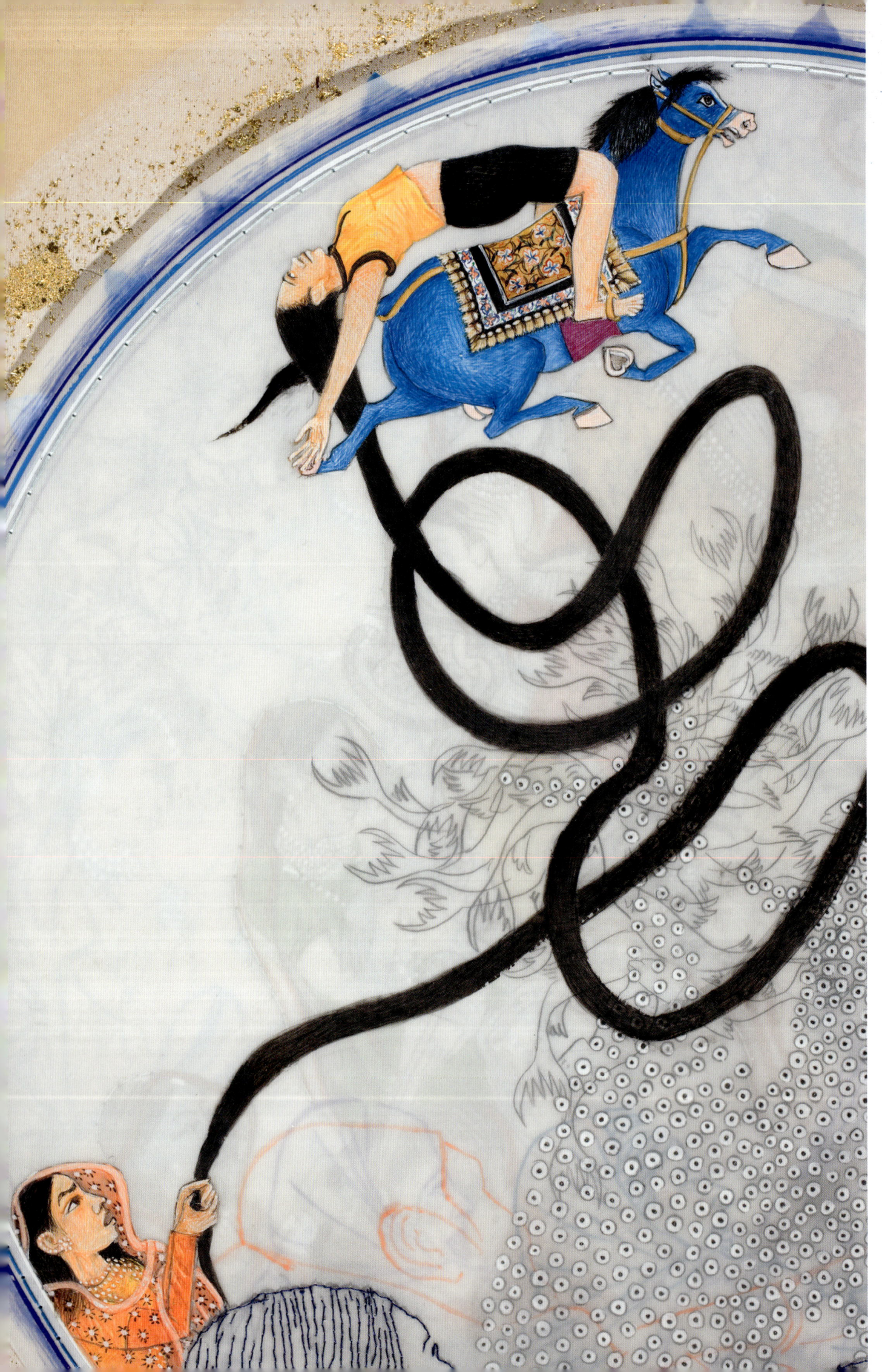

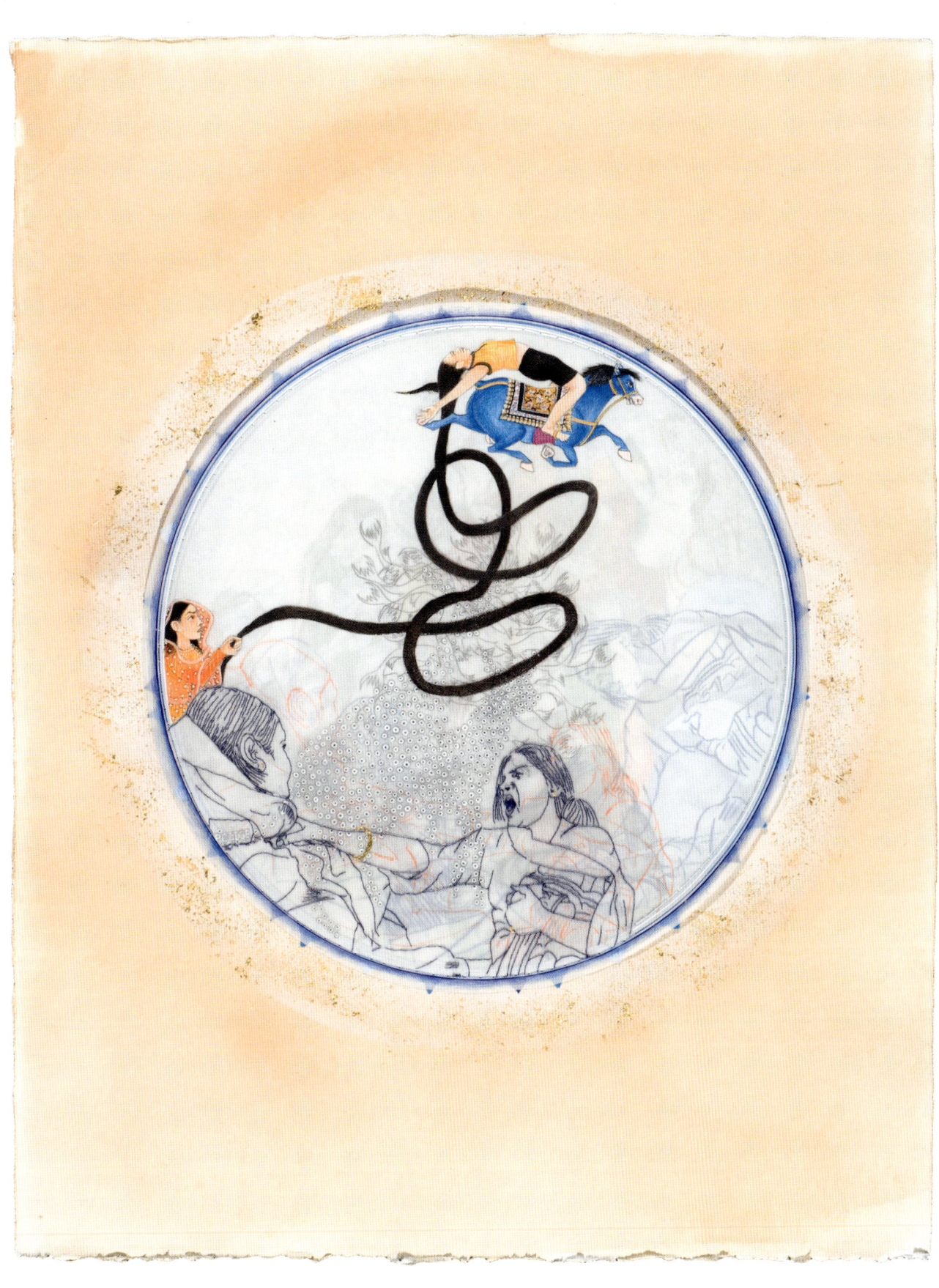

OPPOSITE (DETAIL)/ABOVE **Untitled I** 2008
FROM THE SERIES Dirty Pretty
Pigments, white gouache, text, thread, gold leaf on Mylar
and tea-stained paper, 28 × 20 inches

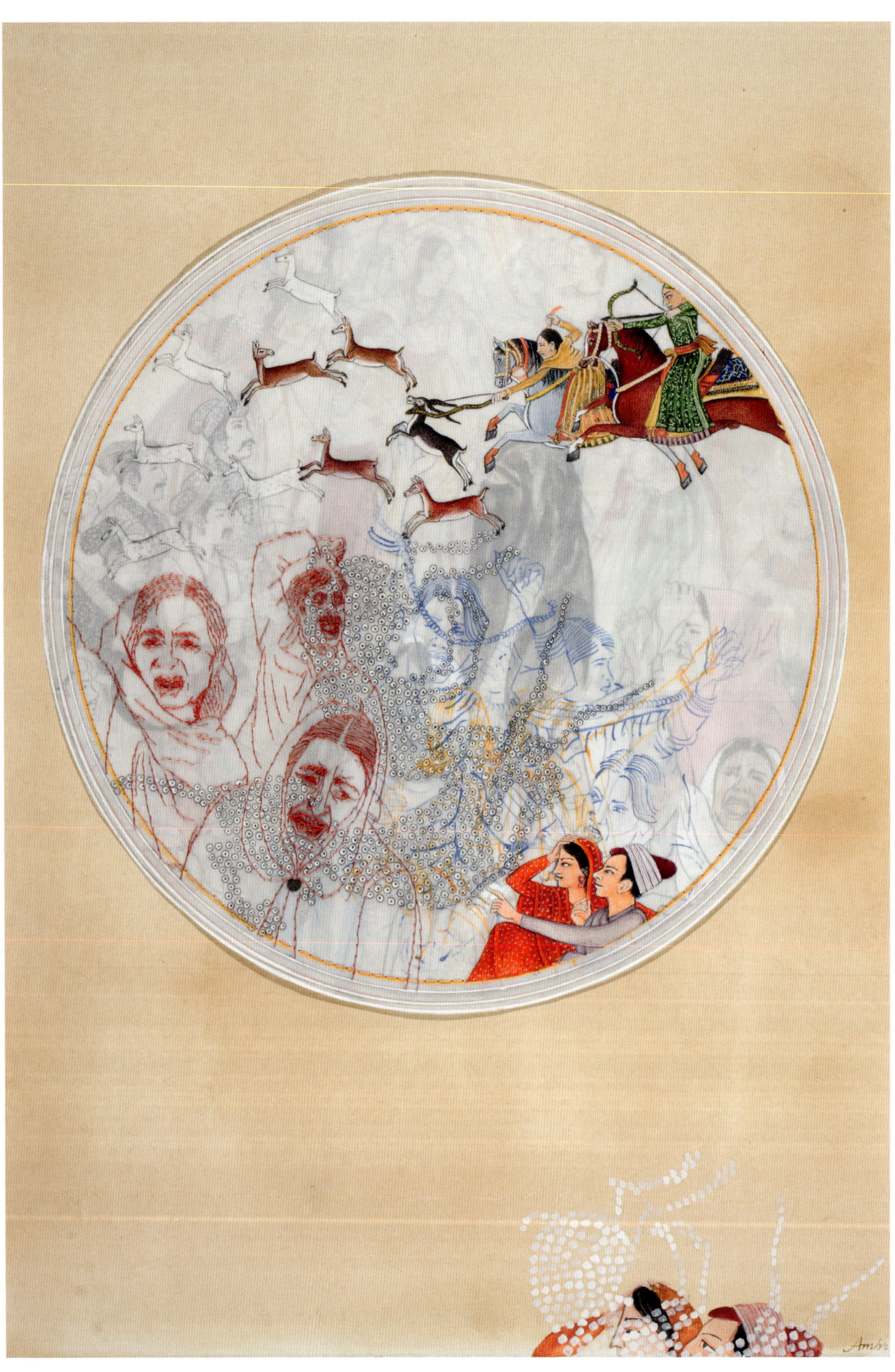

ABOVE/OPPOSITE (DETAIL) *Untitled 2* 2008
FROM THE SERIES Dirty Pretty
Pigments, gouache, text, thread, gold leaf on Mylar
and tea-stained paper, 28 × 20 inches

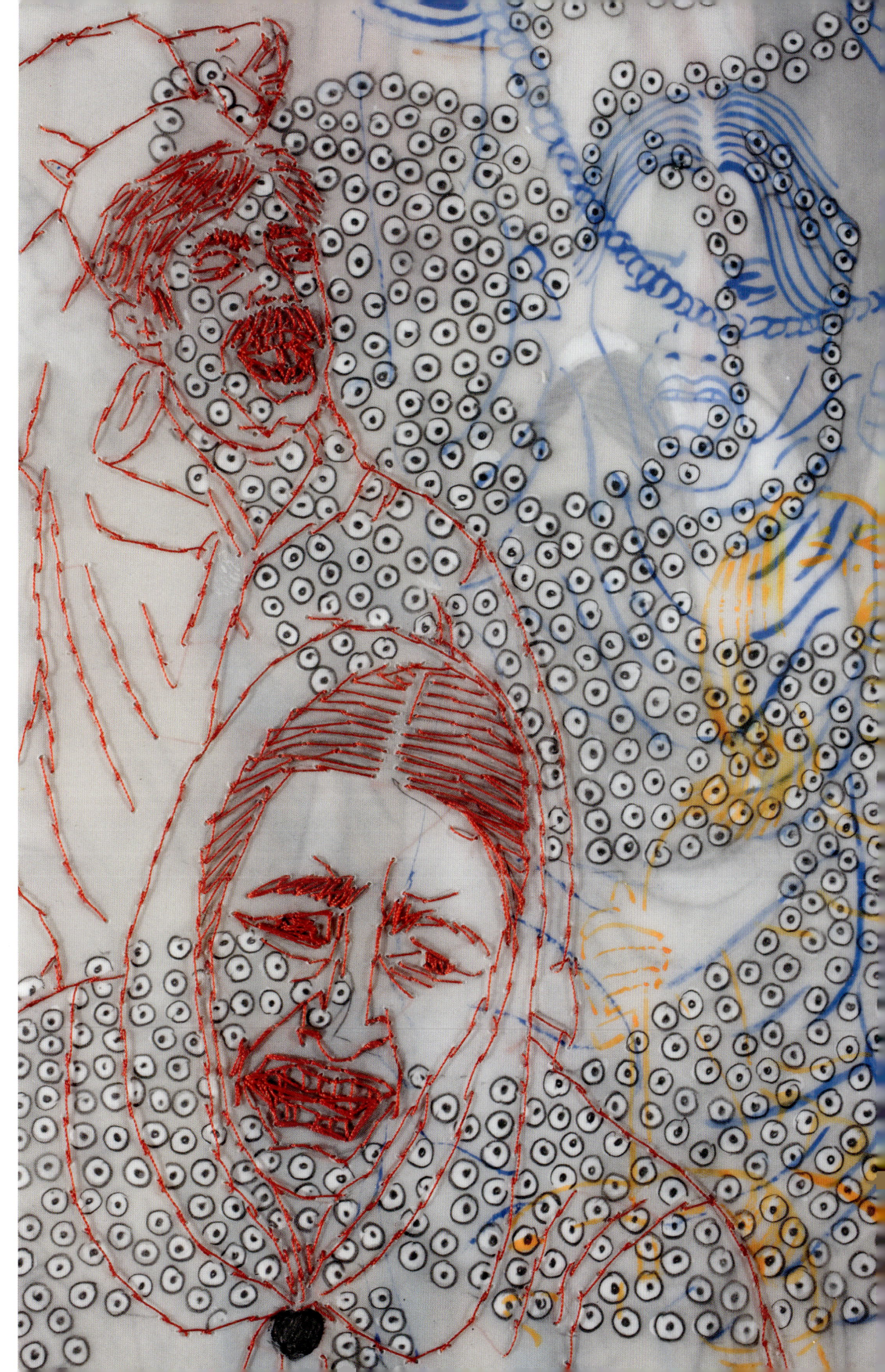

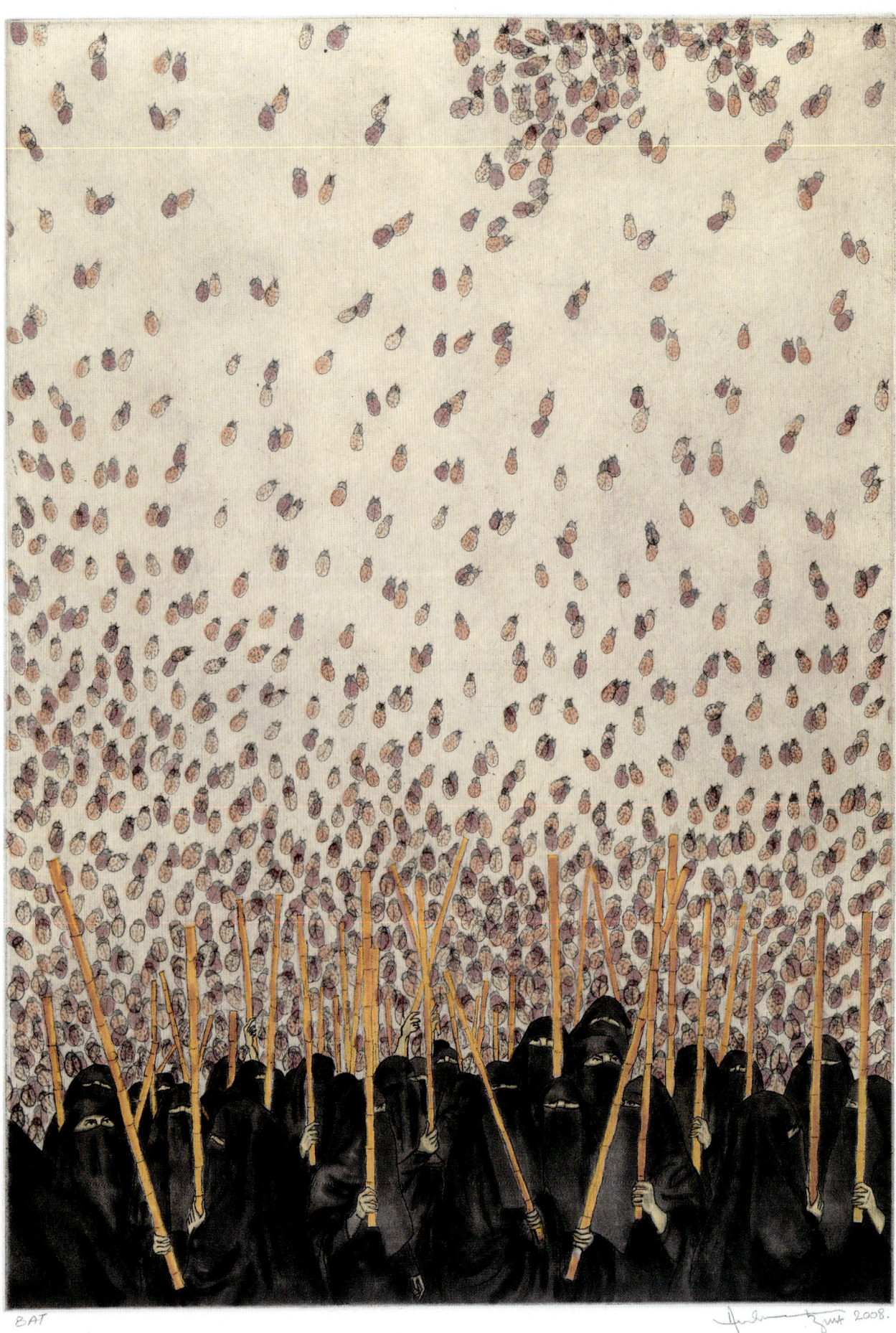

BAT

2008.

Ladybugs 2008
FROM THE SERIES Daughters Of The East
Six plate aquatint etching with chine collé, dry point and spit
bite printed on Torinoku Sekishu Gampi on off-white Rives
BFK backing paper, plate size 13 × 18 inches, paper size 25 × 19
inches, edition of 30

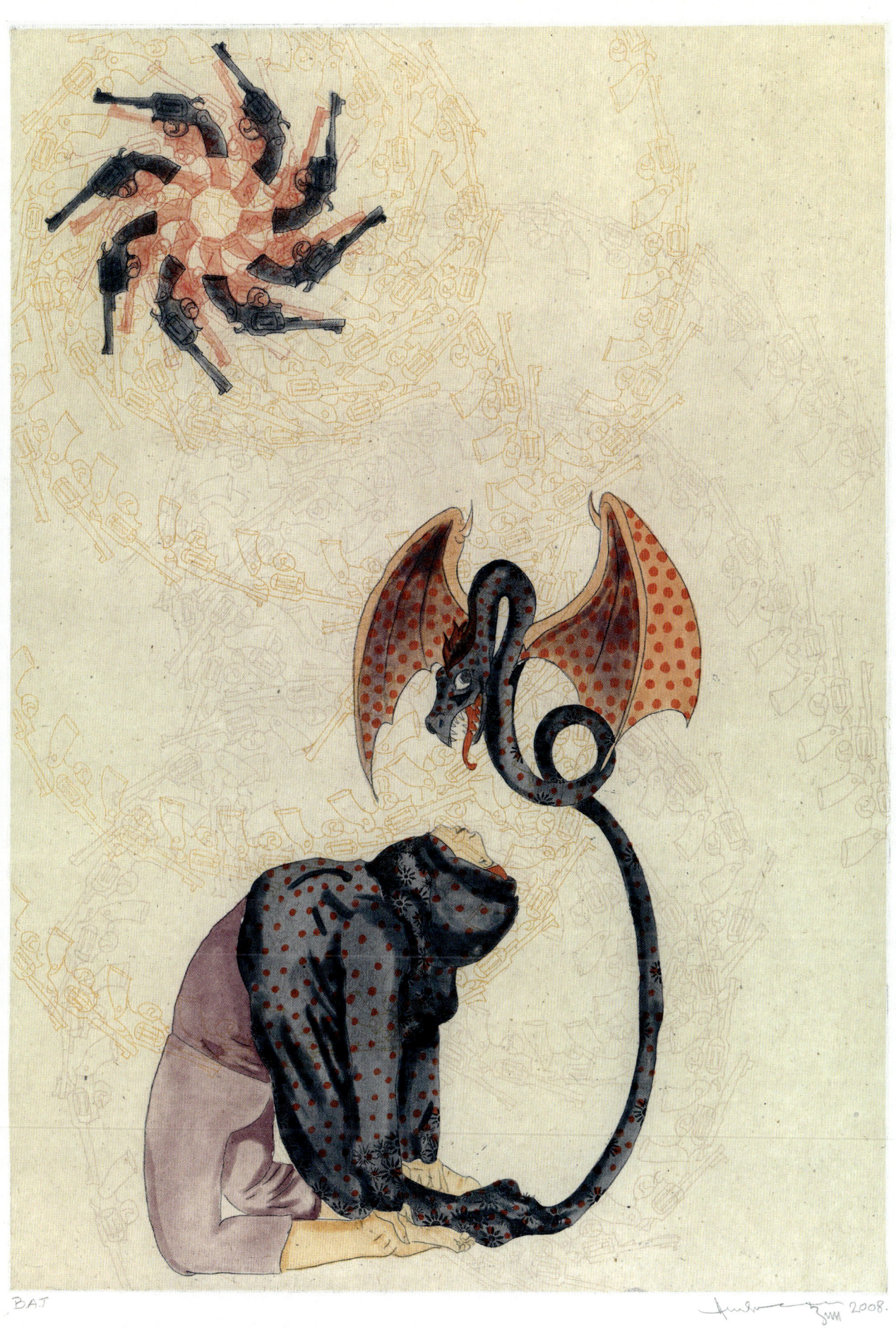

BAT

Untitled 2008
FROM THE SERIES Daughters Of The East
Six plate aquatint etching with chine collé, dry point and
spit bite printed on Kitikata on soft white Somerset textured
backing paper plate size 13 × 18 inches, paper size 25 × 19
inches, edition of 30

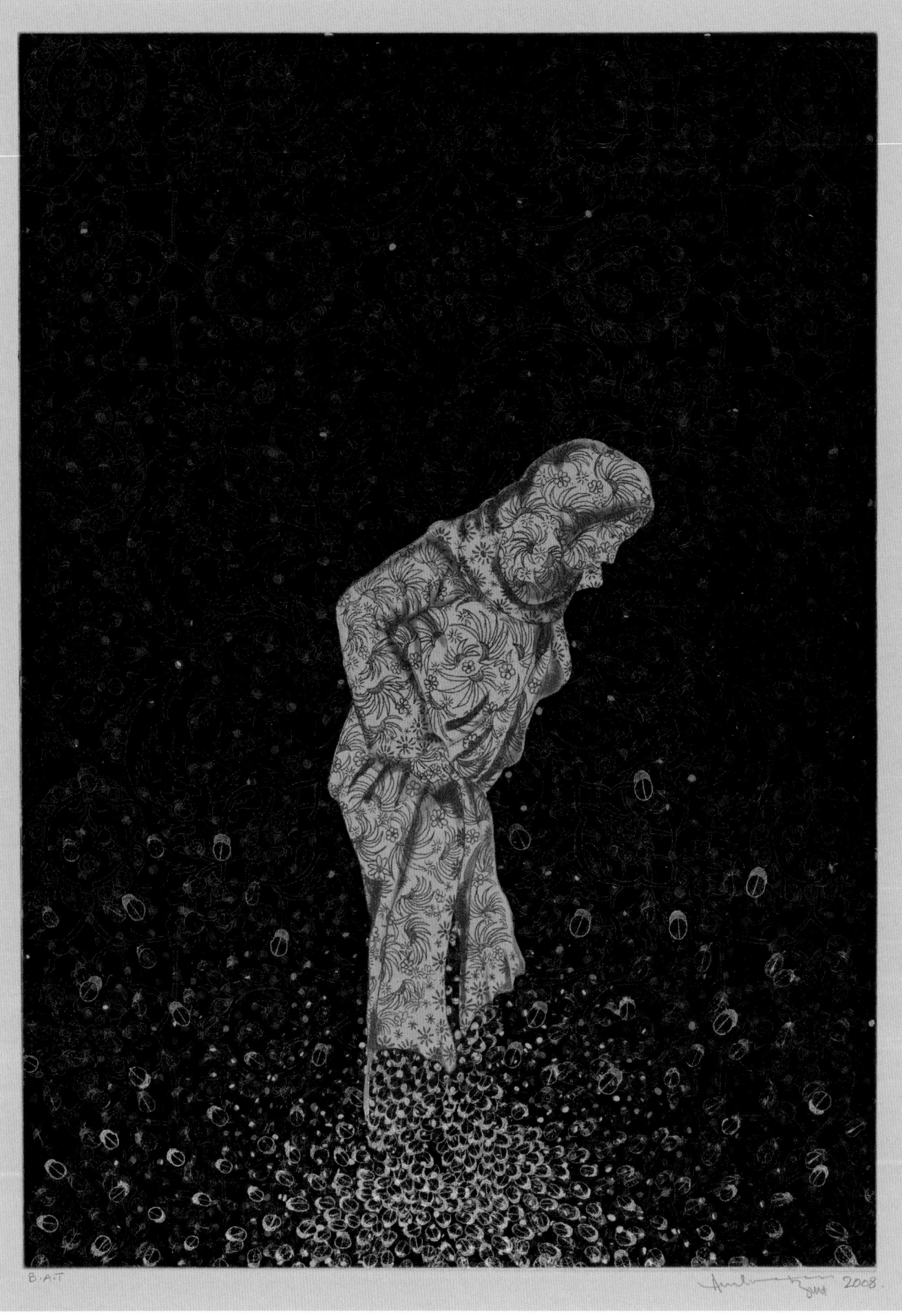

B.A.T

Untitled 2008
FROM THE SERIES Daughters Of The East
Six plate aquatint etching with chine collé, dry point and
spit bite on gray Rives BFK paper, plate size 13×18 inches,
paper size 25×19 inches, edition of 30

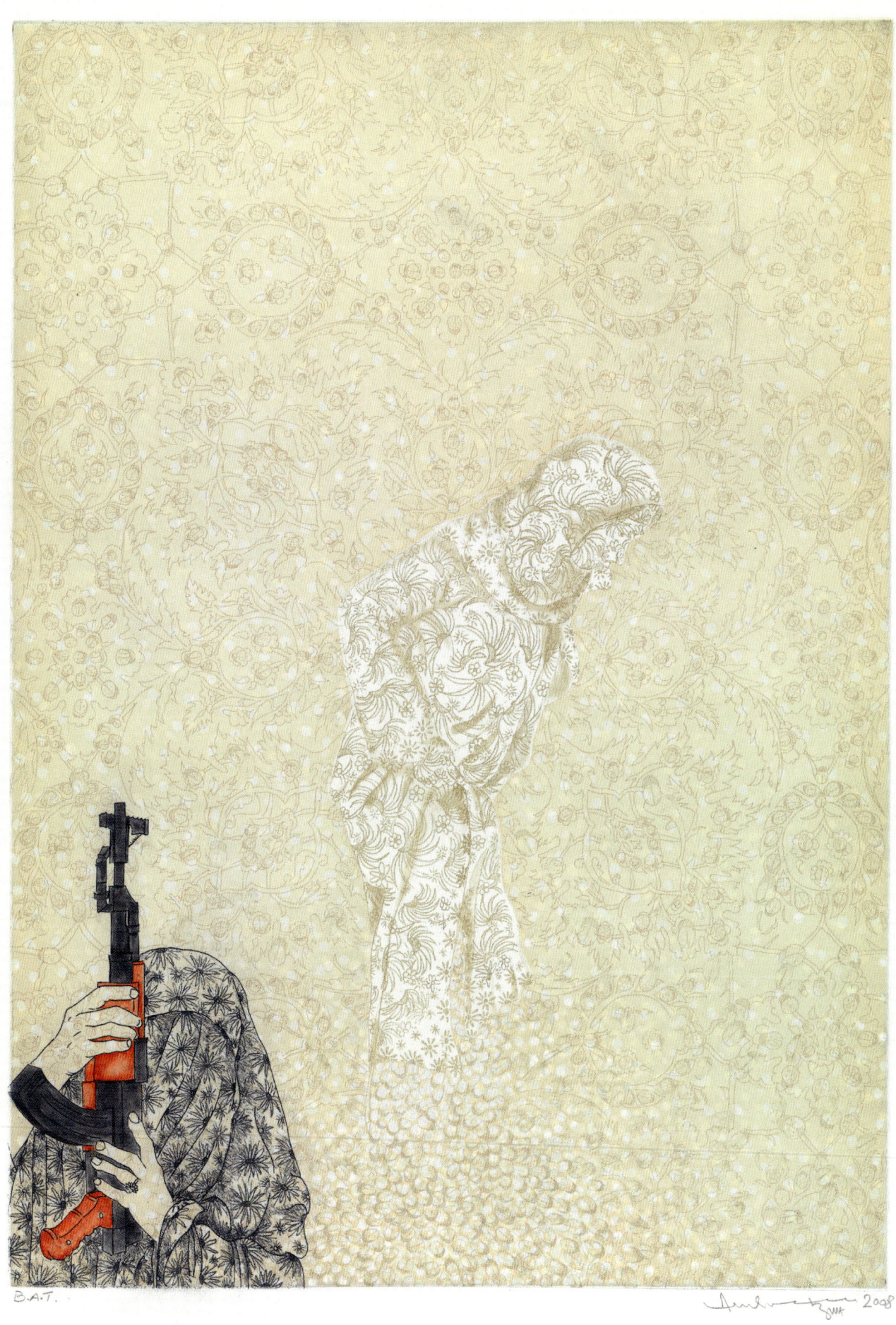

B.A.T.

Untitled 2008
FROM THE SERIES Daughters Of The East
Six plate aquatint etching with chine collé, dry point and spit
bite on soft white Somerset textured paper, plate size 13×18
inches, paper size 25×19 inches, edition of 30

89

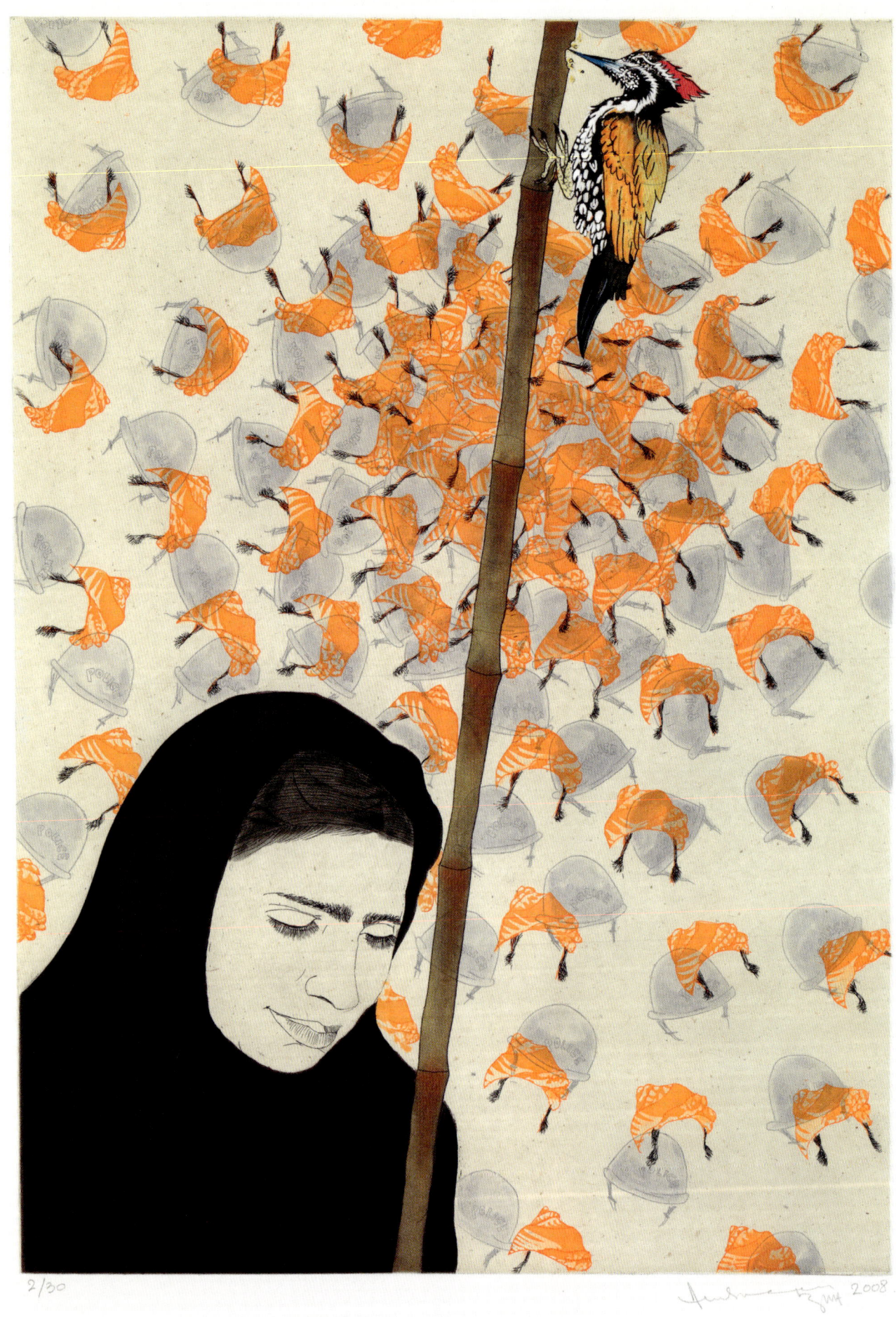

2/30

ABOVE **Untitled** 2008
FROM THE SERIES Daughters Of The East
Six plate aquatint etching with chine collé, dry point and spit
bite printed on Kitikata, on white Rives BFK backing paperplate
size 13 × 18 inches, paper size 25 × 19 inches, edition of 30

OPPOSITE Studio views, 2010

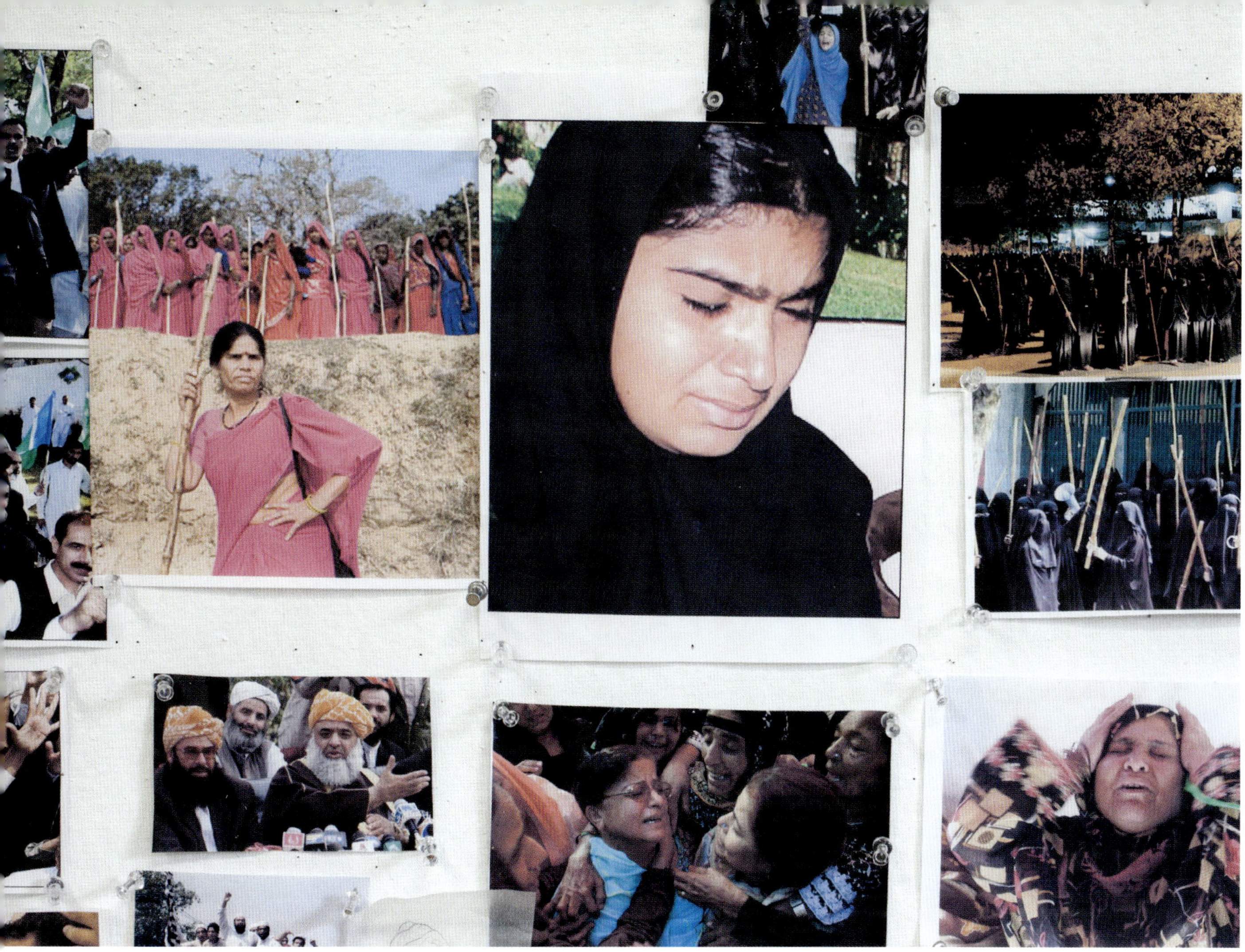

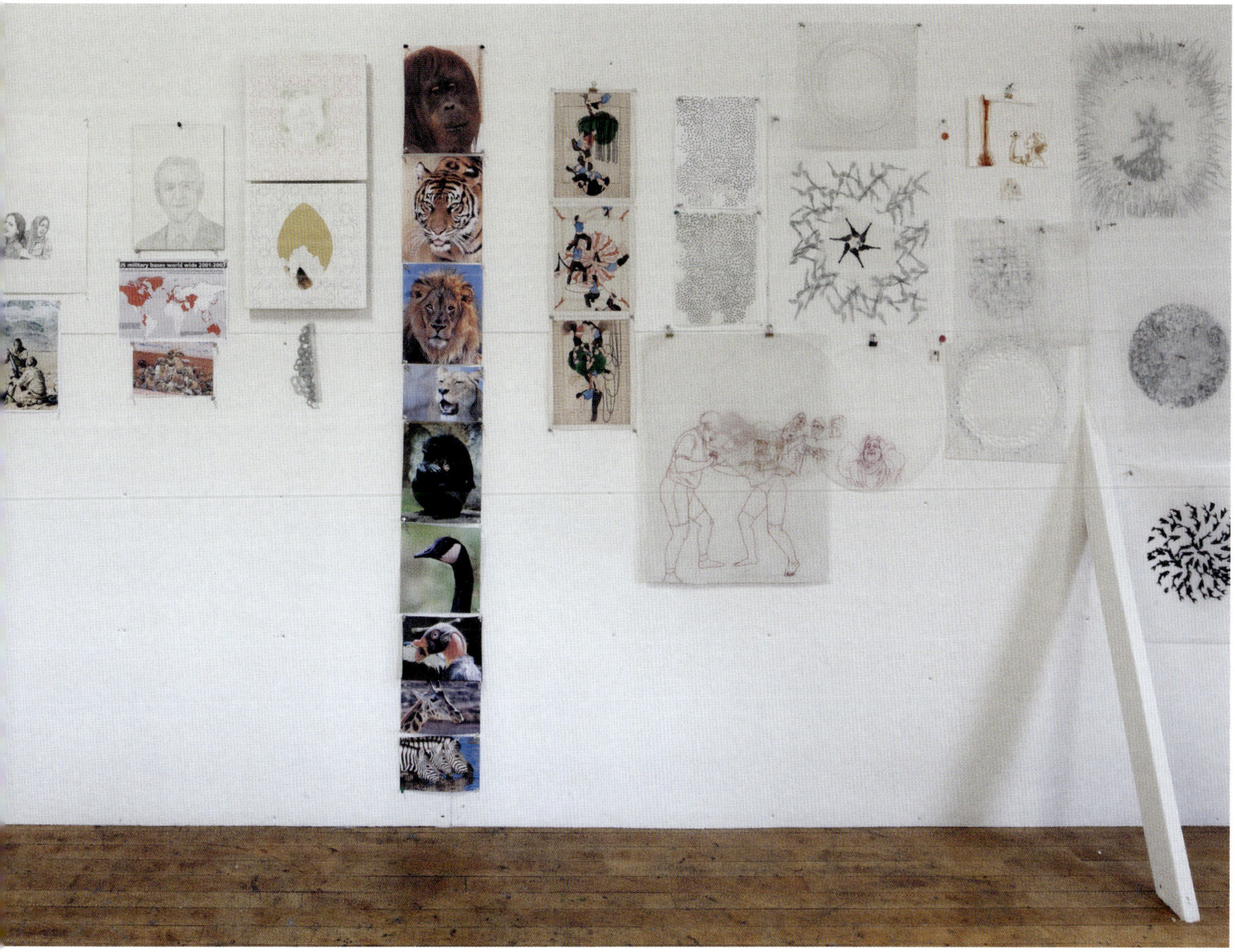
military bases world wide

SPEAK

Speak, your lips are free.
Speak, it is your own tongue.
Speak, it is your own body.
Speak, your life is still yours.

See how in the blacksmith's shop
The flame burns wild, the iron glows red;
The locks open their jaws,
And every chain begins to break.

Speak, this brief hour is long enough
Before the death of body and tongue:
Speak, 'cause the truth is not dead yet,
Speak, speak, whatever you must speak.

Faiz Ahmed Faiz
Translated by Azfar Hussain

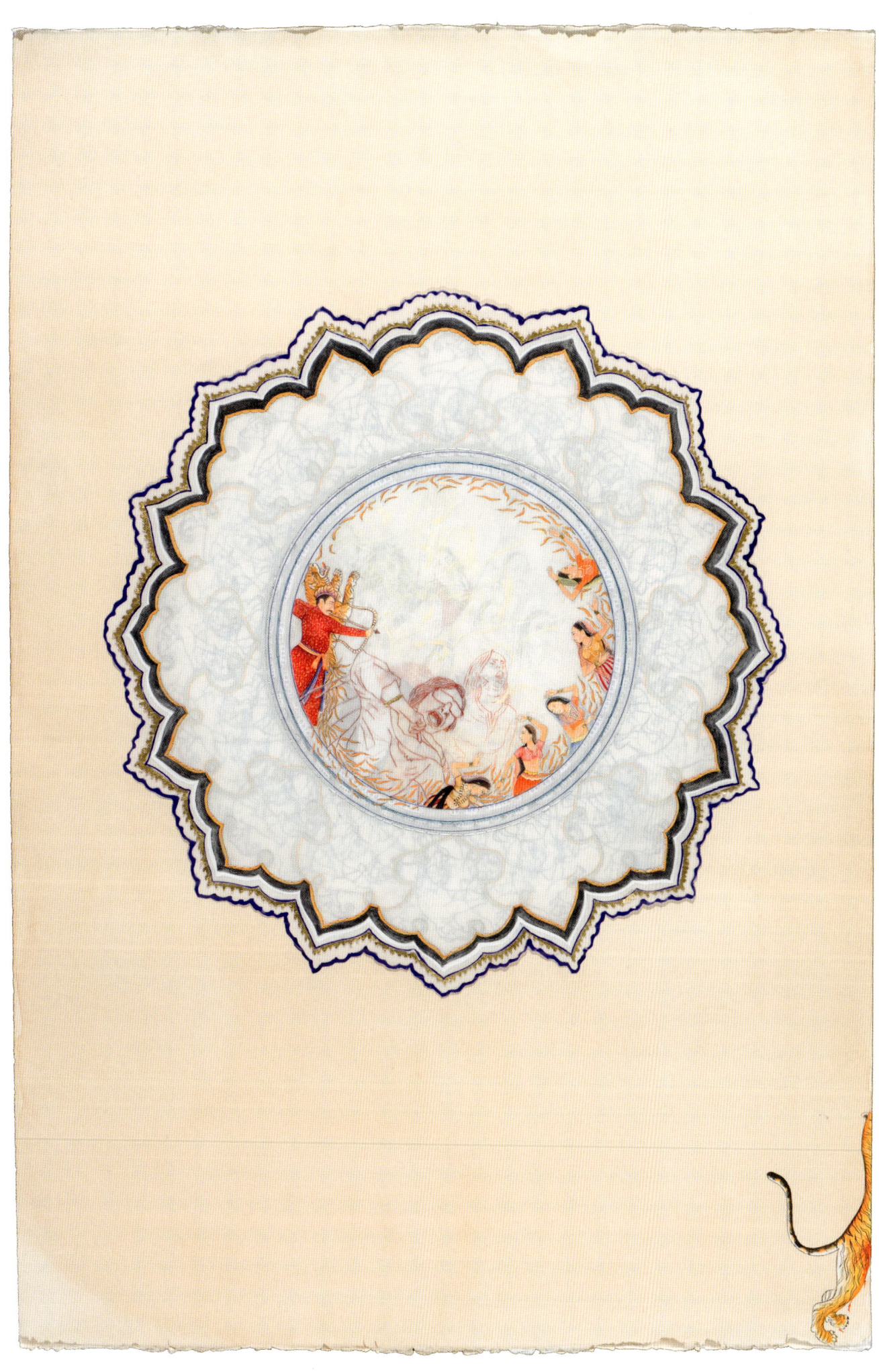

ABOVE/OVERLEAF (DETAIL) *The Great Hunt I* 2008
FROM THE SERIES Dirty Pretty
Pigments, gouache, text, stitching, gold leaf on Mylar and
tea-stained paper, 45 × 30 inches

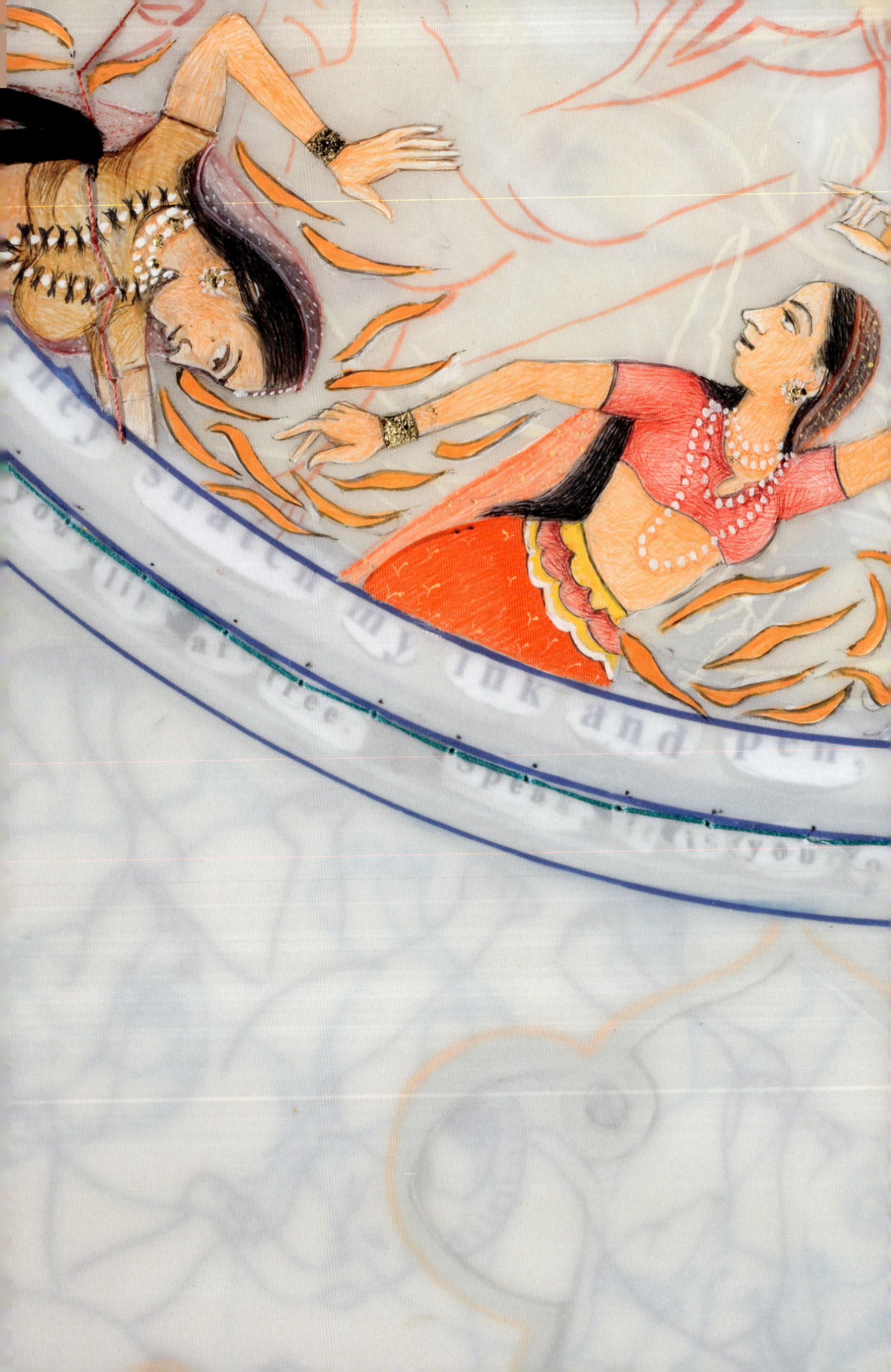

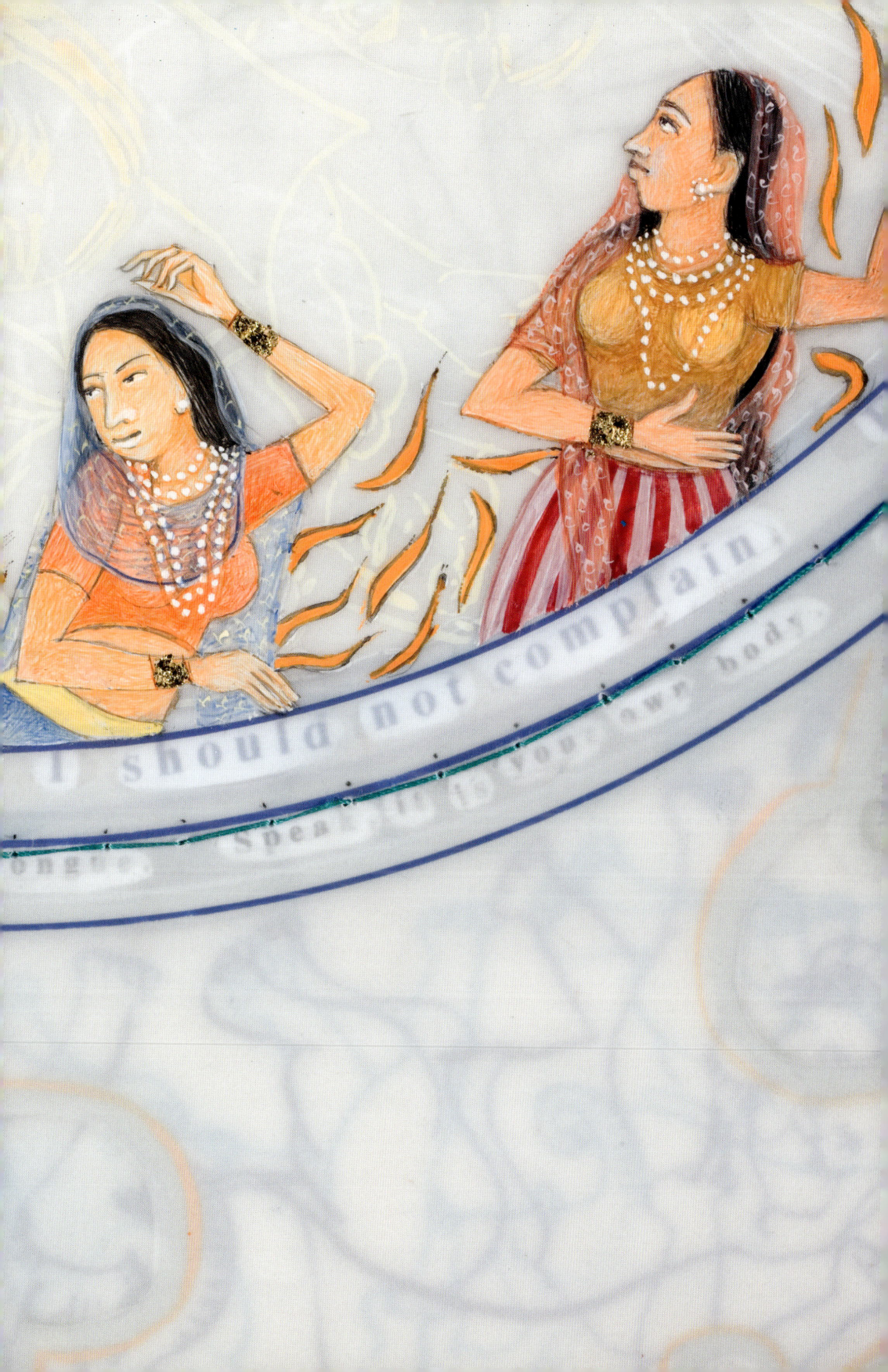

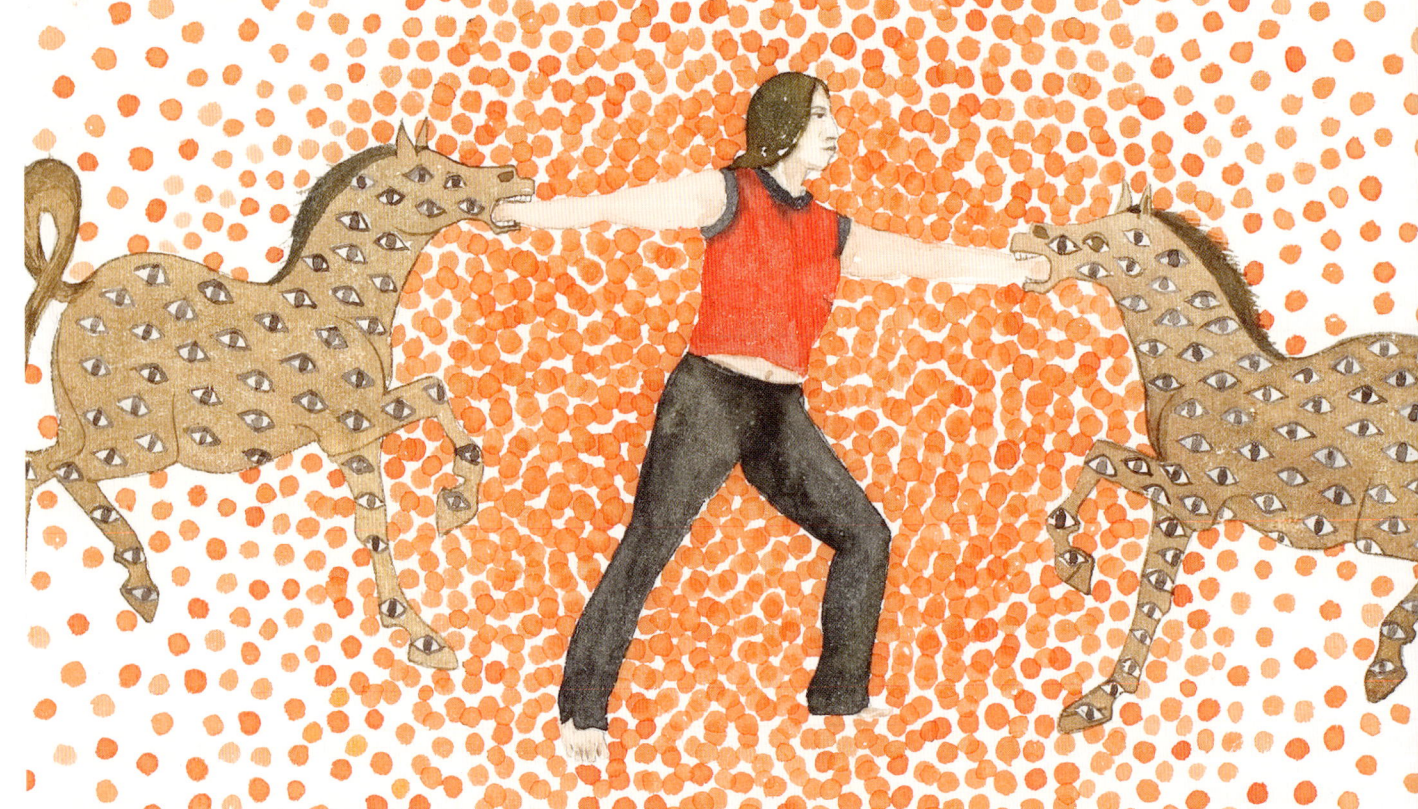

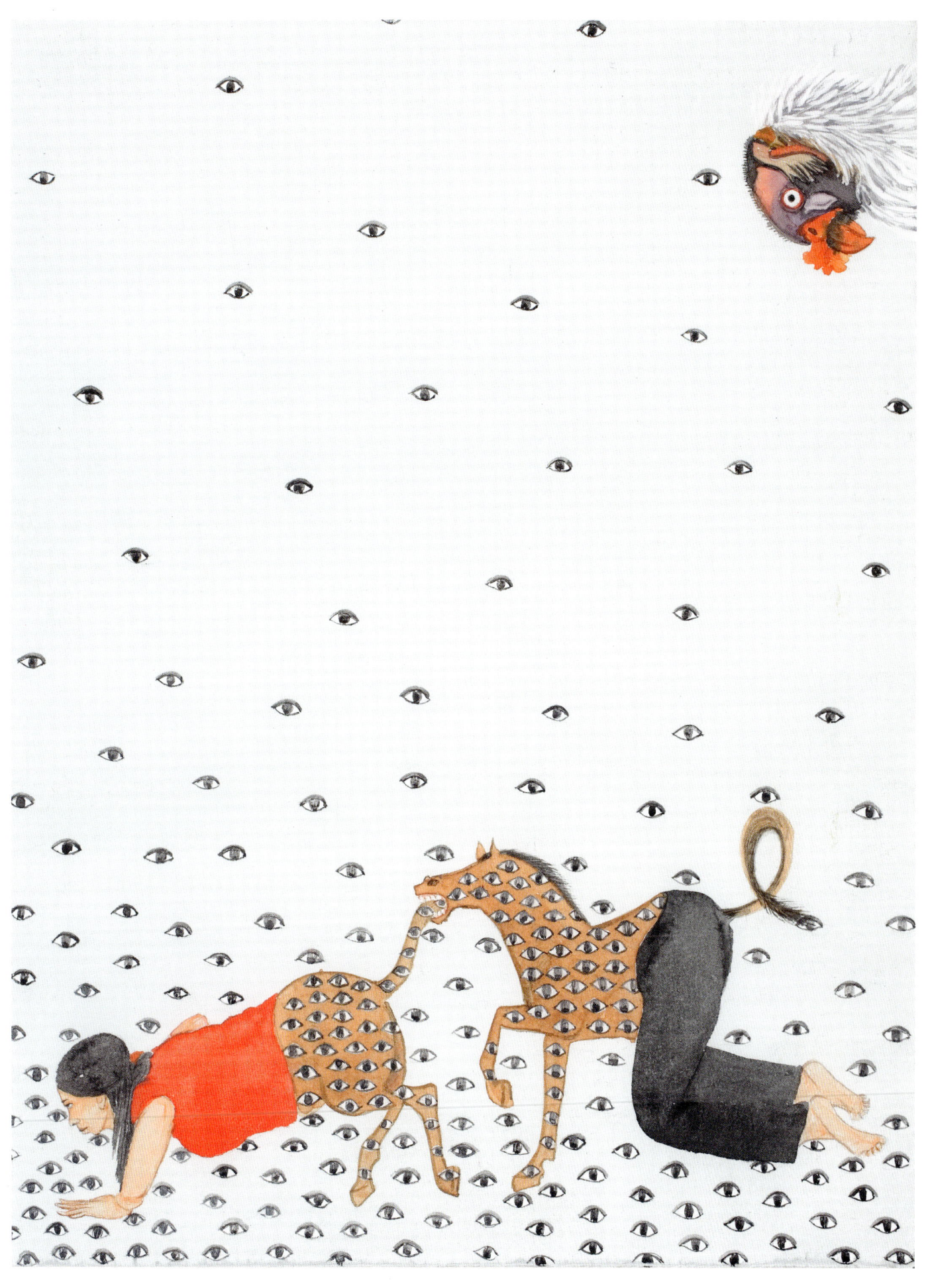

OPPOSITE (DETAIL) **Untitled** 2007
FROM THE SERIES Cirque Du Monde
Watercolor and fruit dye on handmade paper,
20 × 20 inches

ABOVE **Untitled** 2007
FROM THE SERIES Cirque Du Monde
Watercolor with white gouache on handmade paper,
12 × 9 inches

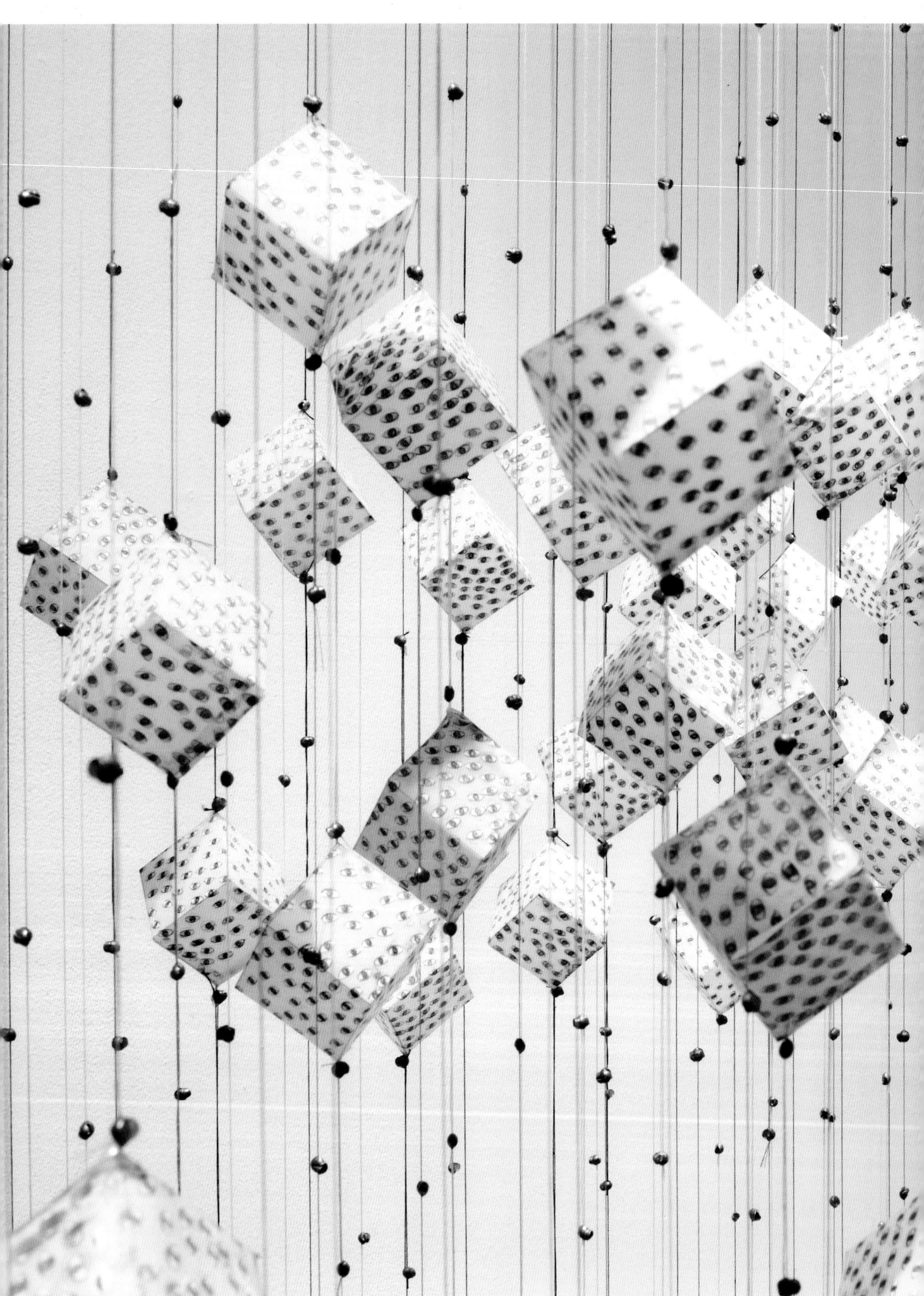

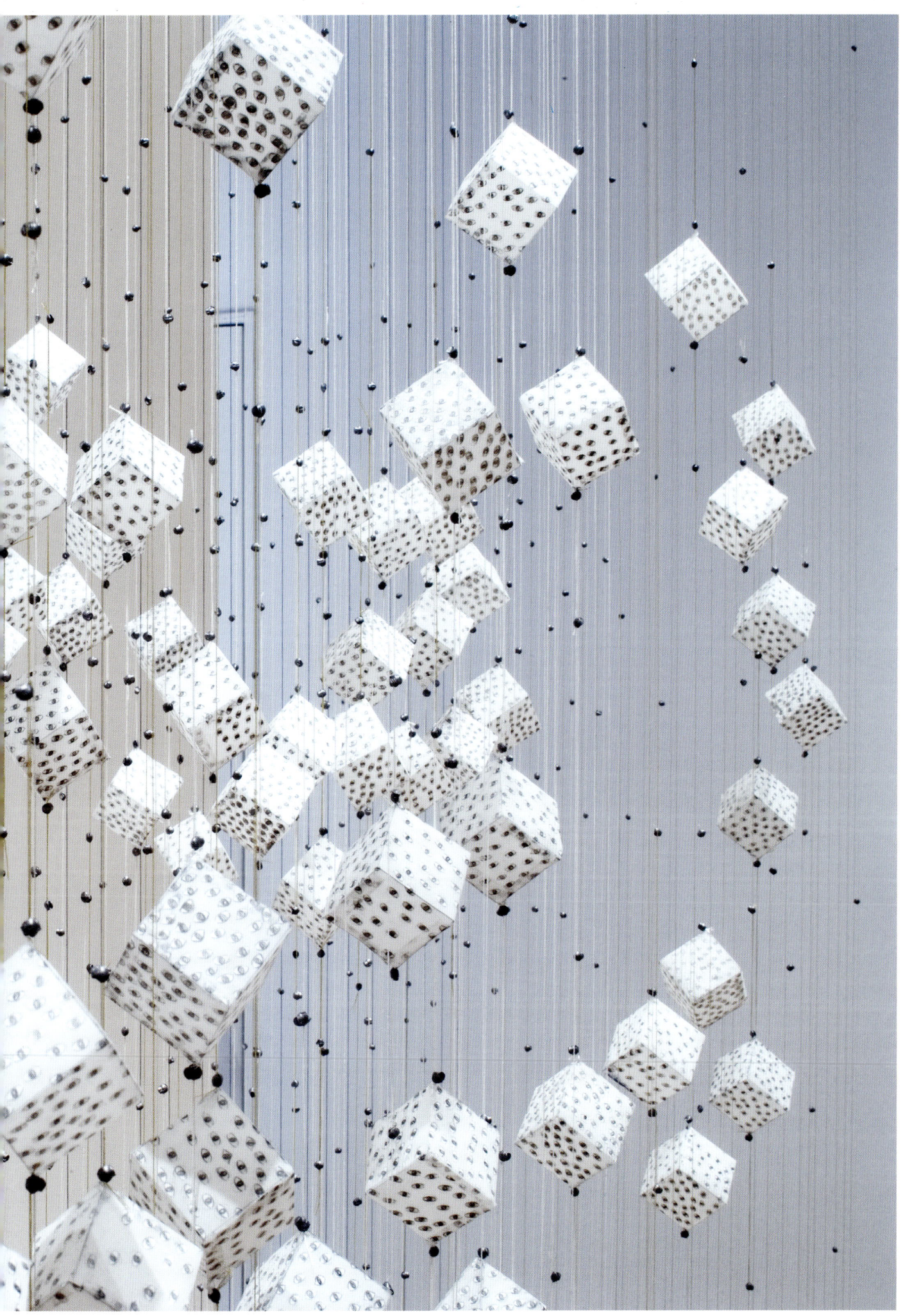

Untitled, 2007
<small>FROM THE SERIES</small> Cirque Du Monde
Mylar, thread, lead, and acrylic, dimensions variable
Installation view, Bernard Toale Gallery, Boston, Massachusetts

99

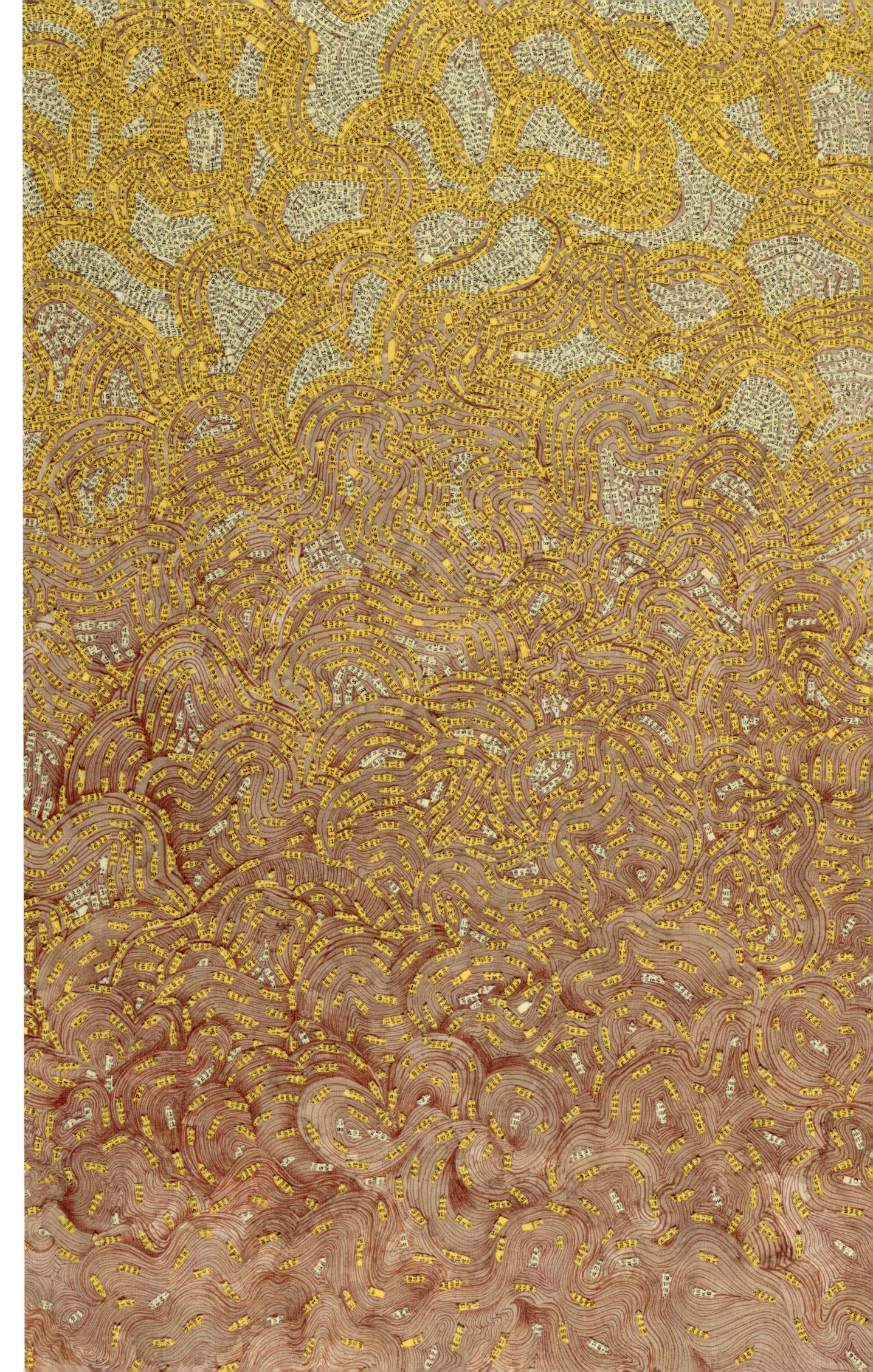

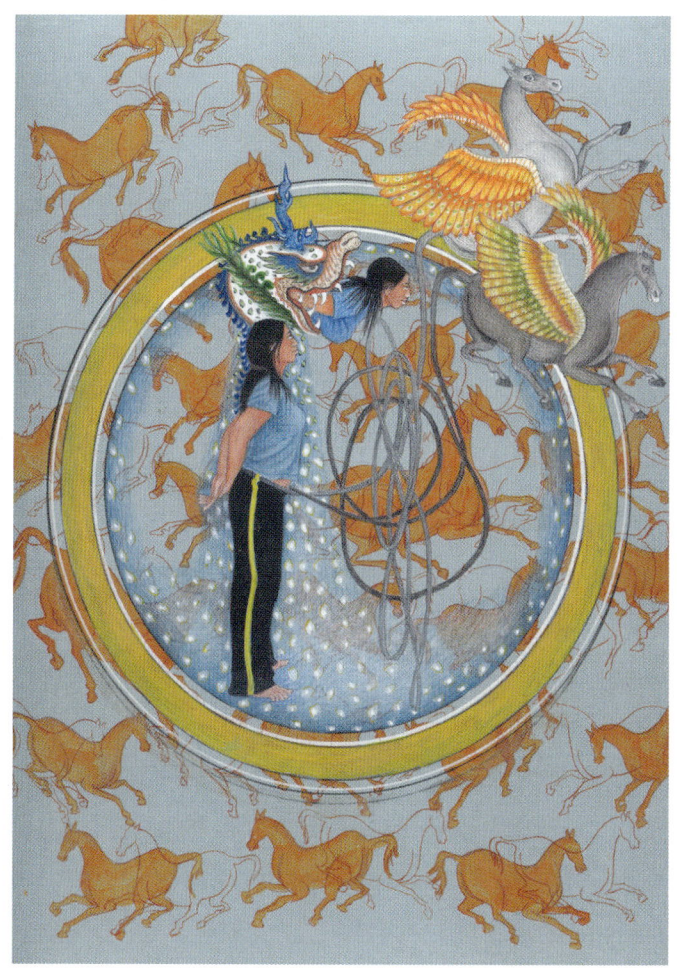

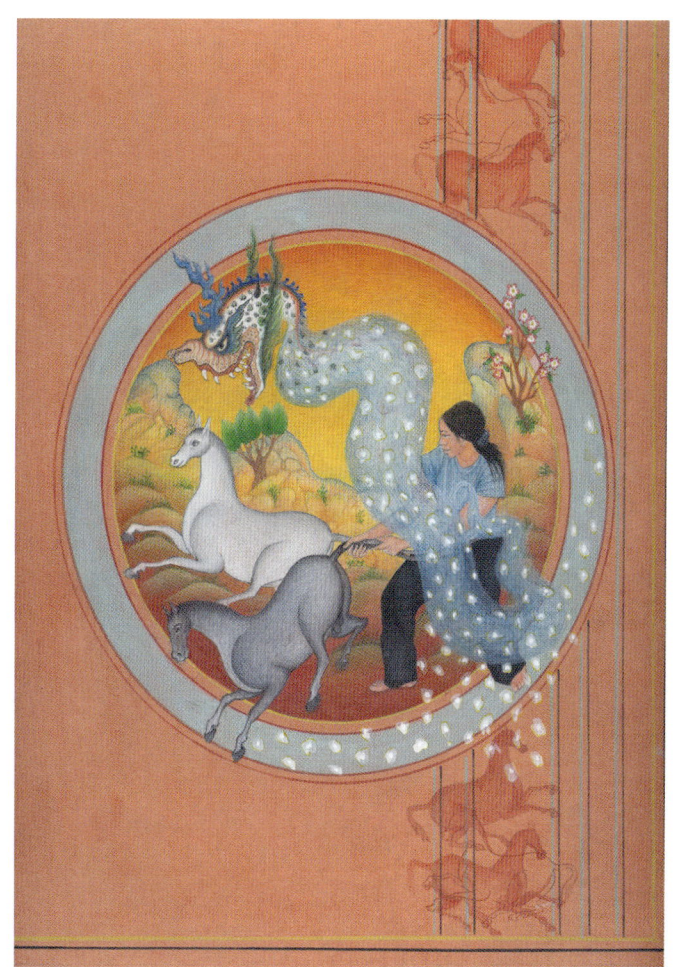

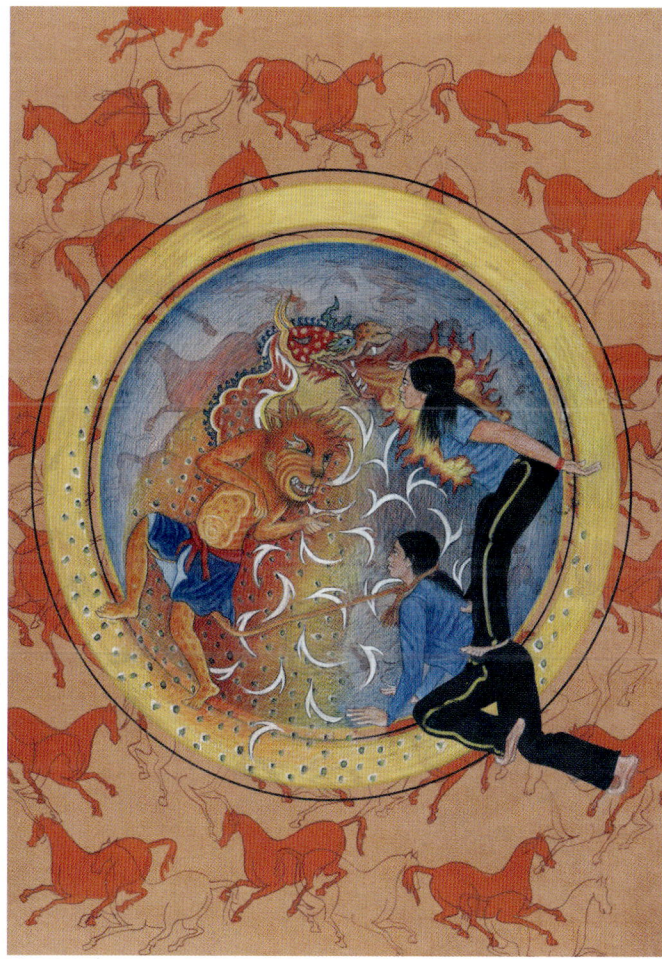

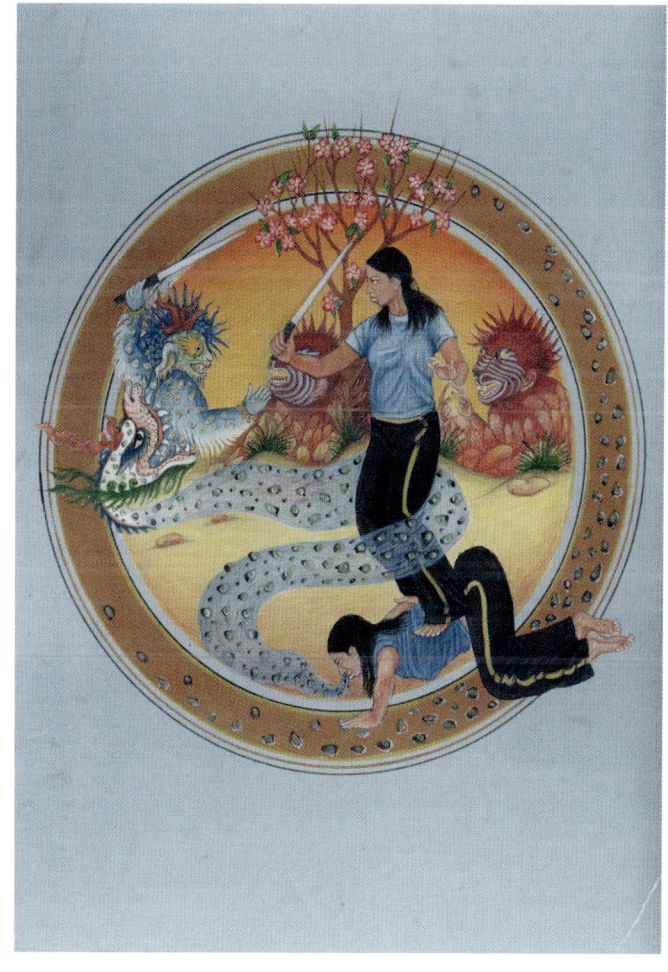

OPPOSITE (DETAIL) **Sultanat Khan (16)** 2020
FROM THE SERIES Say My Name
Pen, collage of text on tea-stained paper, 30 × 20 inches

ABOVE (ALL IMAGES) **Untitled** 2005
FROM THE SERIES Demons
Watercolor with white gouache on handmade wasli
paper, 10½ × 8 inches

101

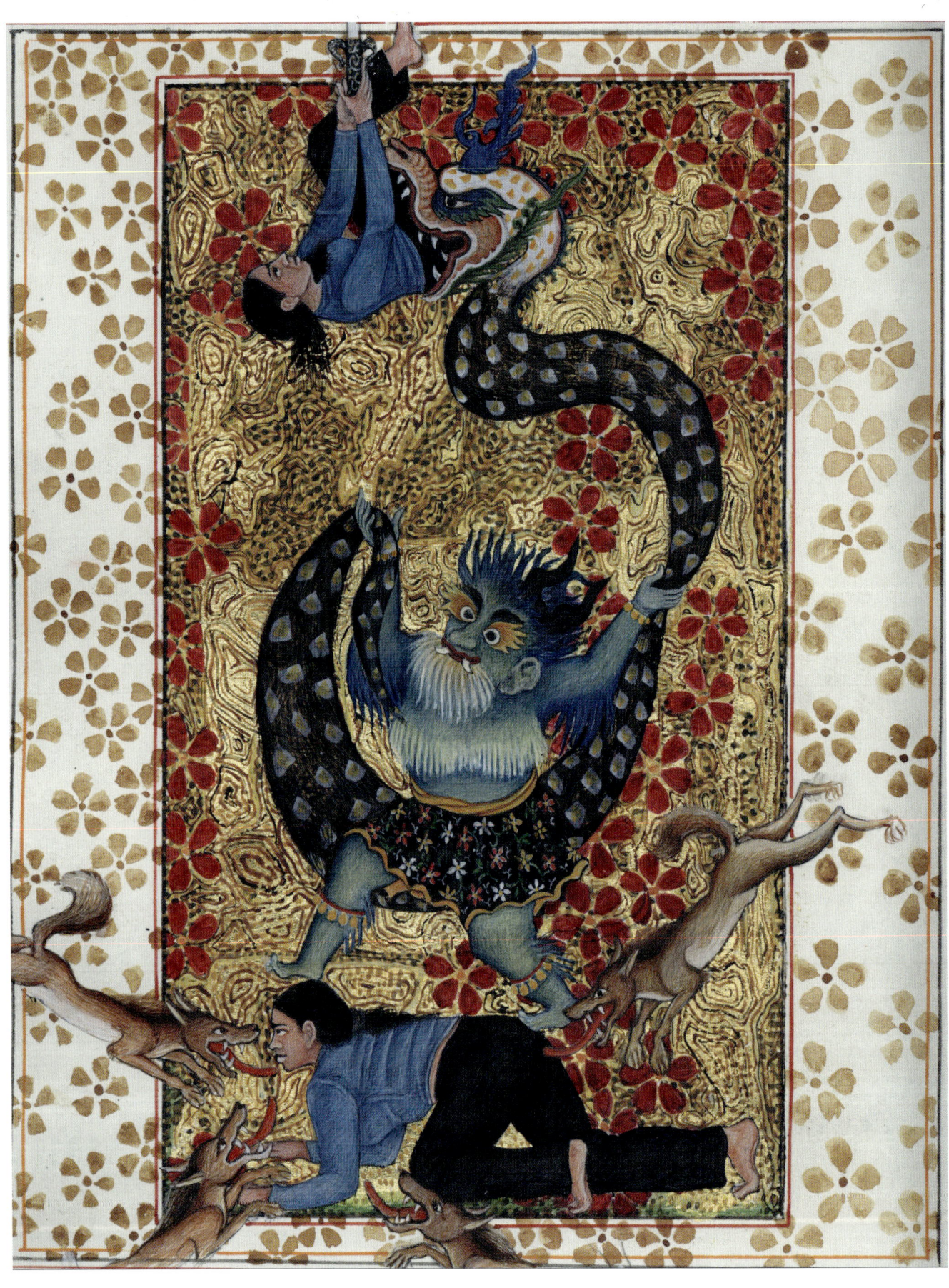

Untitled 2005

FROM THE SERIES **I Need A Hero**
Watercolor, white gouache and gold leaf on handmade wasli
paper, 10½ × 8 inches

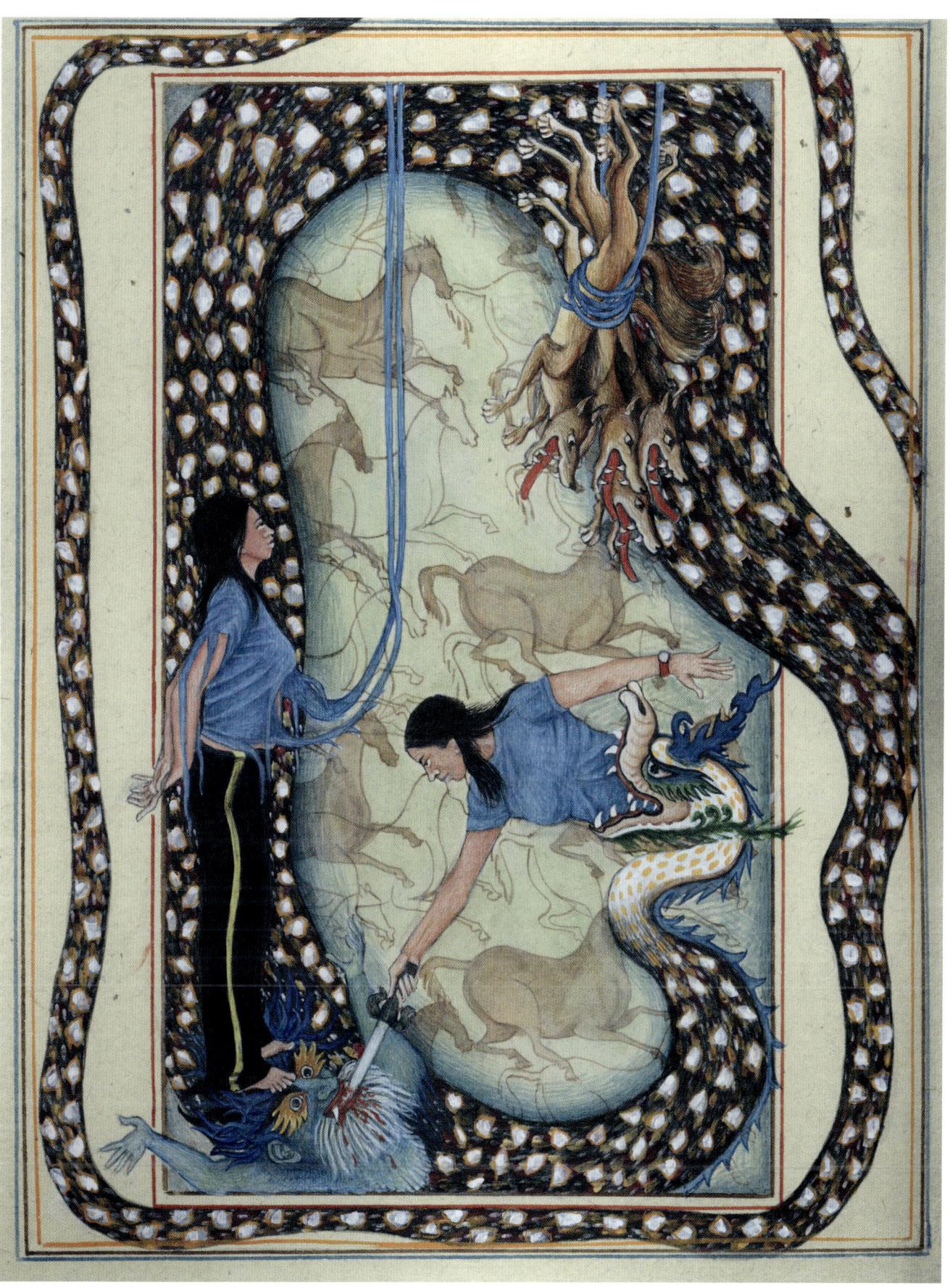

Untitled 2005

FROM THE SERIES I Need A Hero
Watercolor and white gouache on handmade wasli paper,
10½ × 8 inches

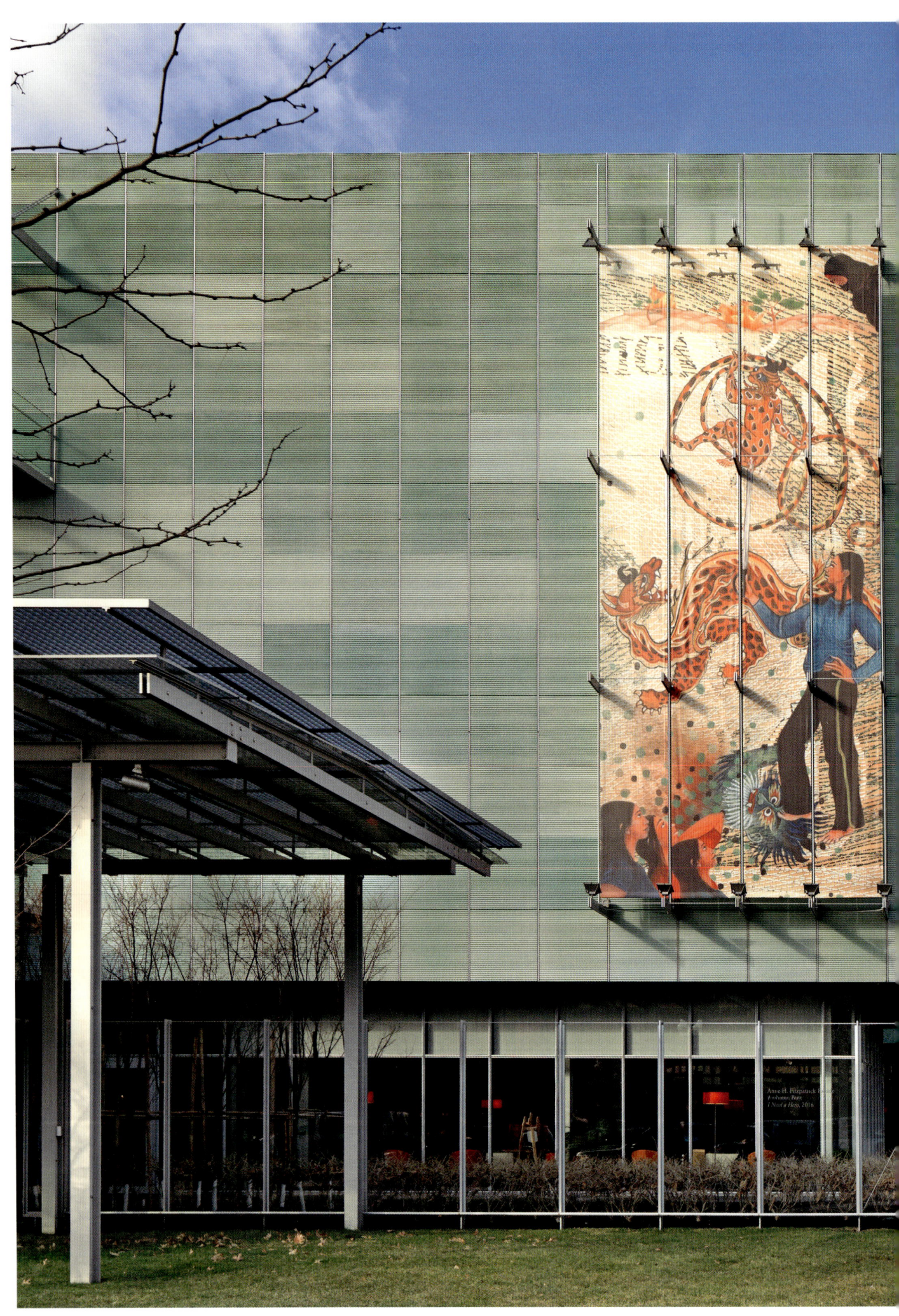

We Need A Hero 2017
Installation view of the Anne H. Fitzpatrick Facade at
Isabella Stewart Gardner Museum, Boston, Massachusetts

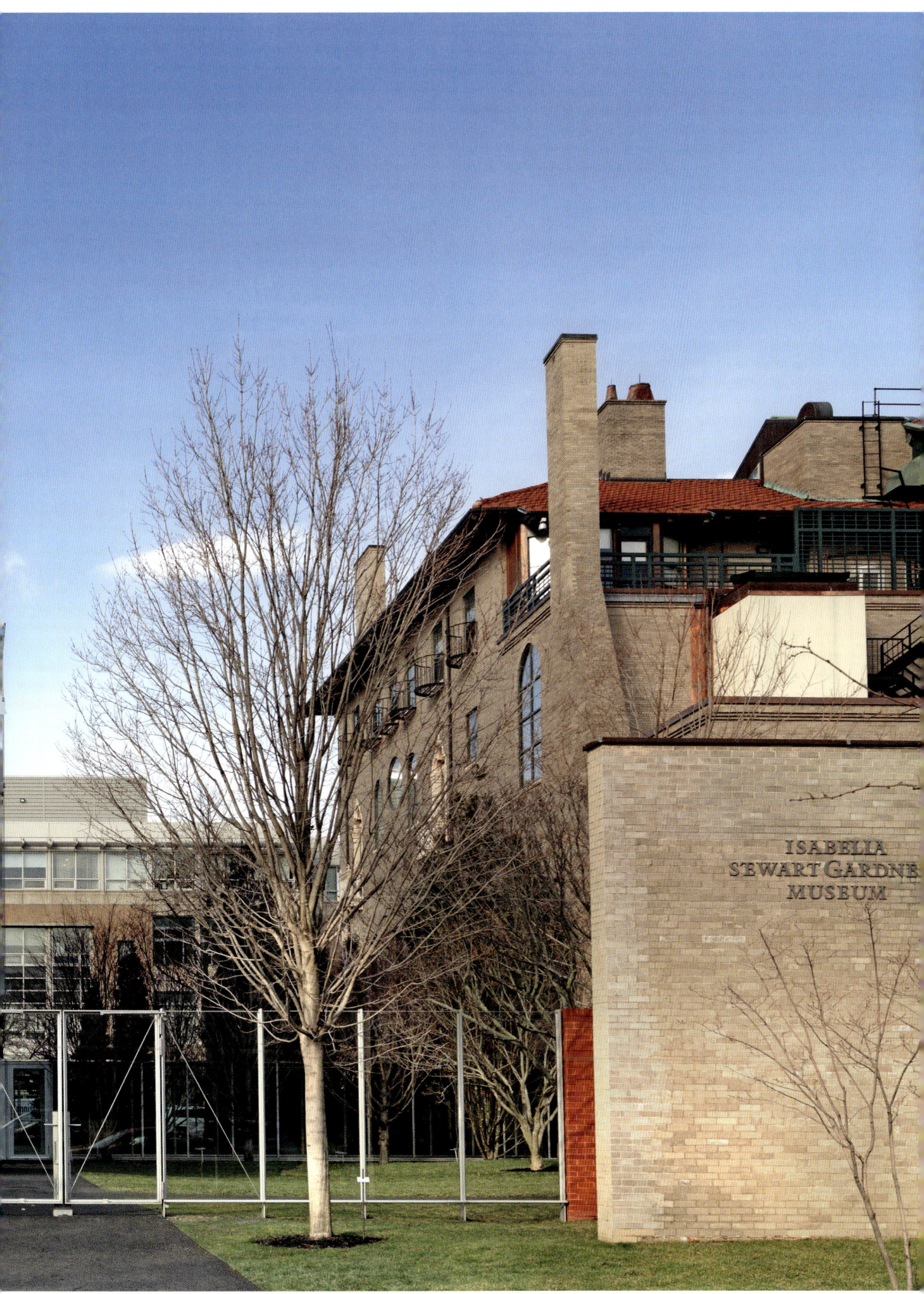

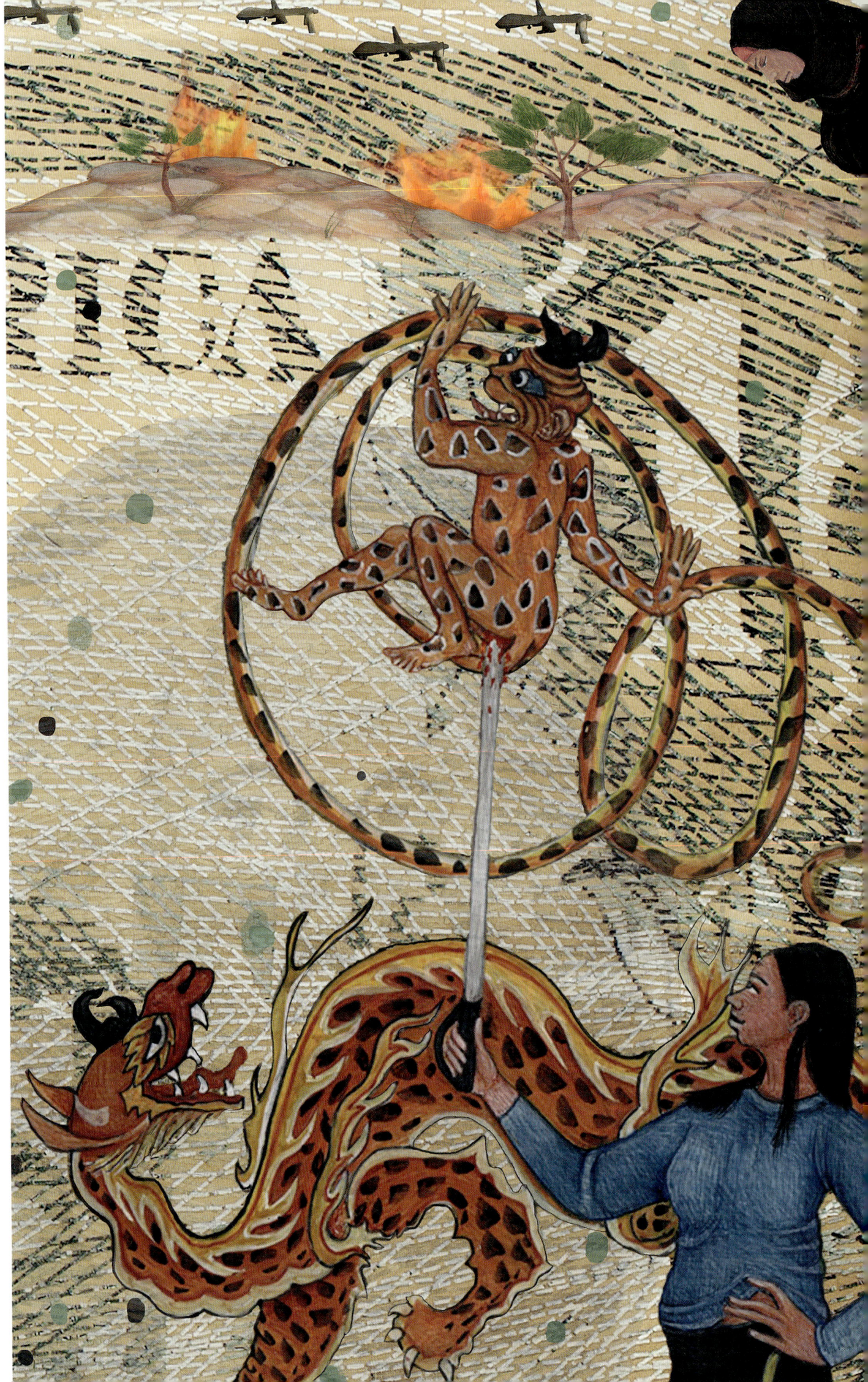

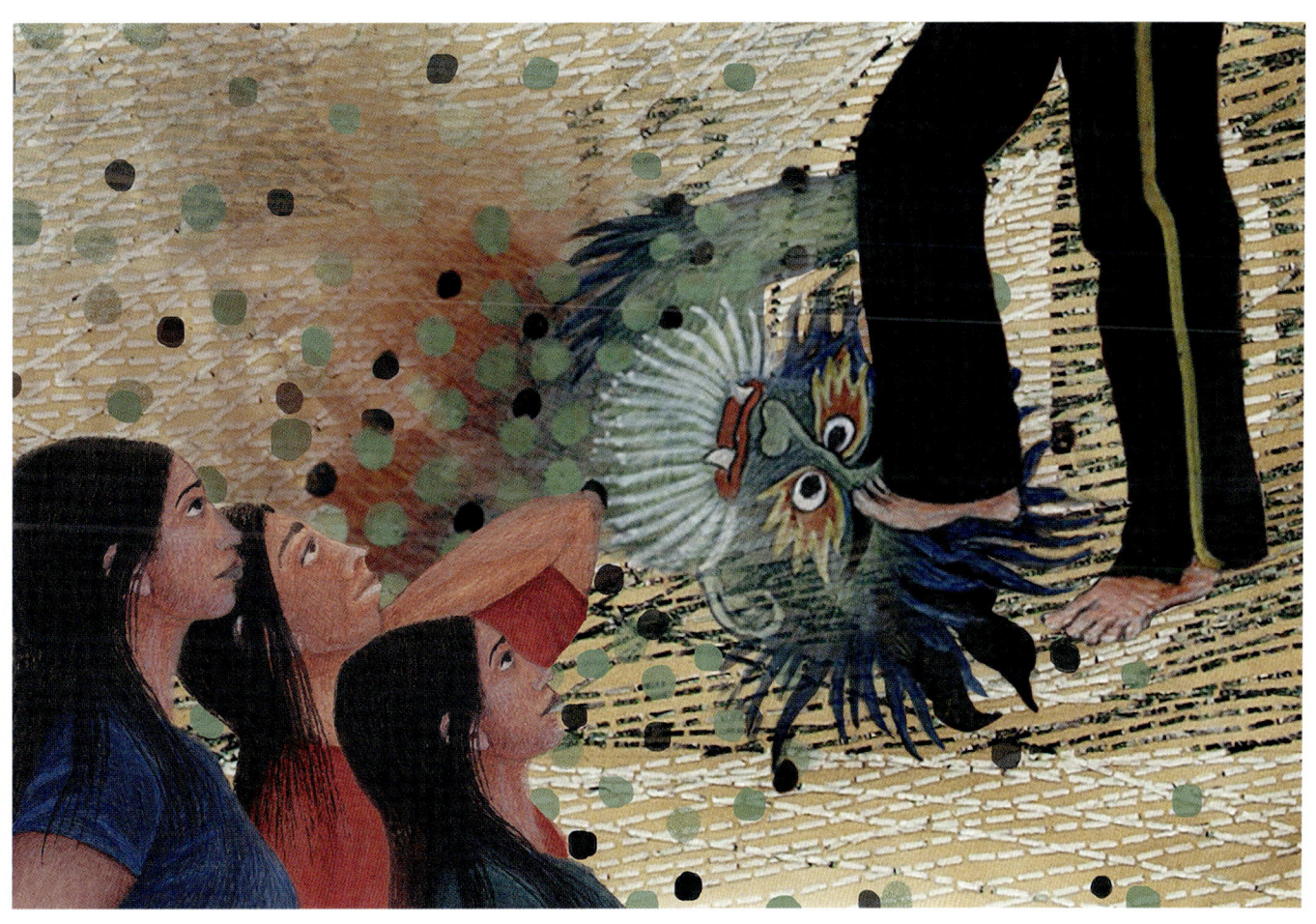

OPPOSITE AND ABOVE (DETAILS) *We Need A Hero* 2017
Inkjet print on vinyl, 16 × 36 feet

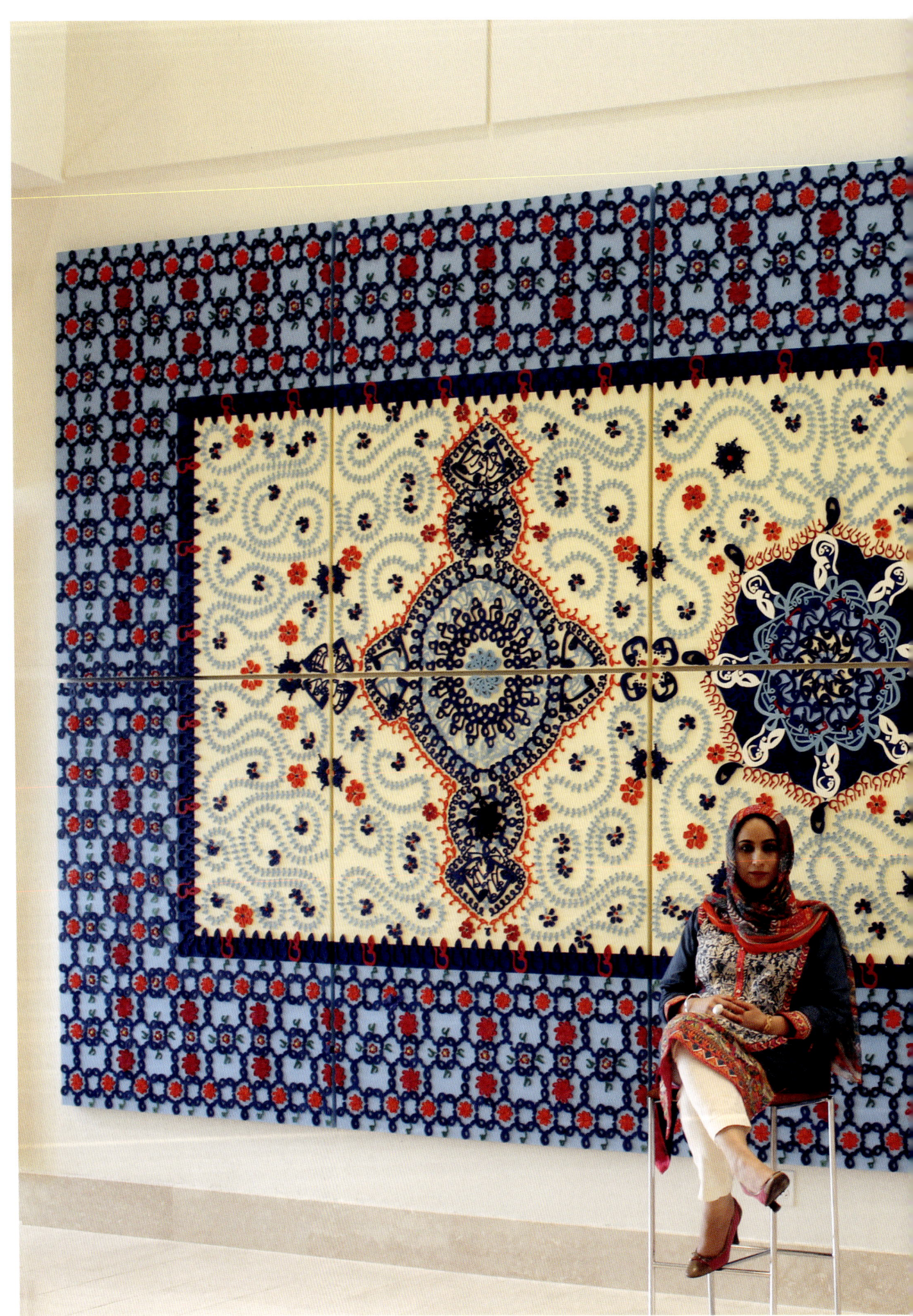

Untitled 2016
Resin with pigments, acrylic on wood, 120 × 240 inches
Commissioned by Art in Embassies Program for the
U.S. Embassy, Islamabad, Pakistan

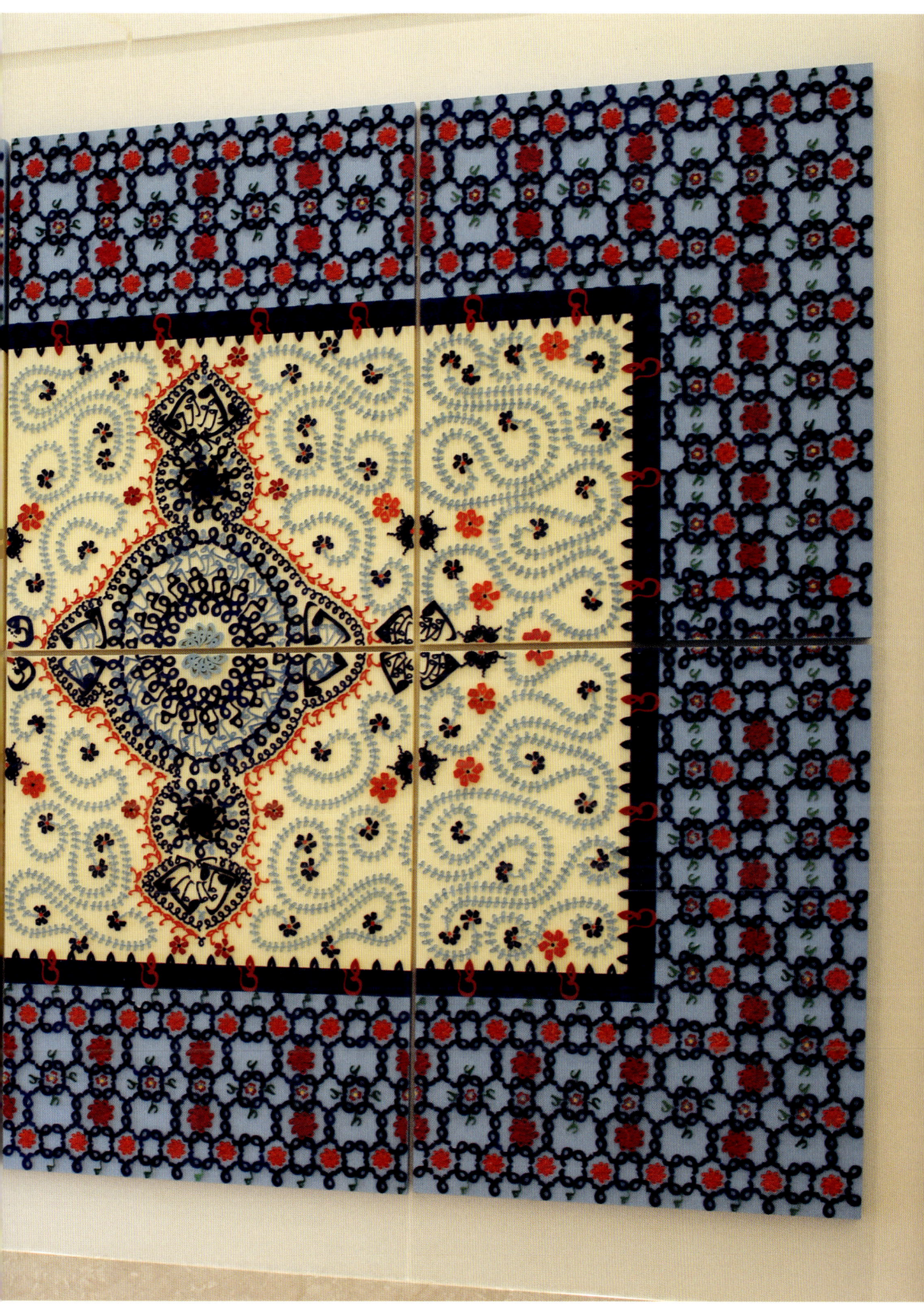

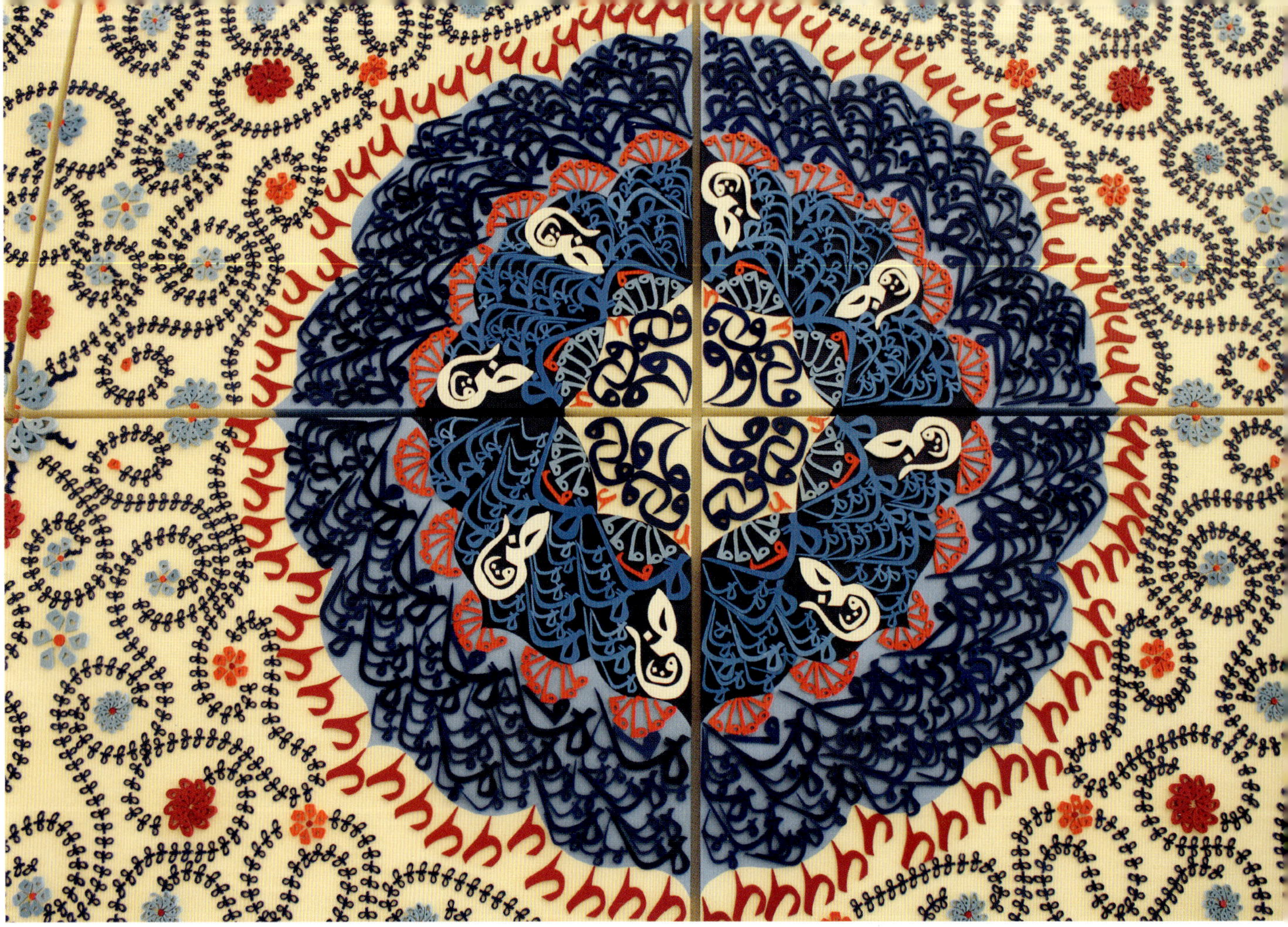

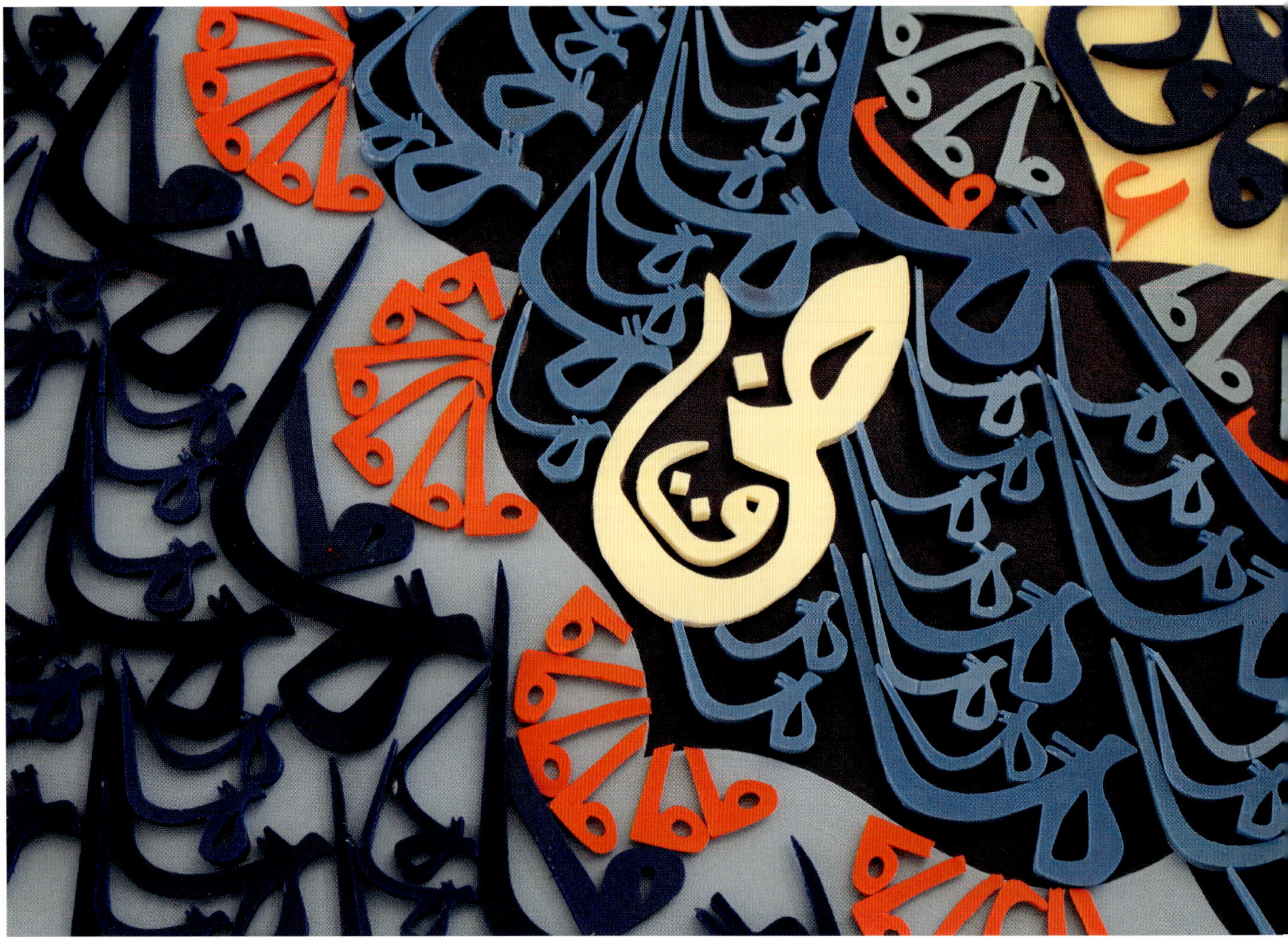

TOP, BOTTOM AND OPPOSITE (DETAILS) *Untitled* 2016
Resin with pigments, acrylic on wood, 120 × 240 inches.
Commissioned by Art in Embassies Program fo the U.S.
Embassy, Islamabad Pakistan

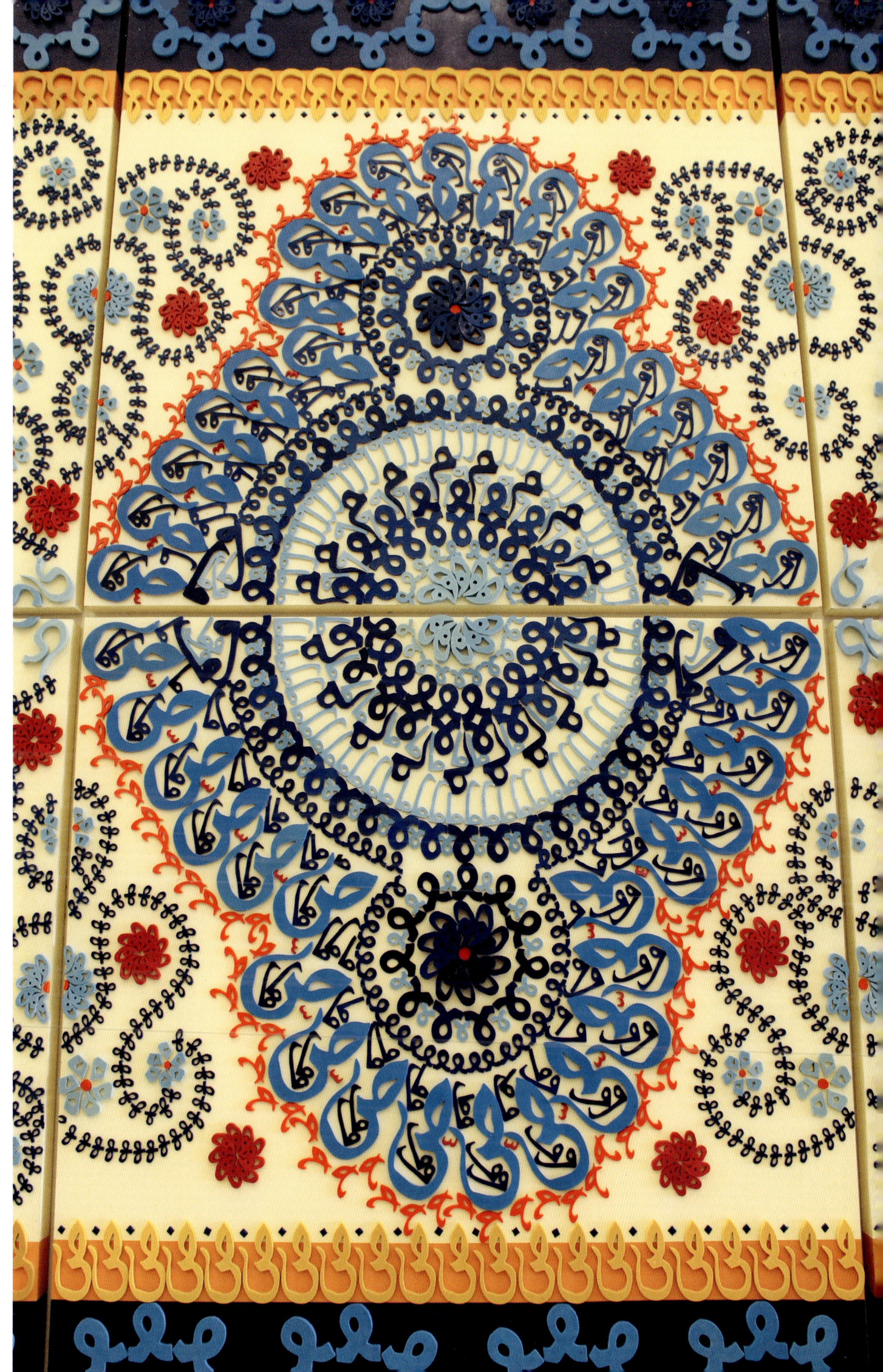

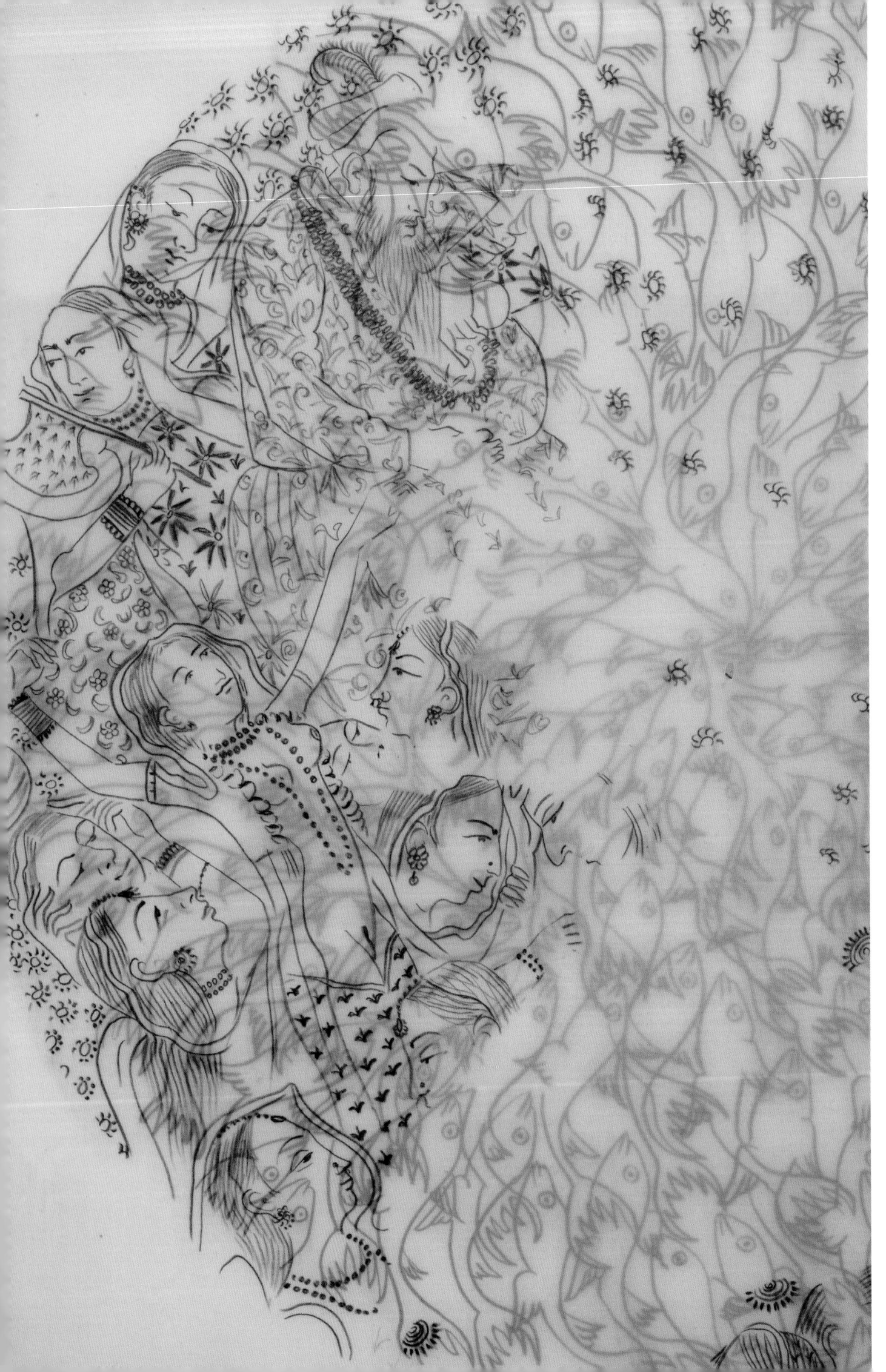

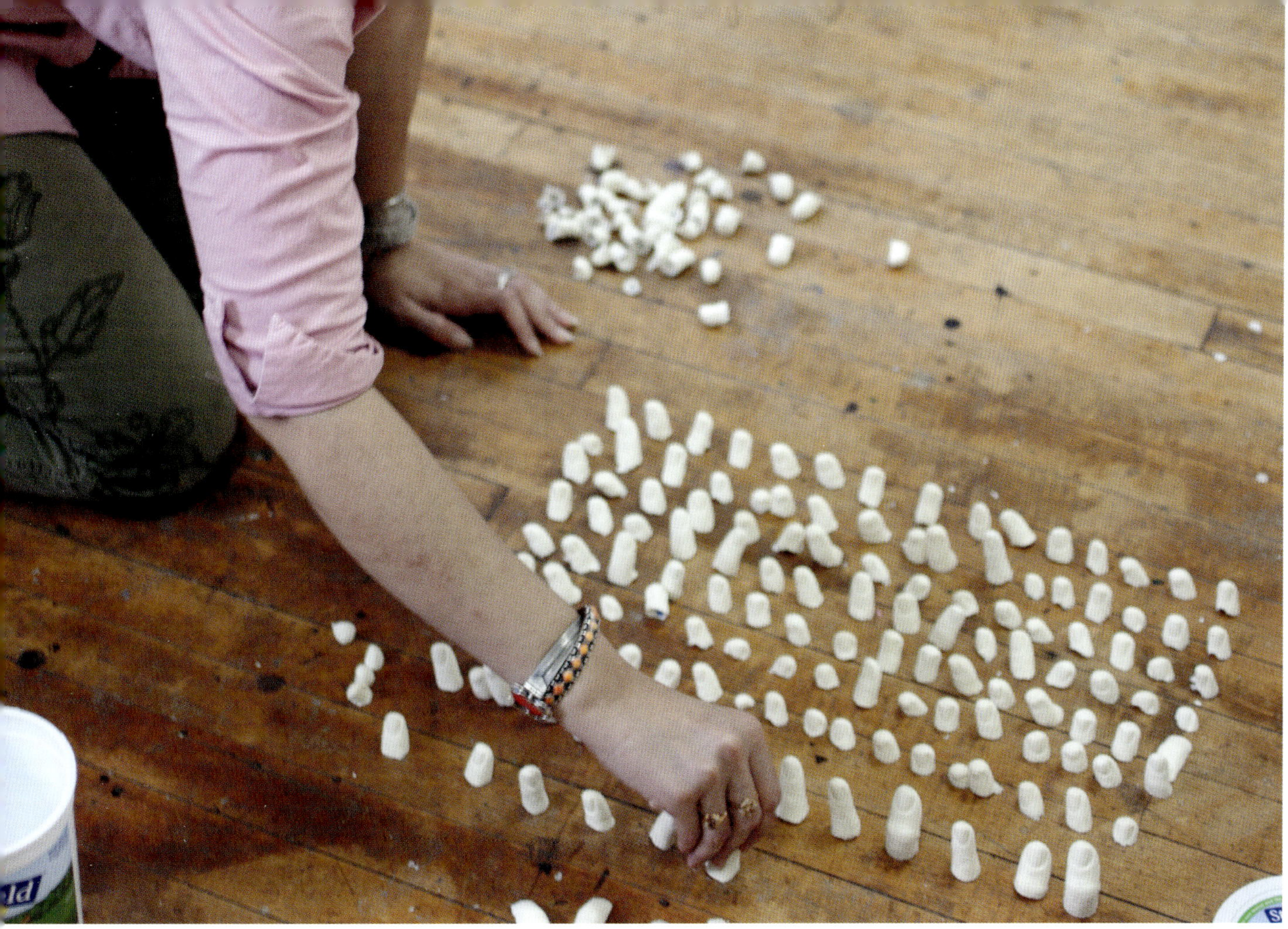

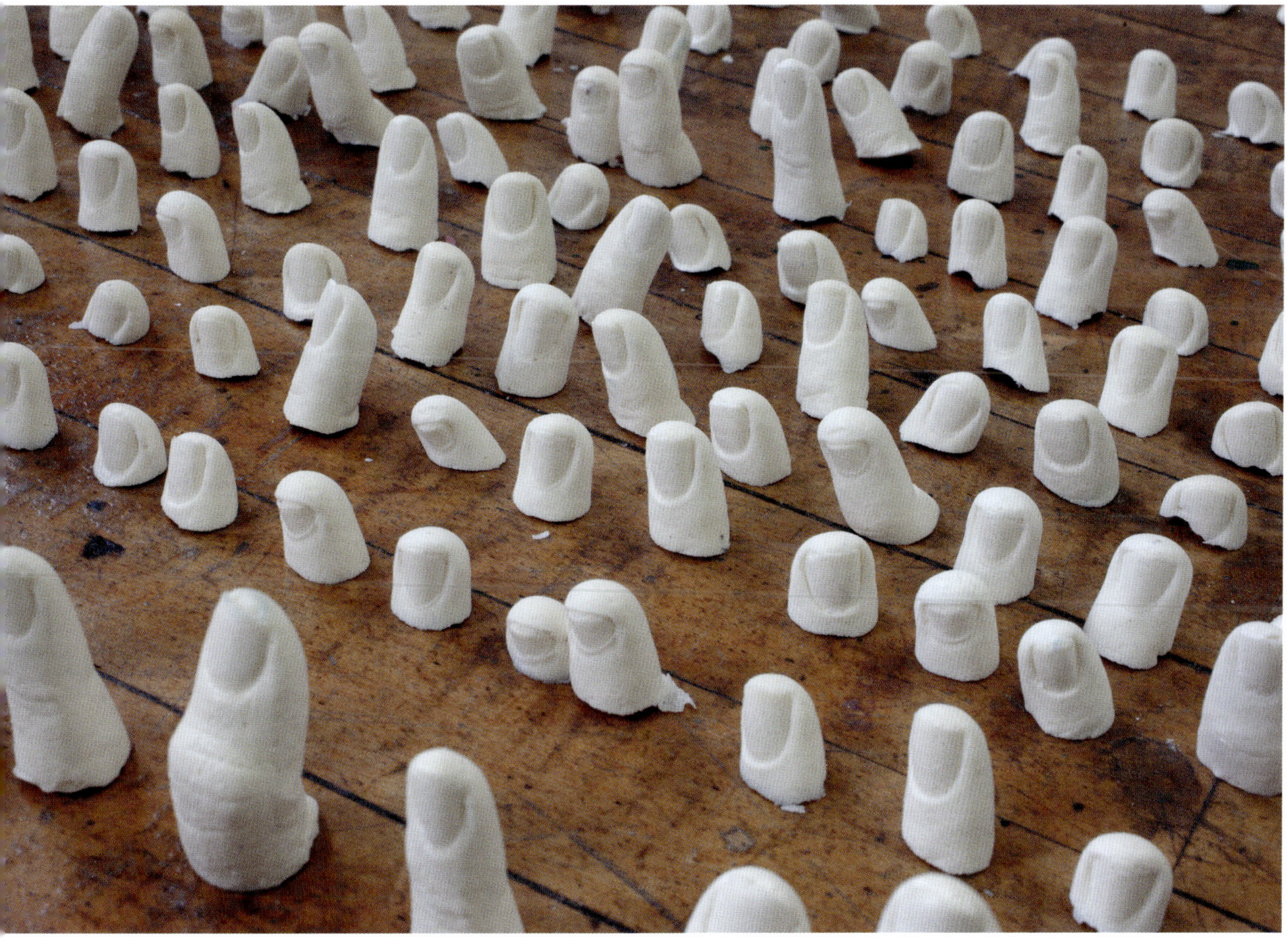

OPPOSITE (DETAIL) Studio photograph of a drawing for print project Dirty Pretty 2008

TOP AND BOTTOM Studio views, Lexington, Massachusetts 2010

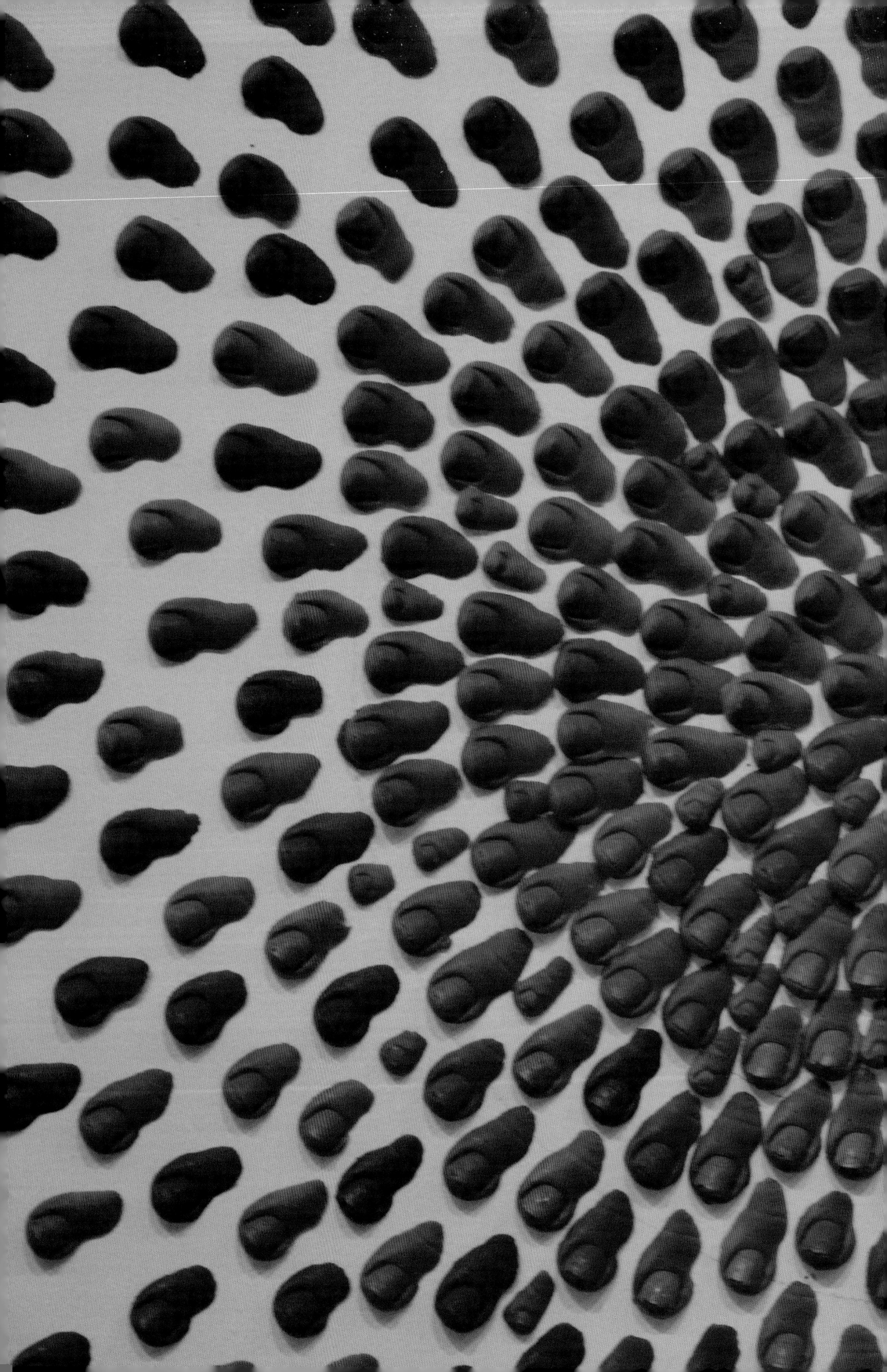

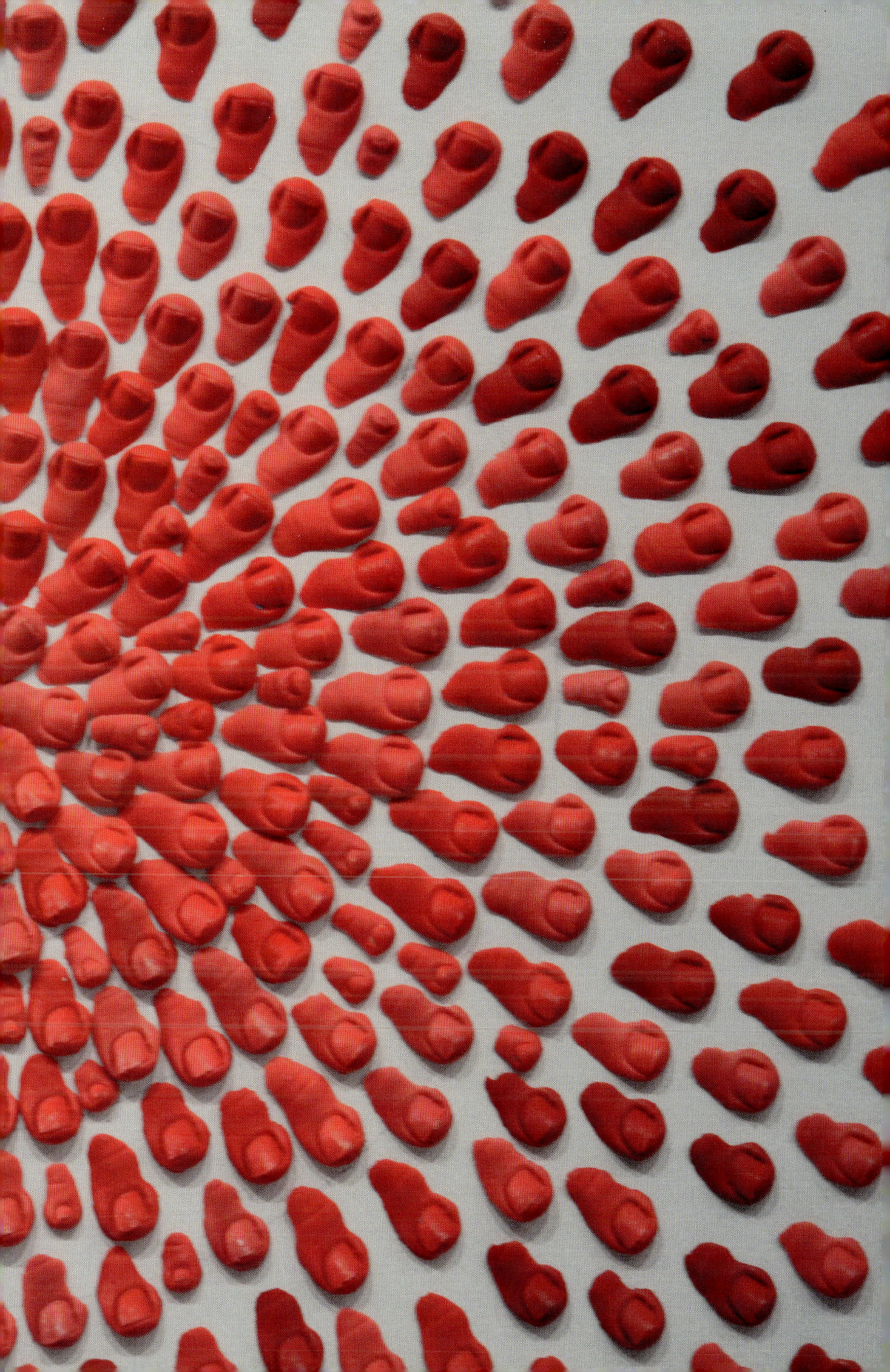

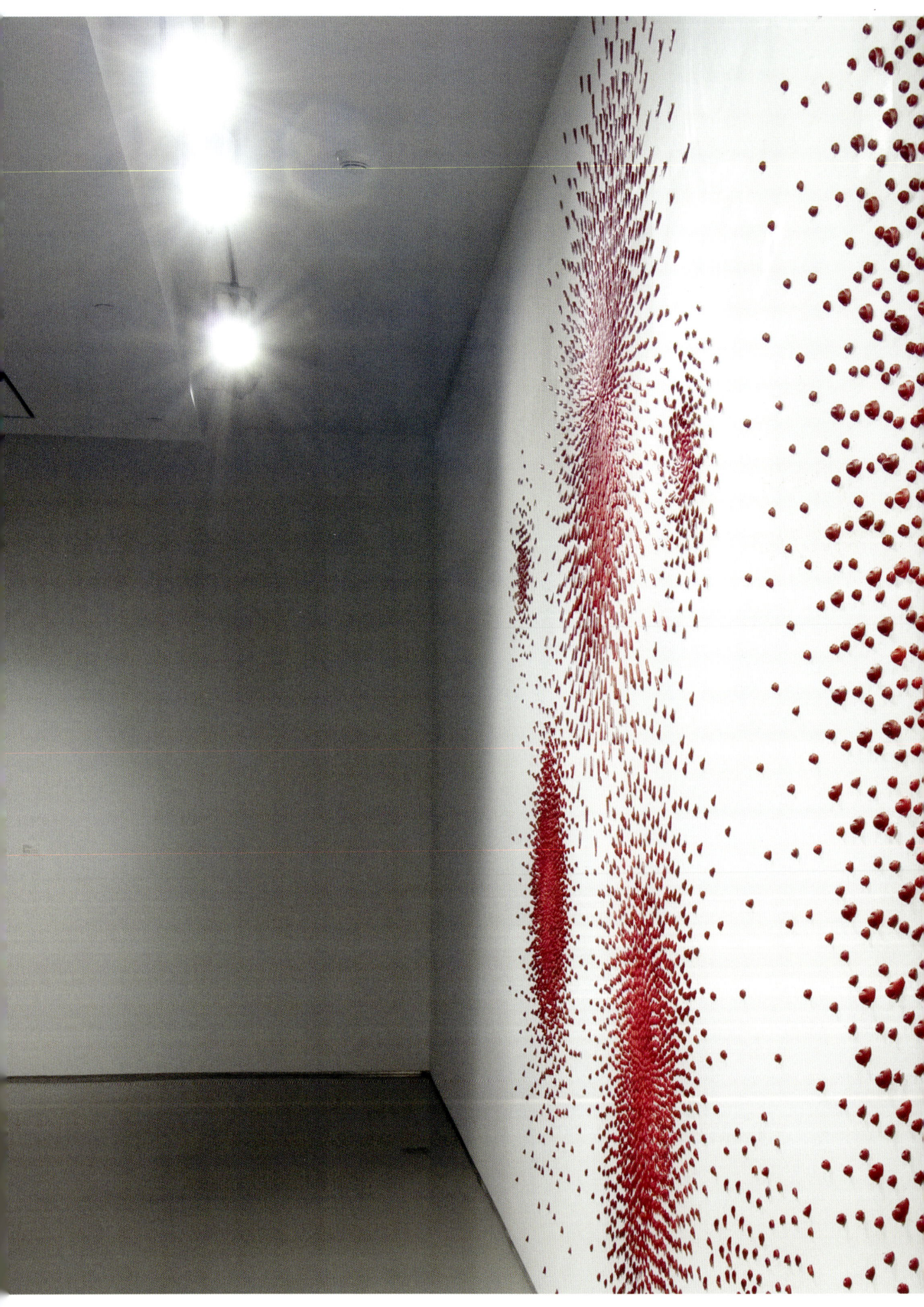

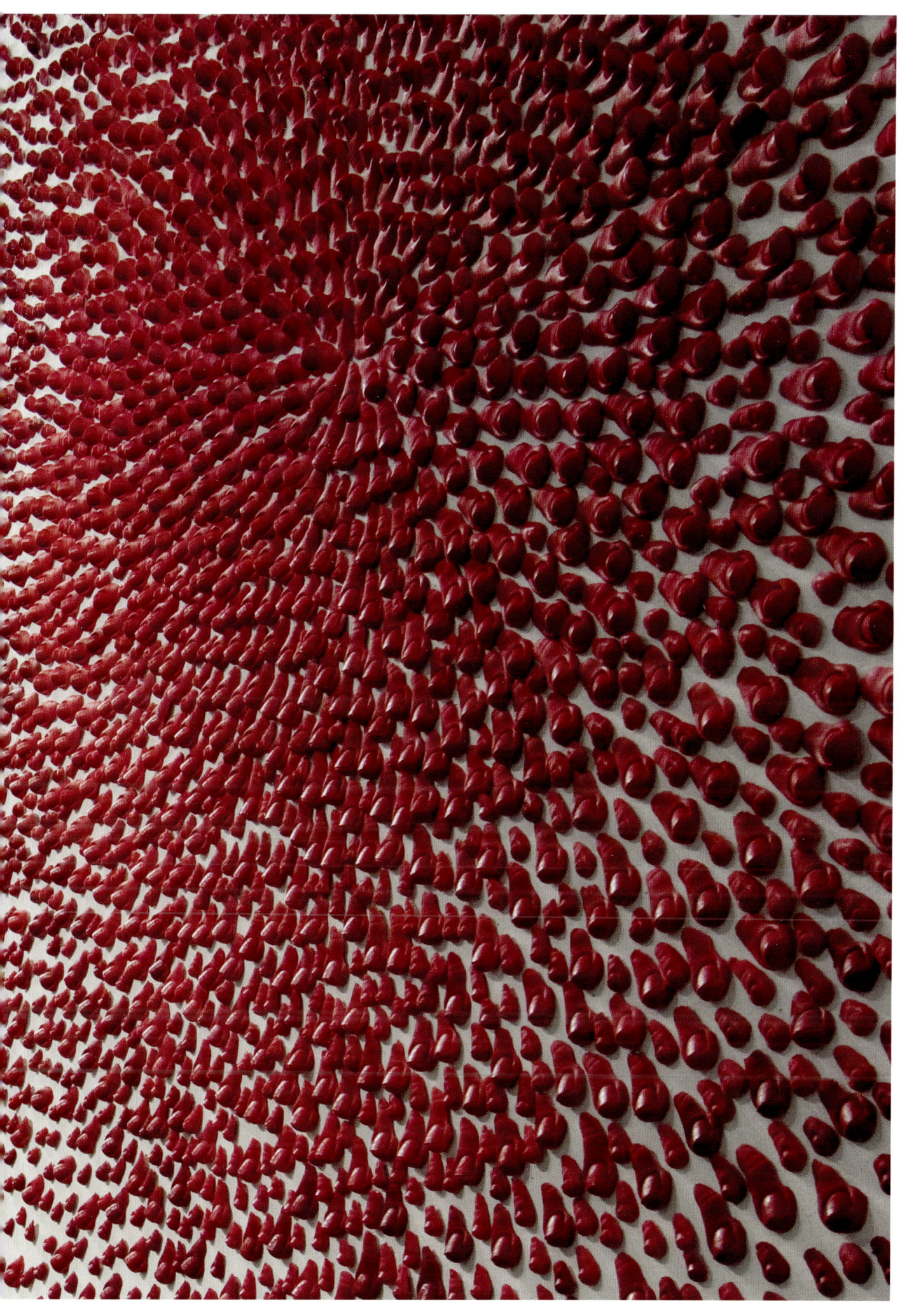

PREVIOUS PAGES (DETAIL)/ABOVE *I Am My Lost Diamond* 2011
Resin cast digits and pins on wall, dimensions variable.
Installation view, Contemporary Arts Center, Cincinnati, Ohio

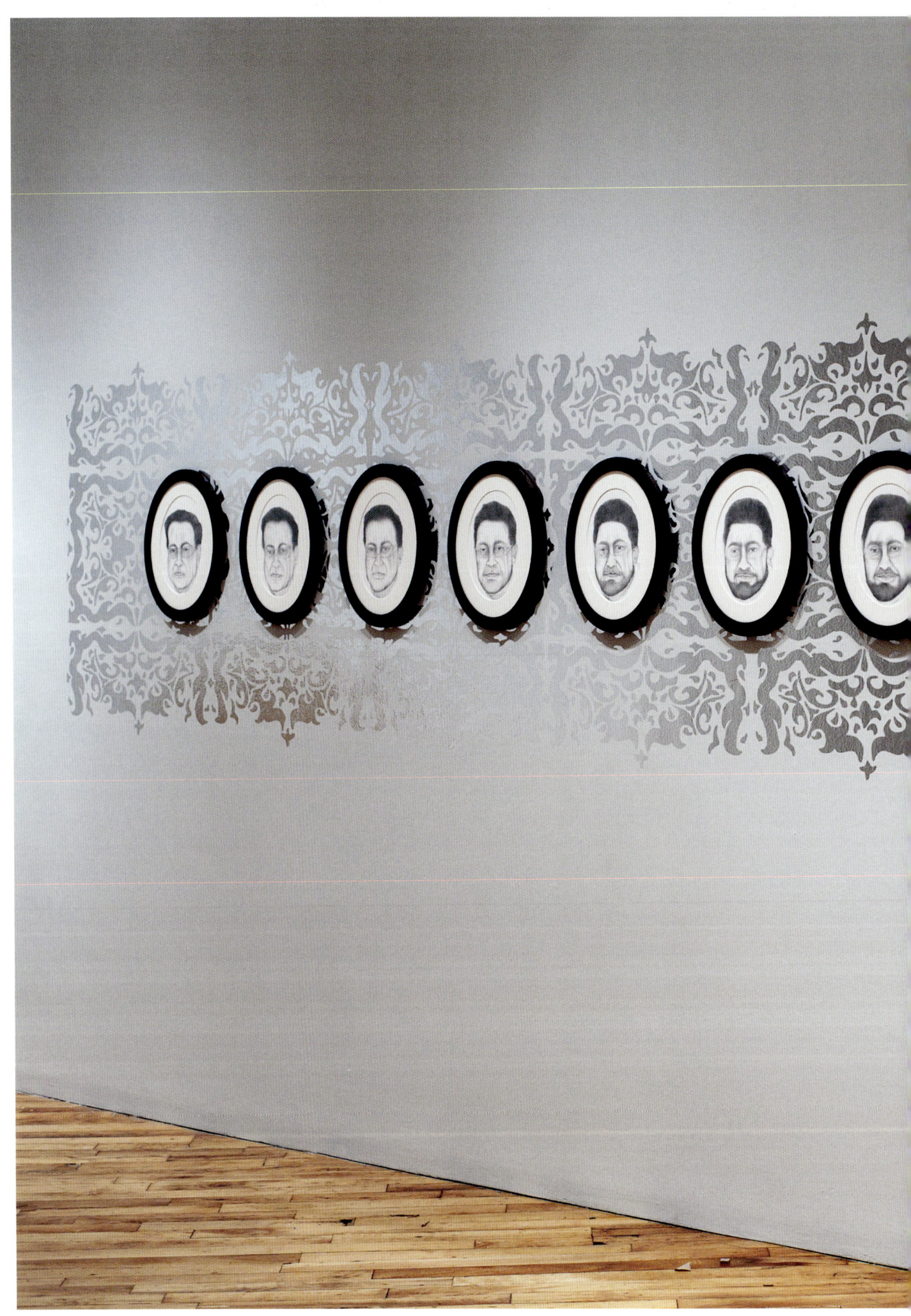

*Out Beyond The Ideas Of Rightness & Wrongness, There Is
A Place, I'll Meet You There* 2012
Pencil on paper and paper cut-out on wall, each 16 × 13 inches
Installation view

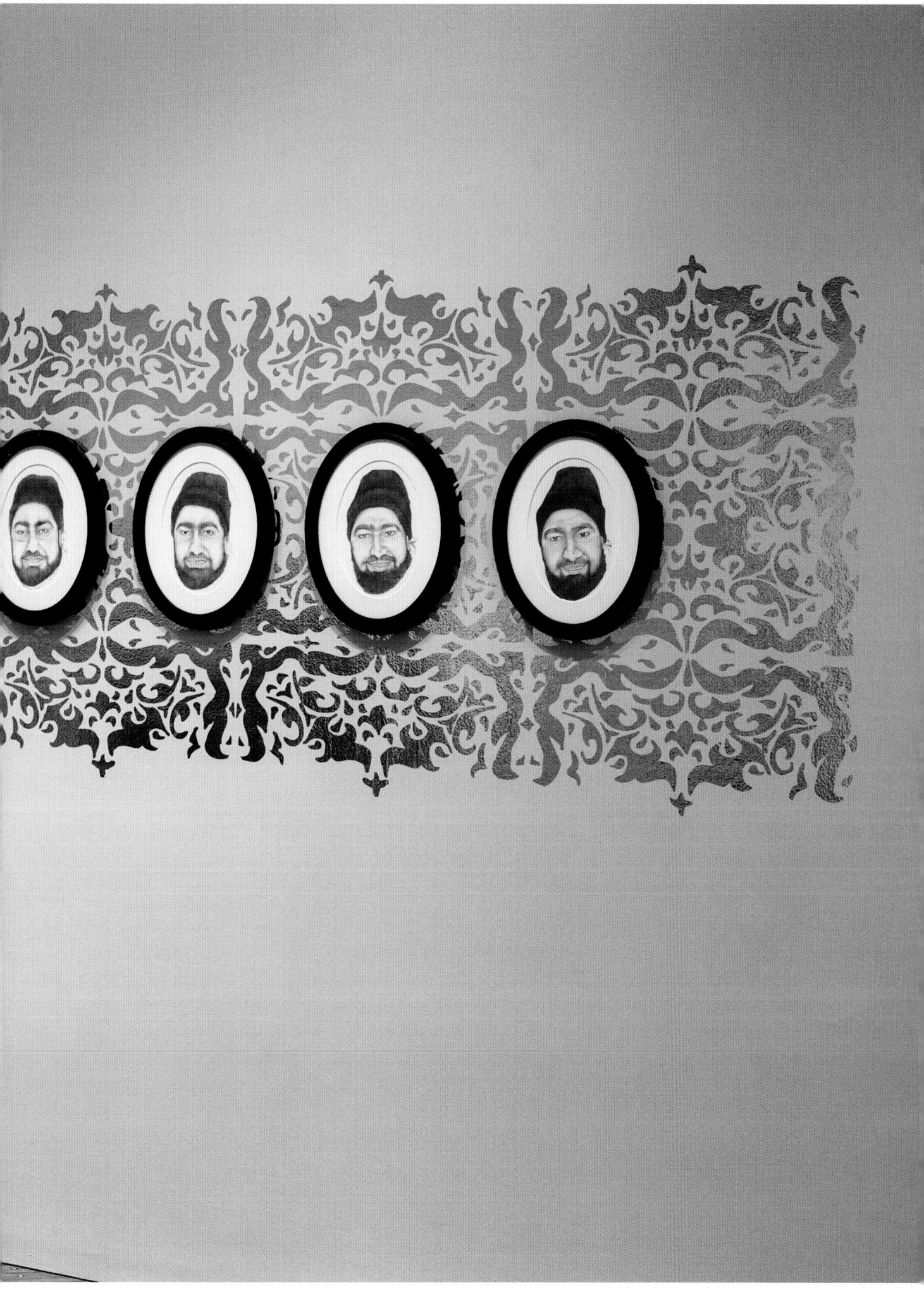

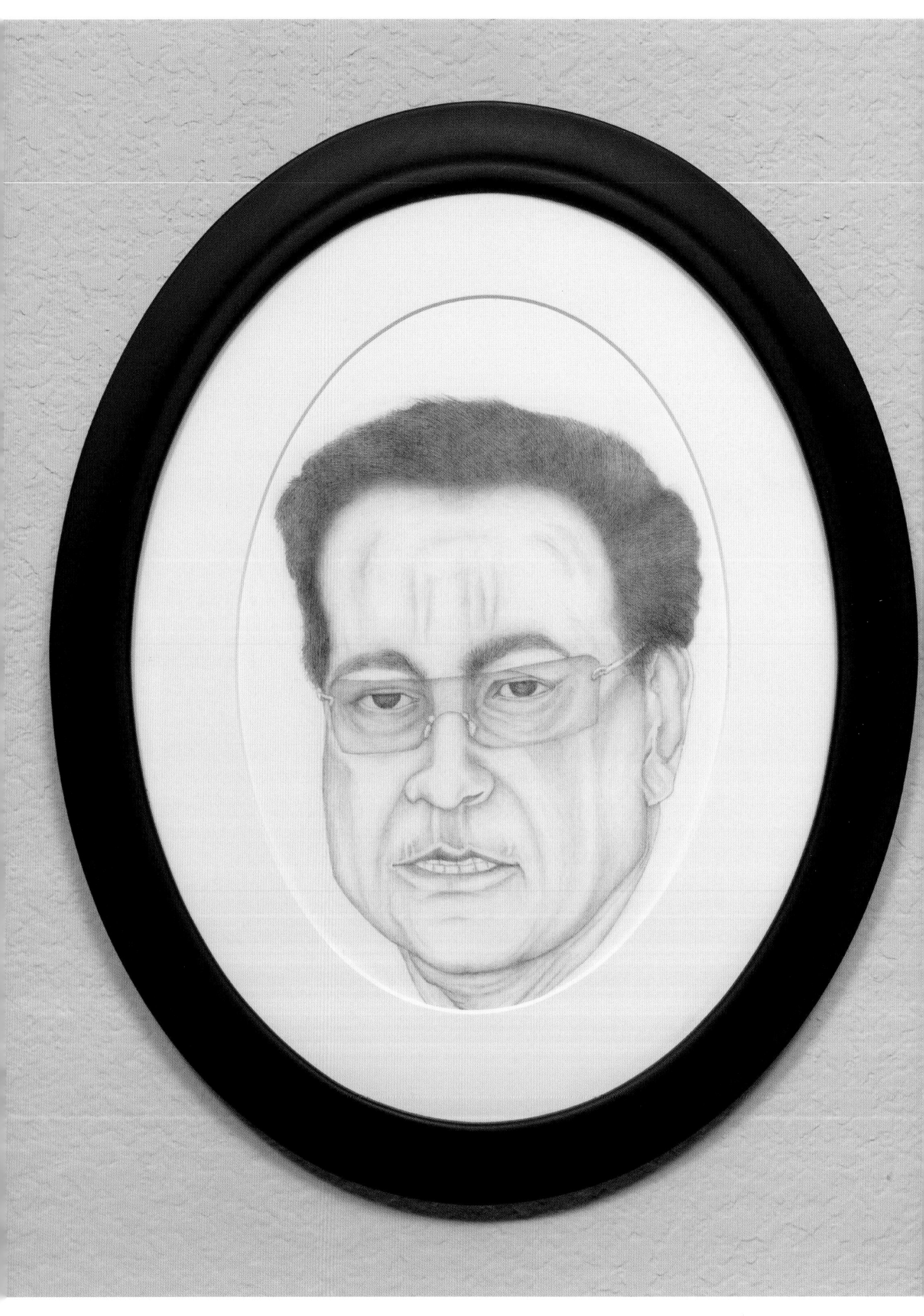

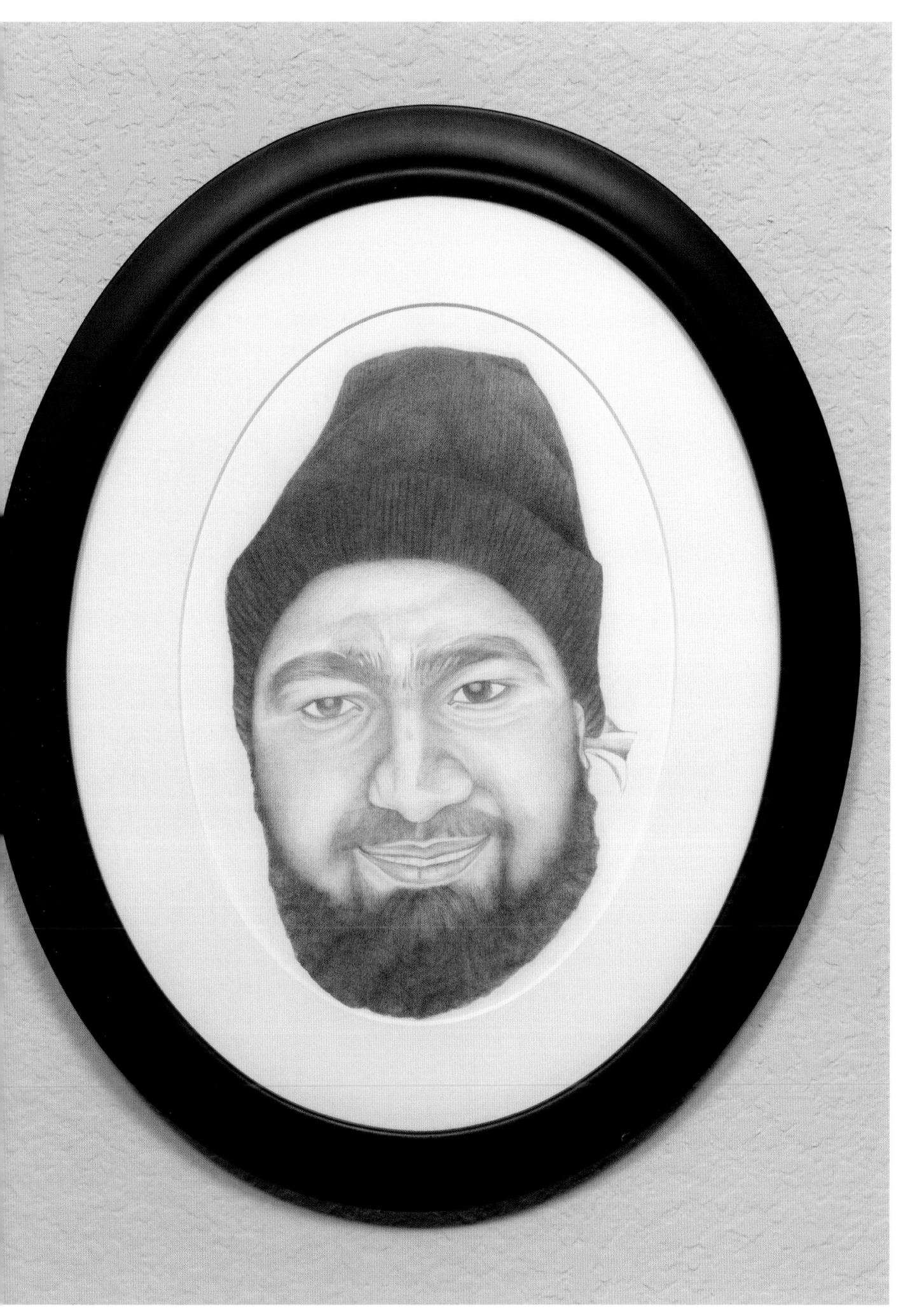

(DETAIL) *Out Beyond The Ideas Of Rightness & Wrongness,*
There Is A Place, I'll Meet You There 2012
Pencil on paper and paper cut-out on wall, each 16×13 inches

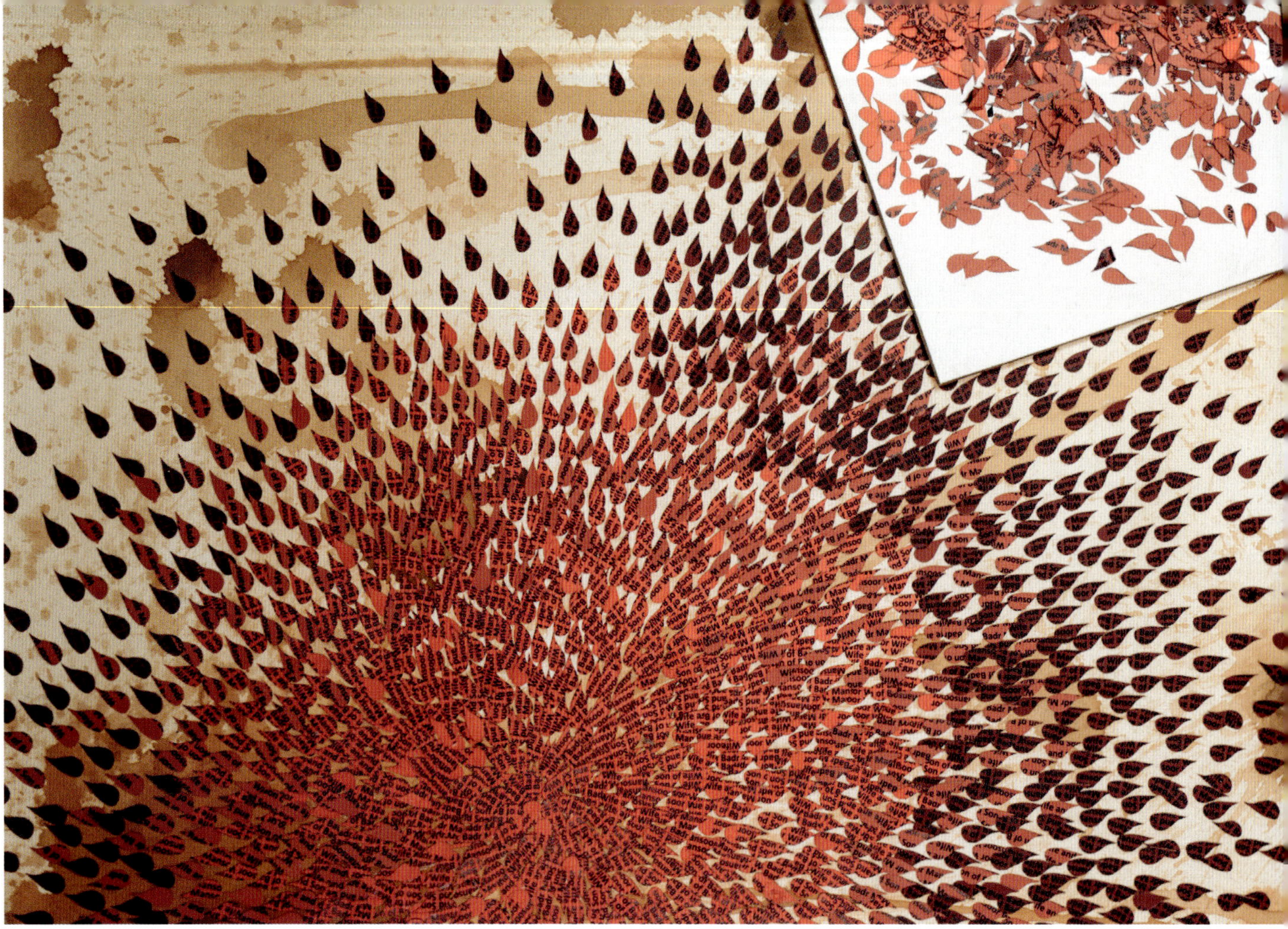

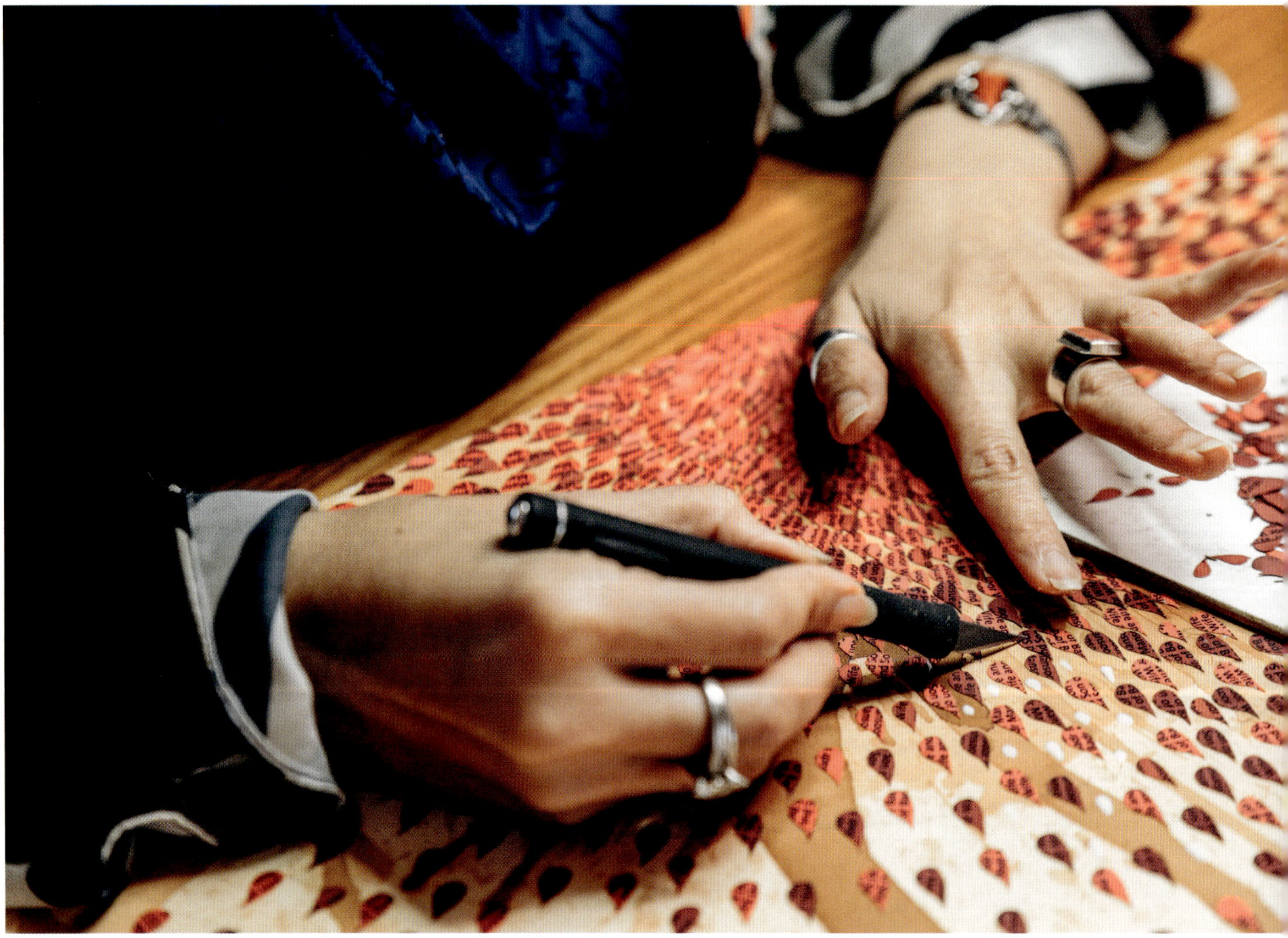

TOP AND BOTTOM **Wife And Son Of Badr Mansoor** 2020
Printed text on tea-stained paper, each 55 × 30 inches,
together 55 × 90 inches
Work in progress studio photographs

OPPOSITE (DETAIL) **Wife And Son Of Badr Mansoor** 2020
Printed text on tea-stained paper, each 55 × 30 inches,
together 55 × 90 inches

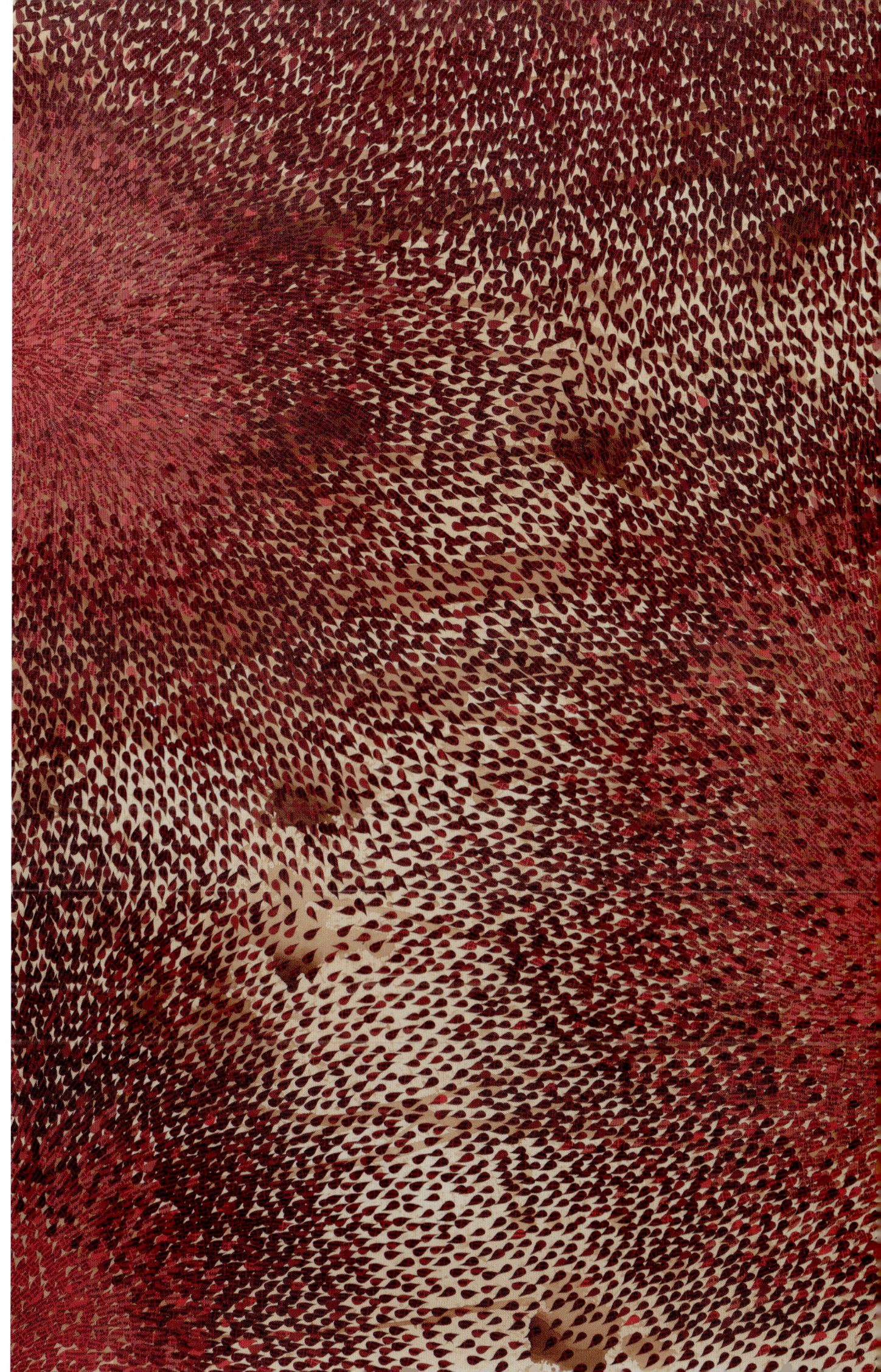

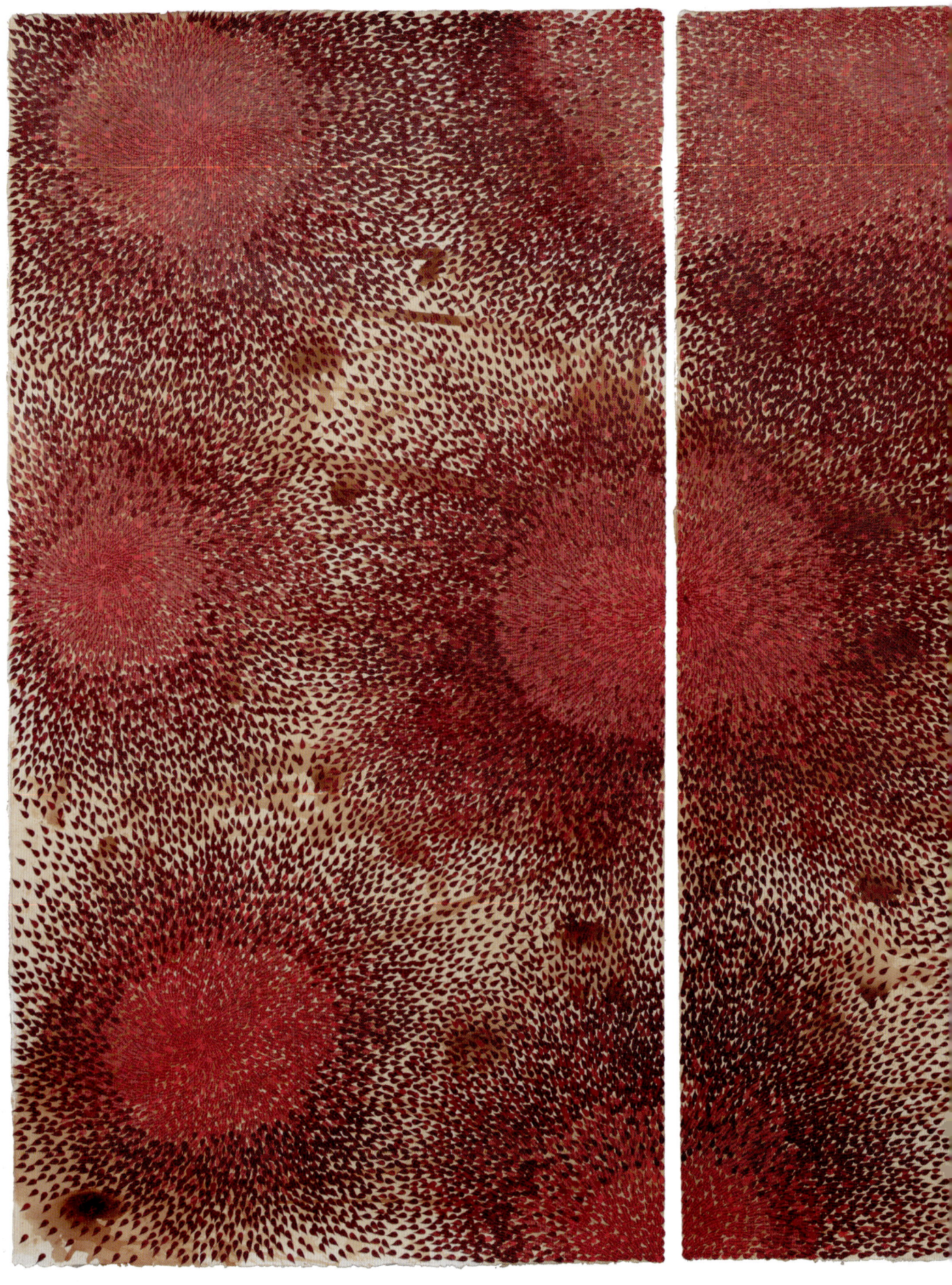

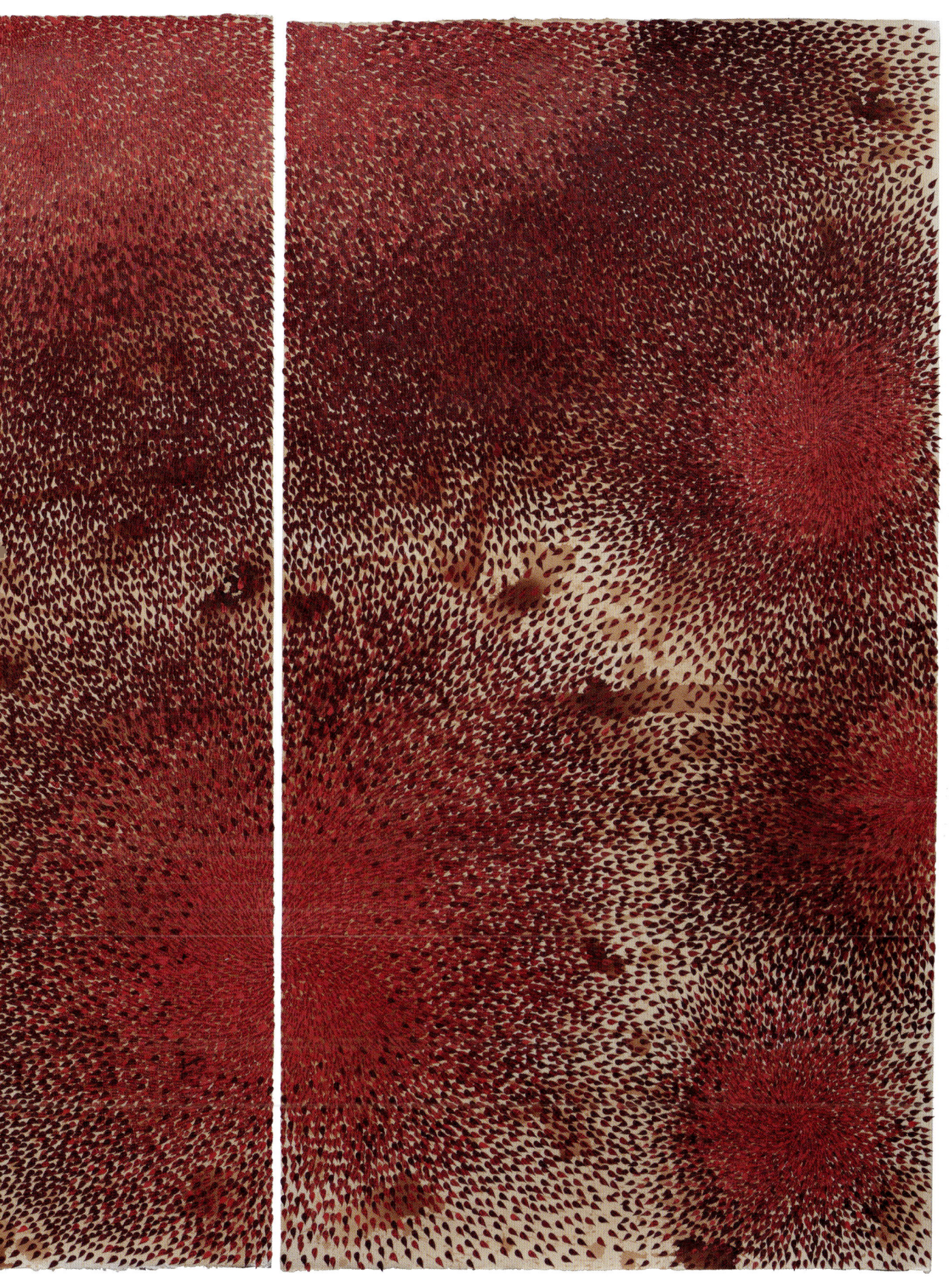

Wife And Son Of Badr Mansoor 2020
Printed text on tea-stained paper, each 55×30 inches,
together 55×90 inches

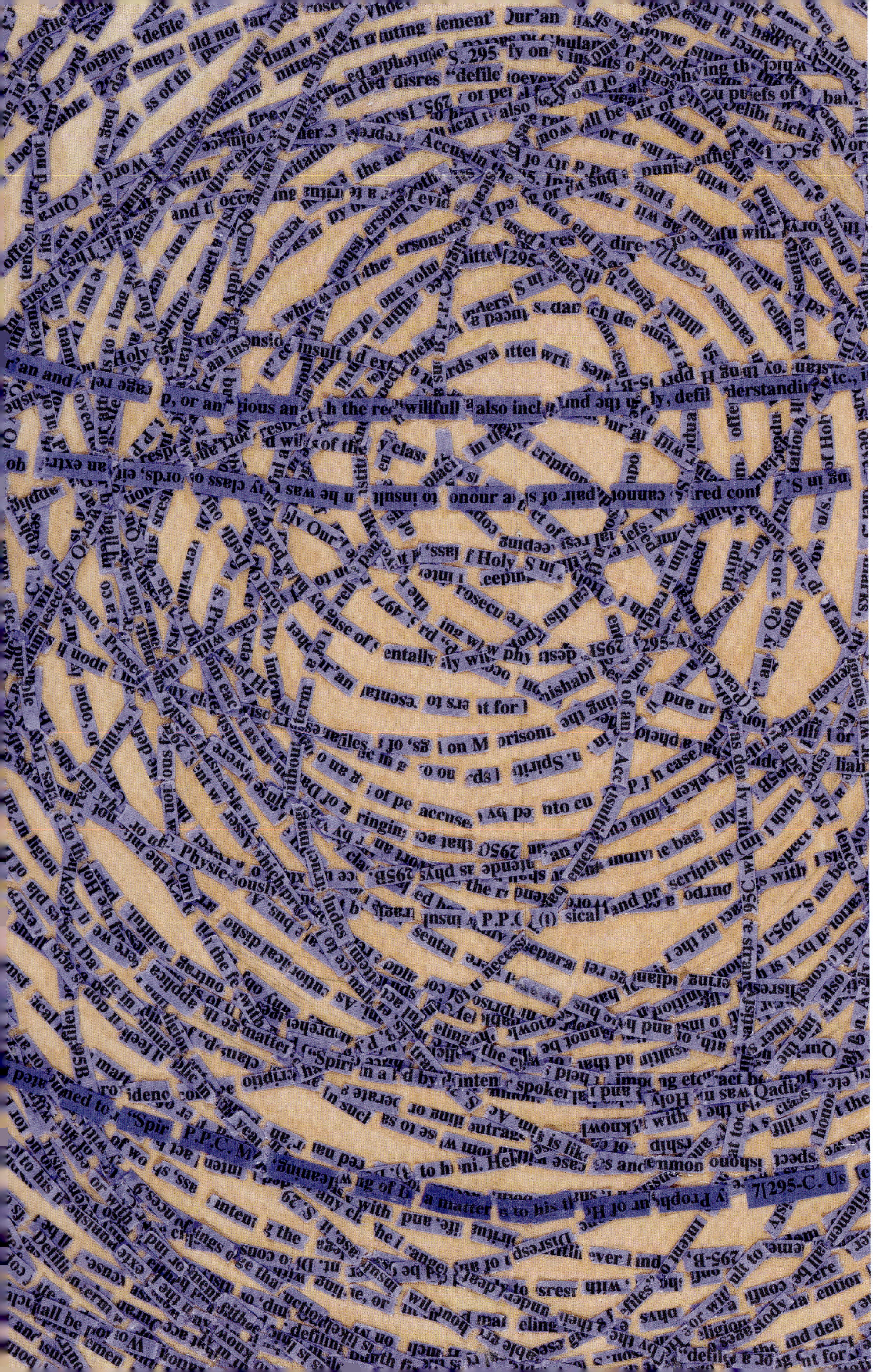

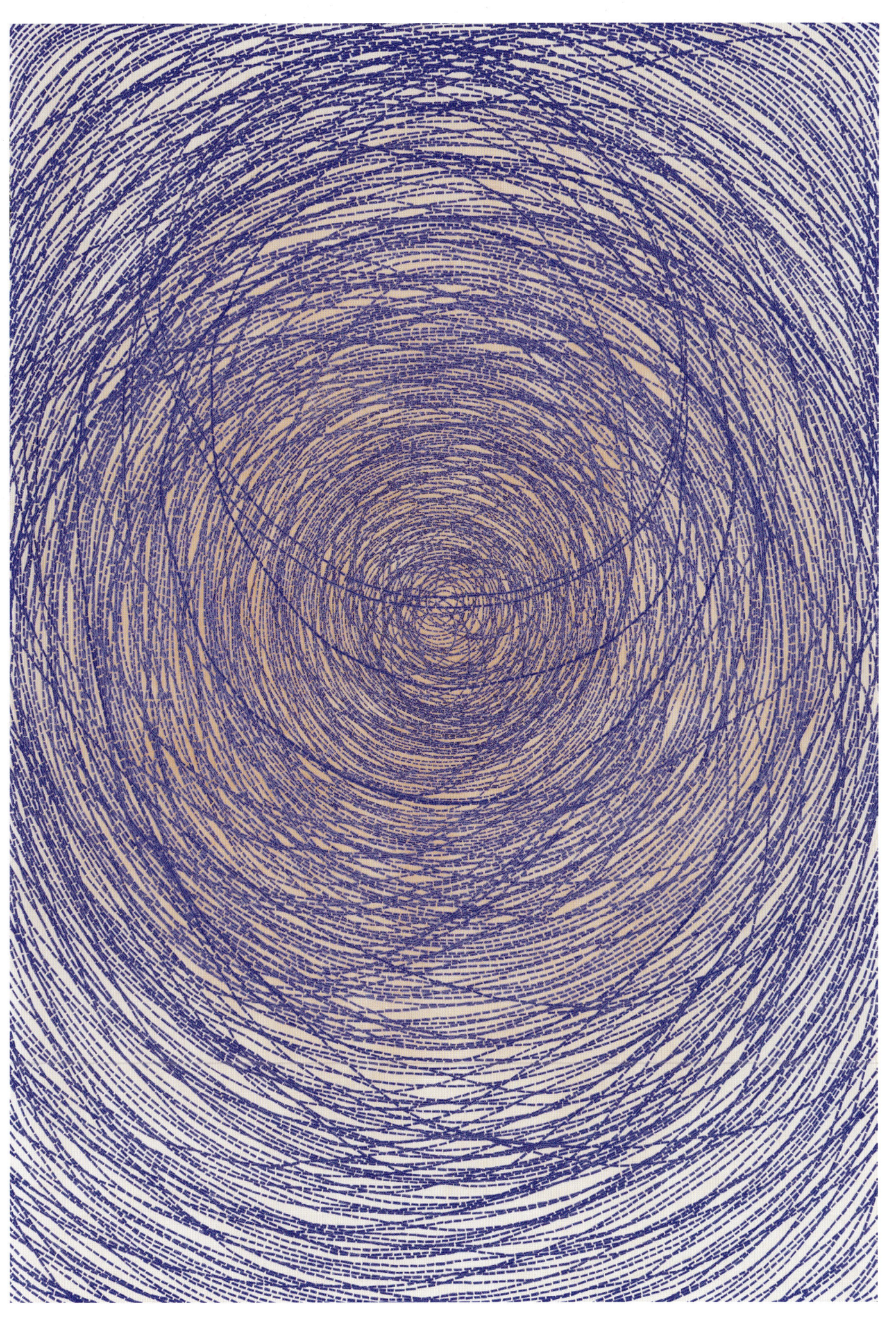

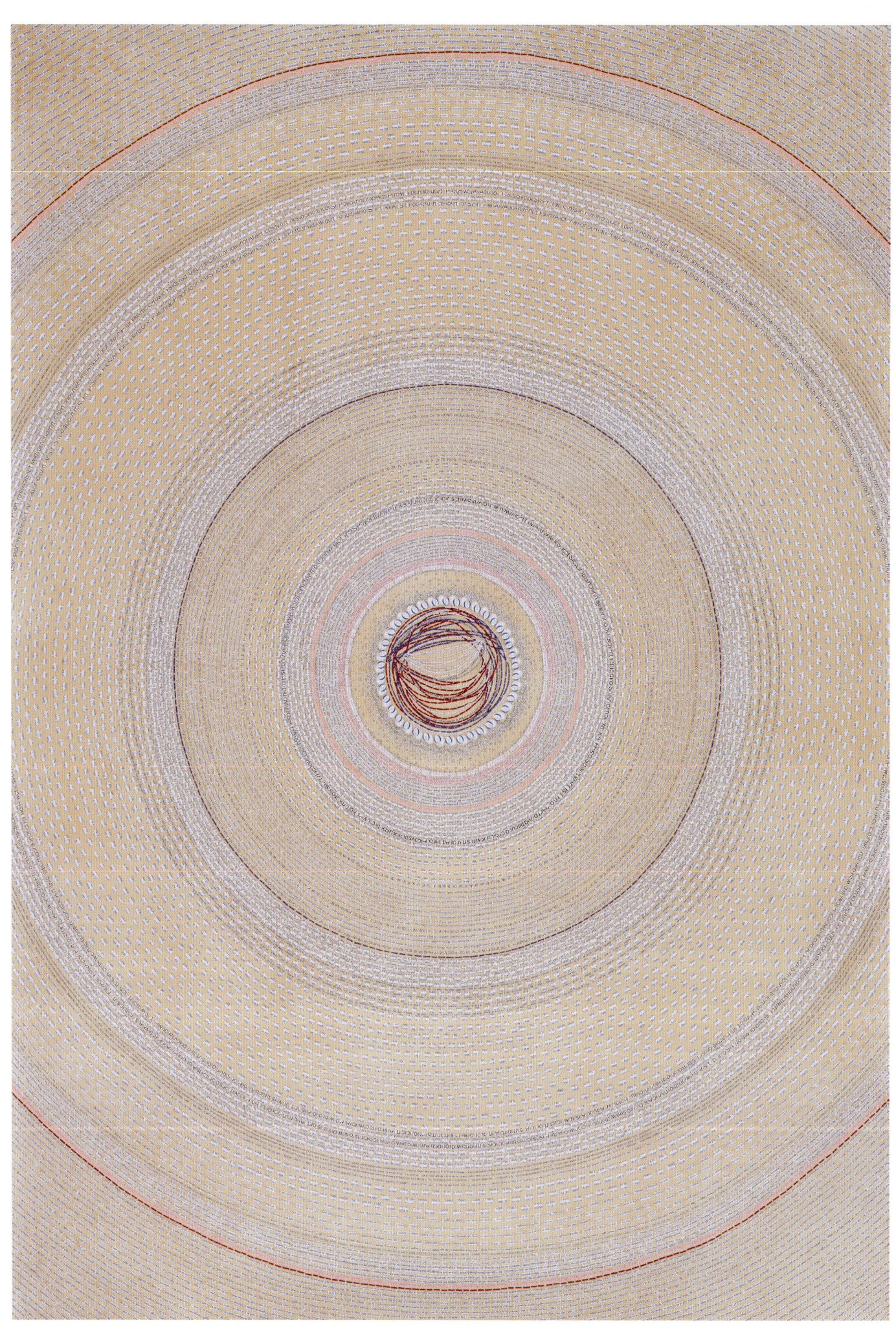

ABOVE/OPPOSITE (DETAIL) *I Am The Rejection Of You* 2011
Collage of text on tea-stained paper, 78×57 inches

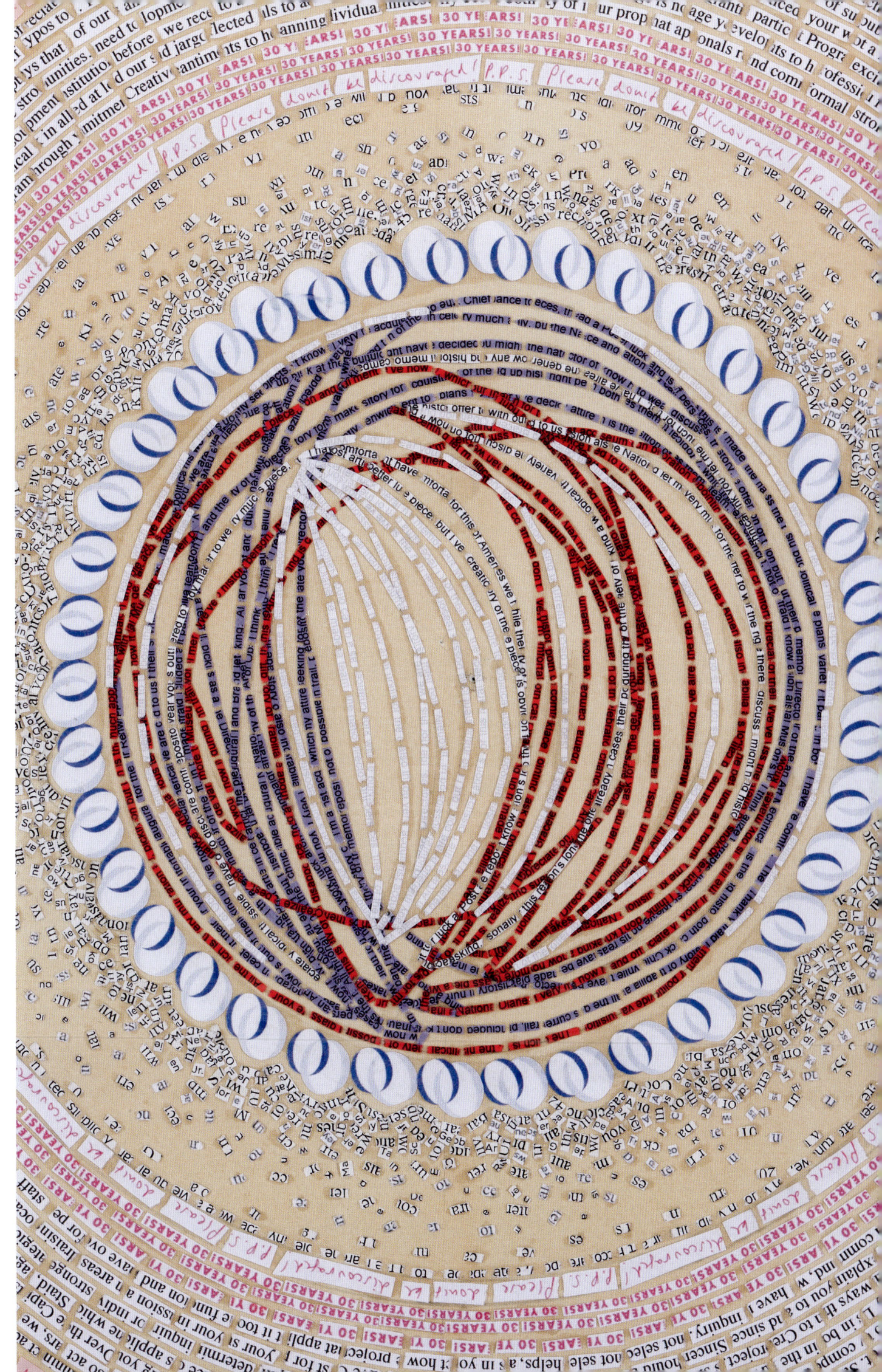

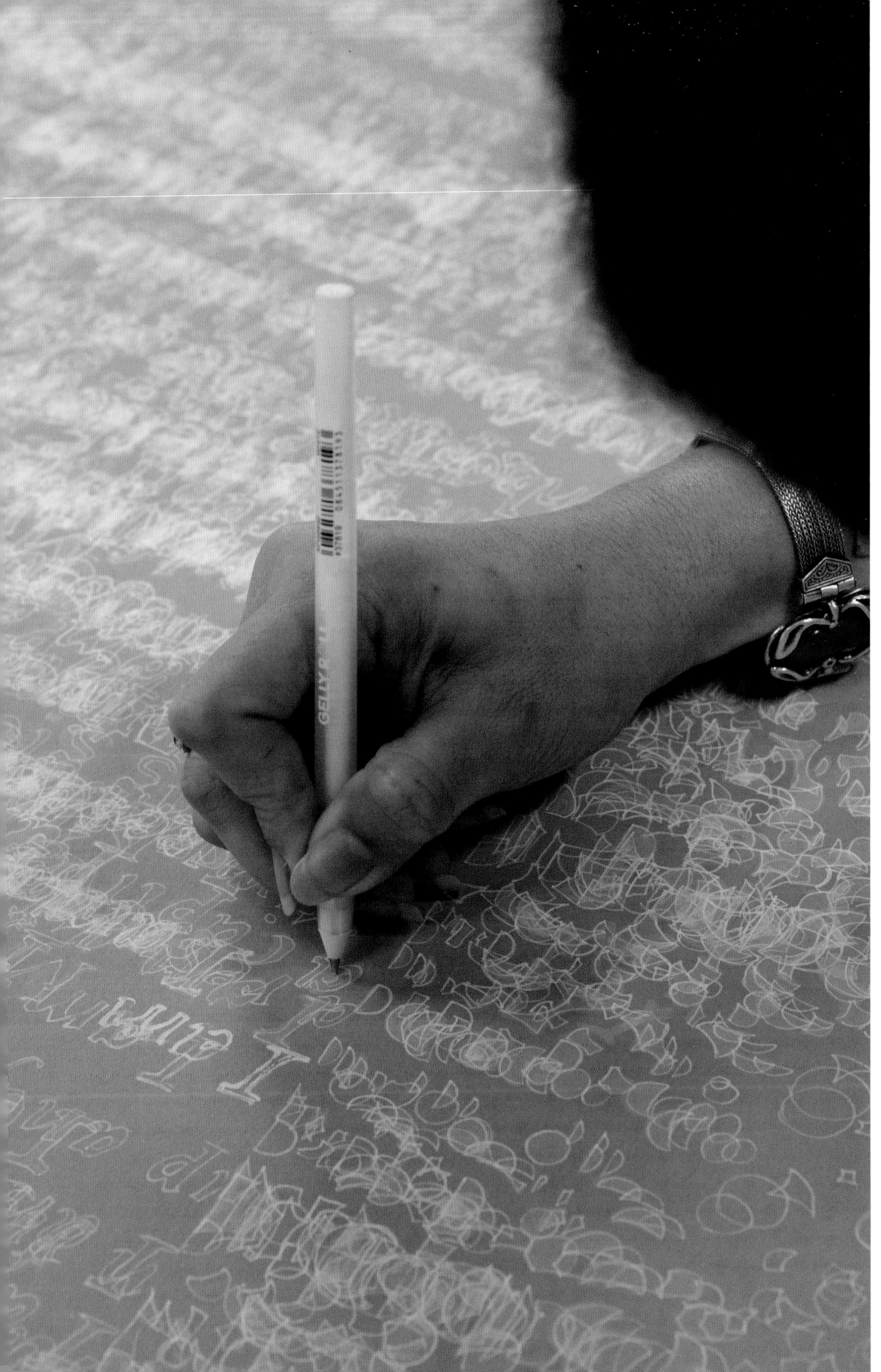

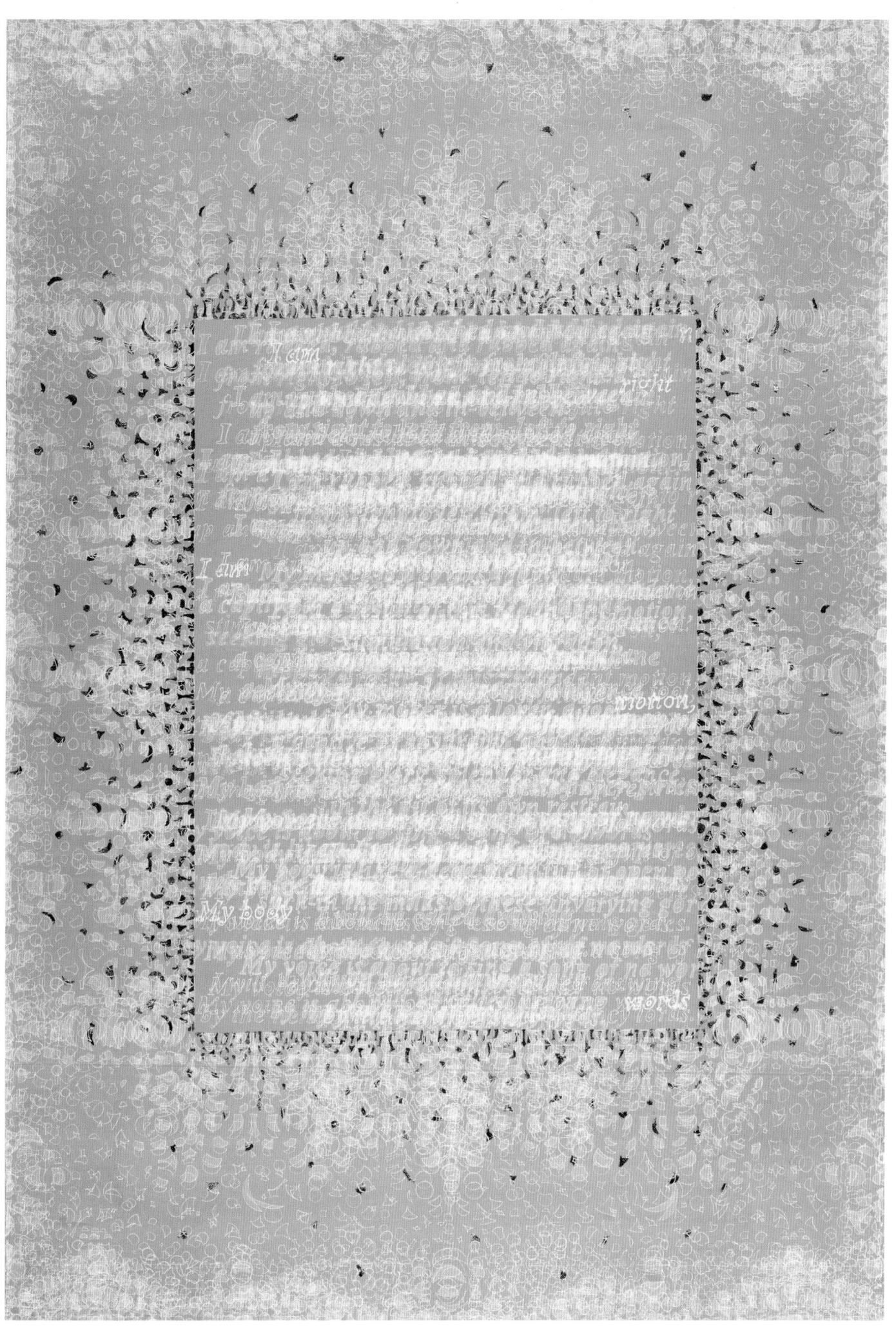

OPPOSITE (DETAIL) *I Will Be Called Drawing* 2010
Pen and gold leaf on tea-stained paper, 45×30 inches
Work in progress studio photograph

ABOVE *I Will Be Called Drawing* 2010
Pen and gold leaf on tea-stained paper, 45×30 inches

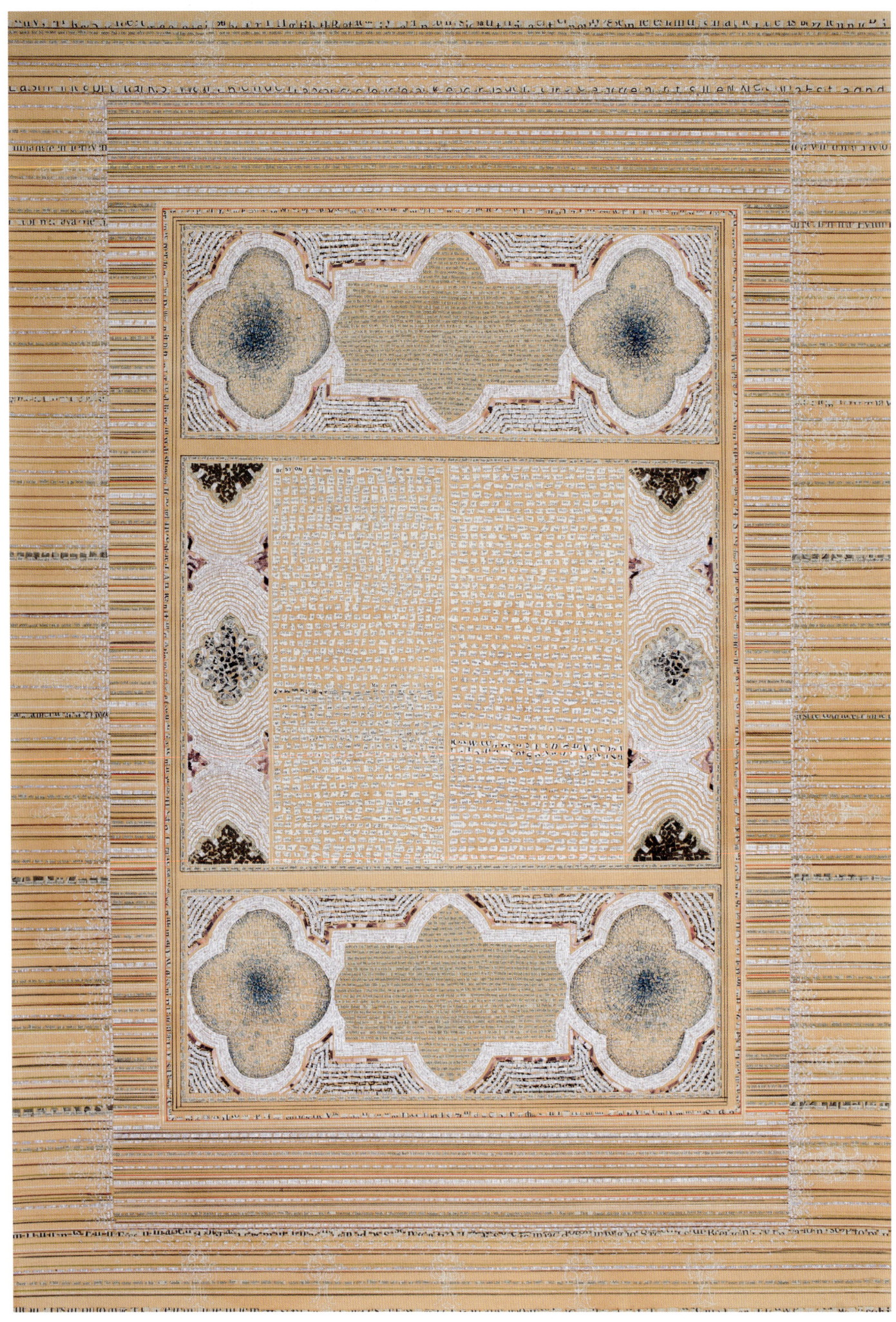

ABOVE/OPPOSITE (DETAIL) *I Am All What Is Left Of Me* 2010
Collage of text on tea-stained paper, 45×30 inches

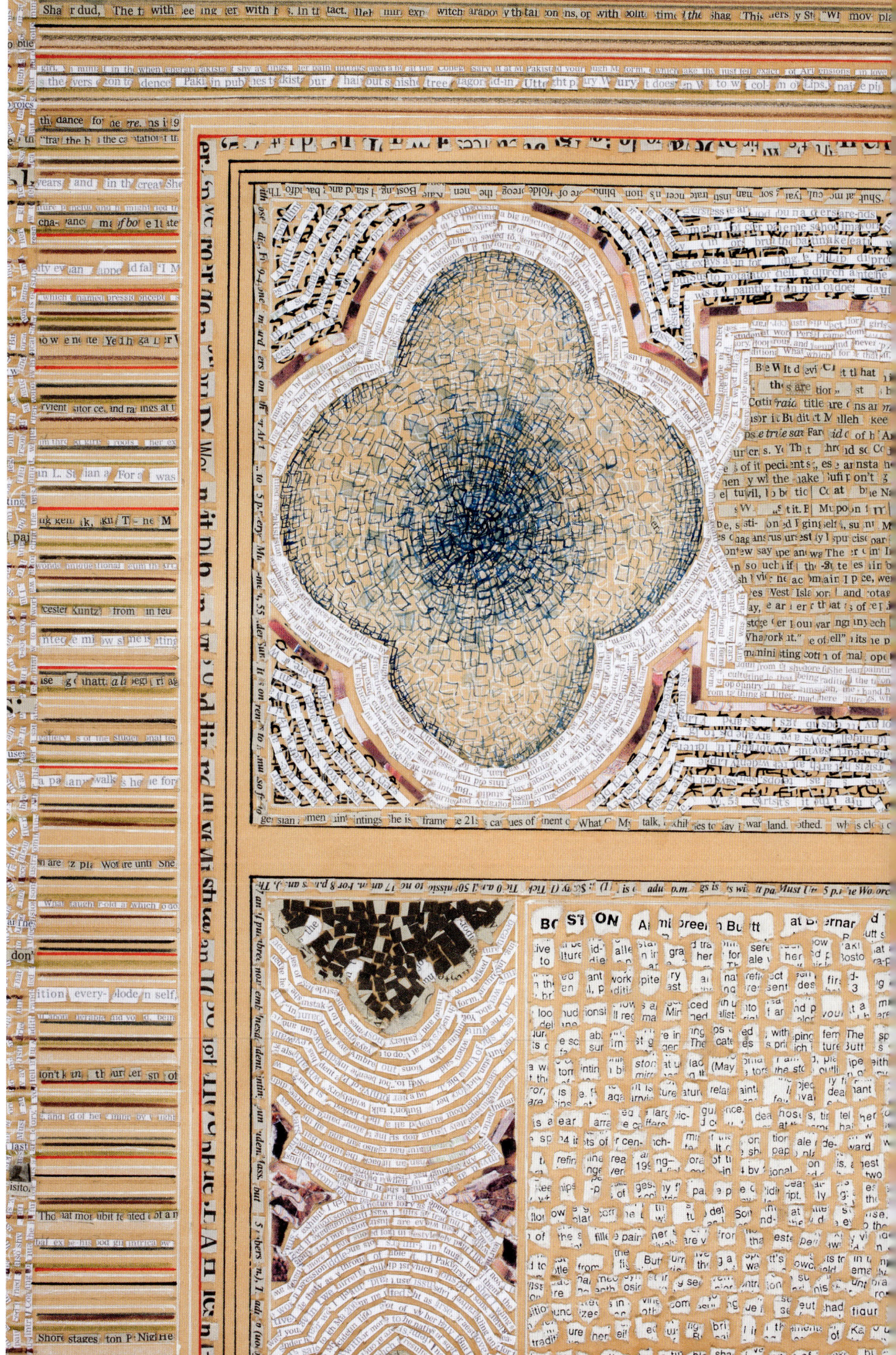

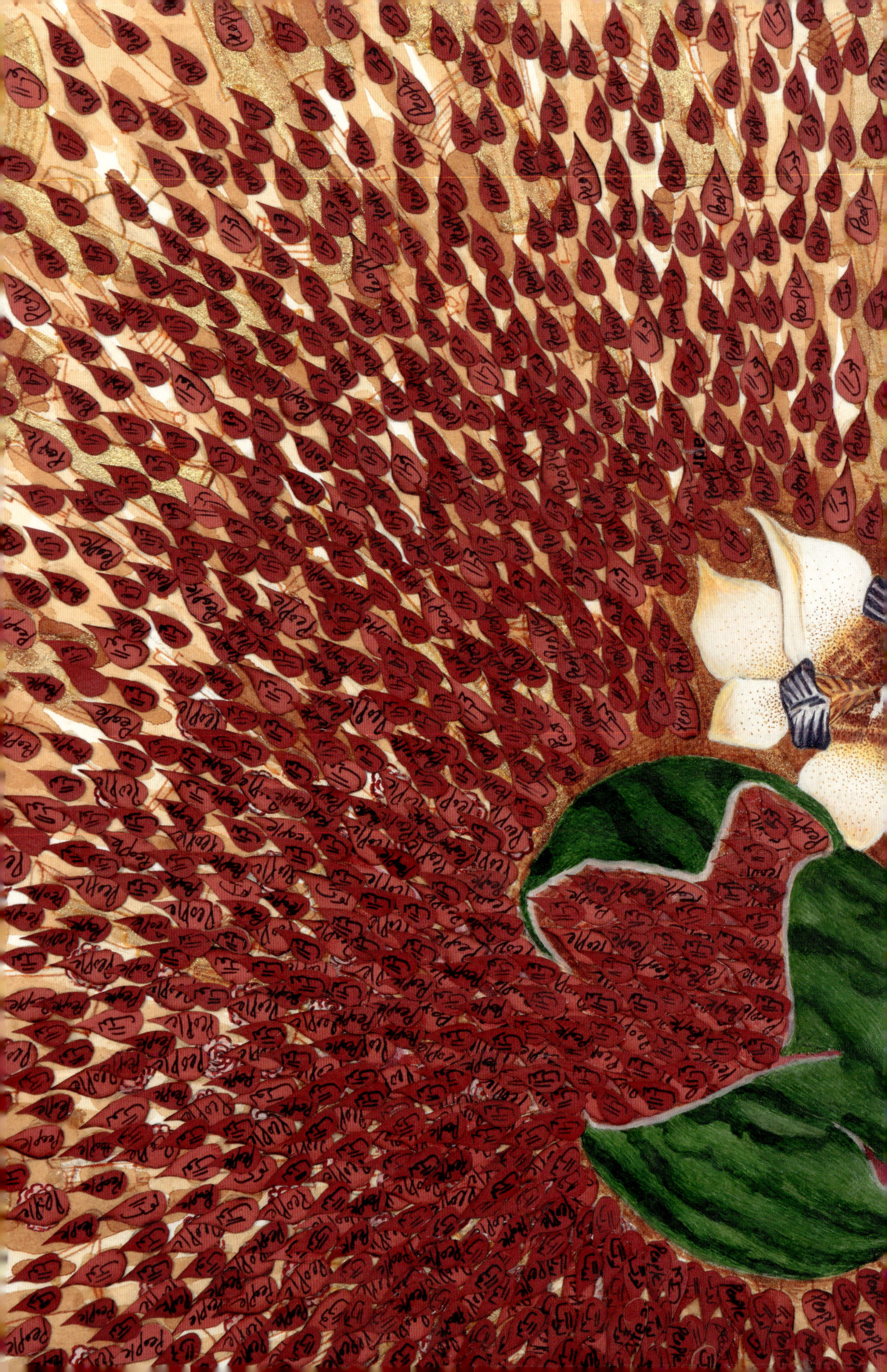

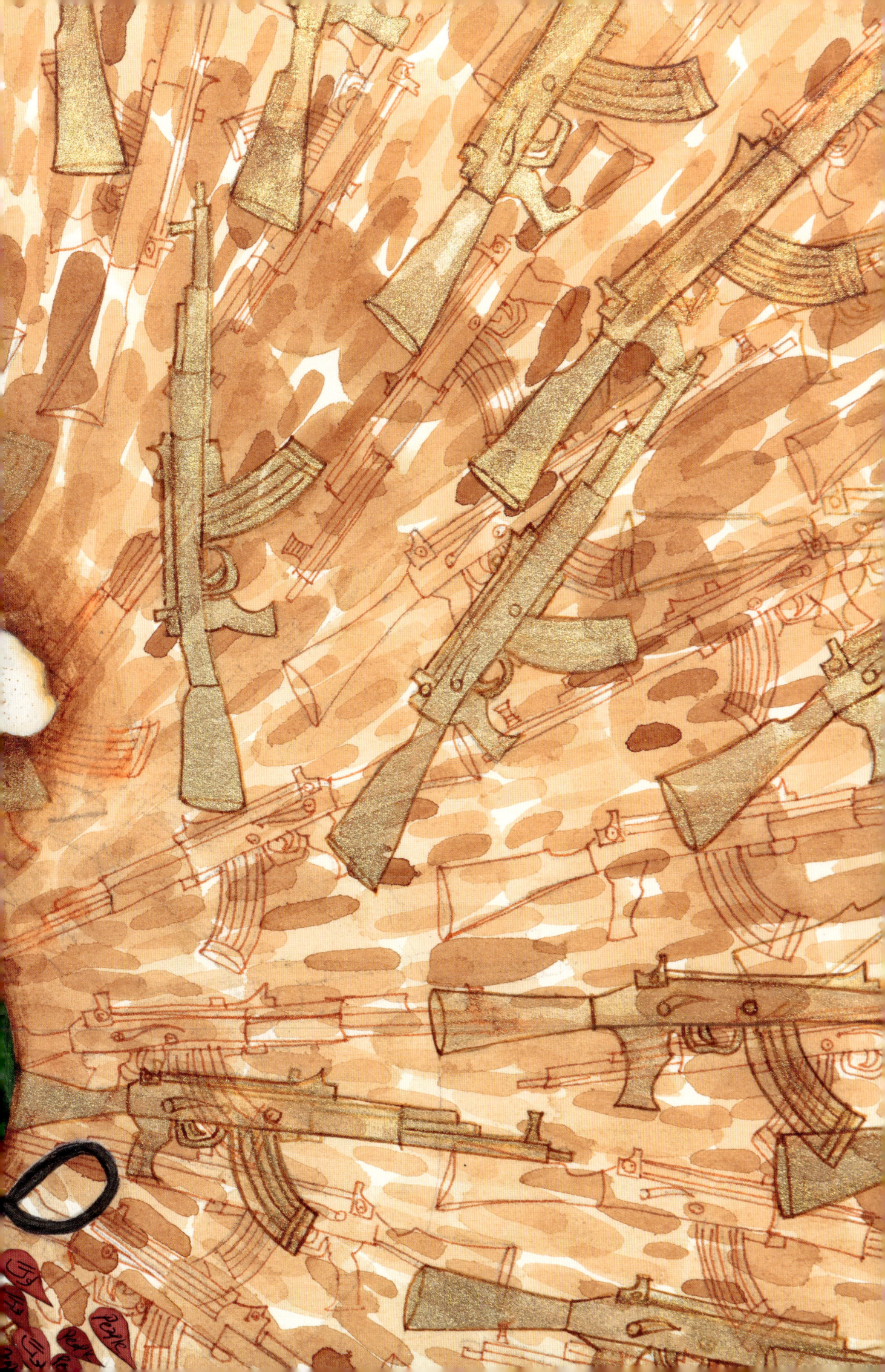

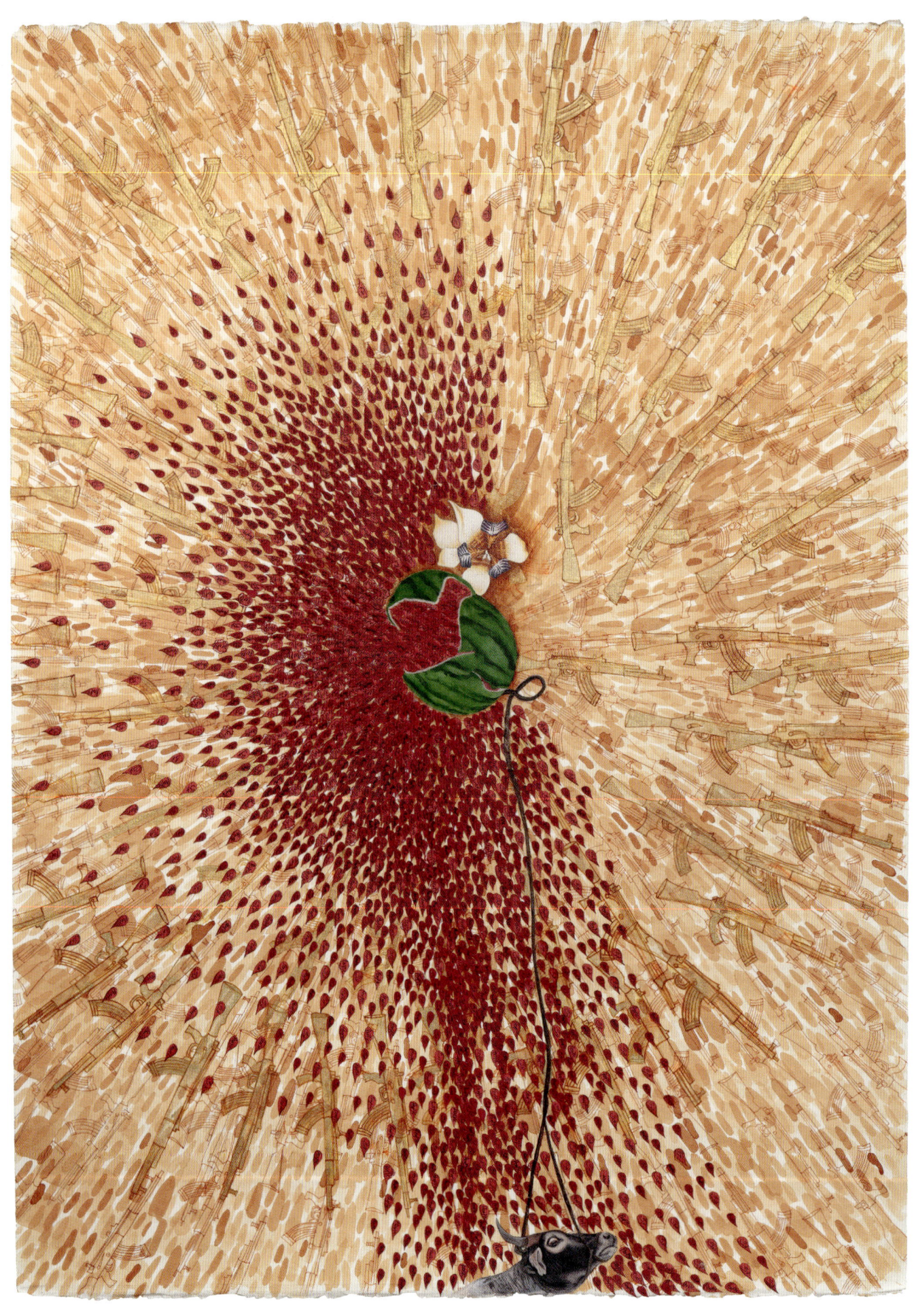

PREVIOUS PAGE (DETAIL)/ABOVE **Untitled** 2023
Collage of text, pen, water-based pigments and white
gouache on tea-stained paper, 30×22 inches

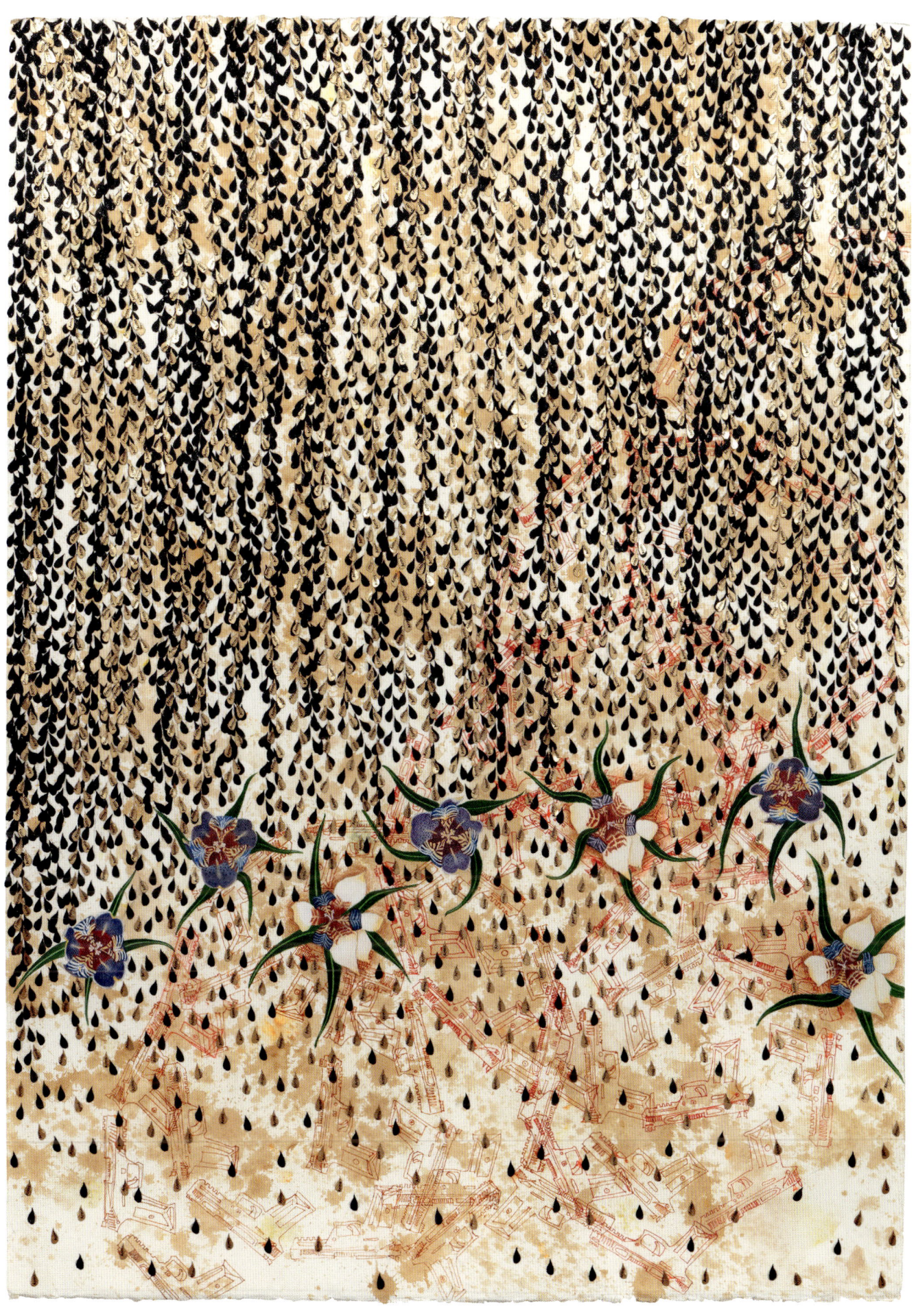

ABOVE/OVERLEAF (DETAIL) **Untitled** 2023
Collage of text, pen, water-based pigments and white
gouache on tea-stained paper, 30×22 inches

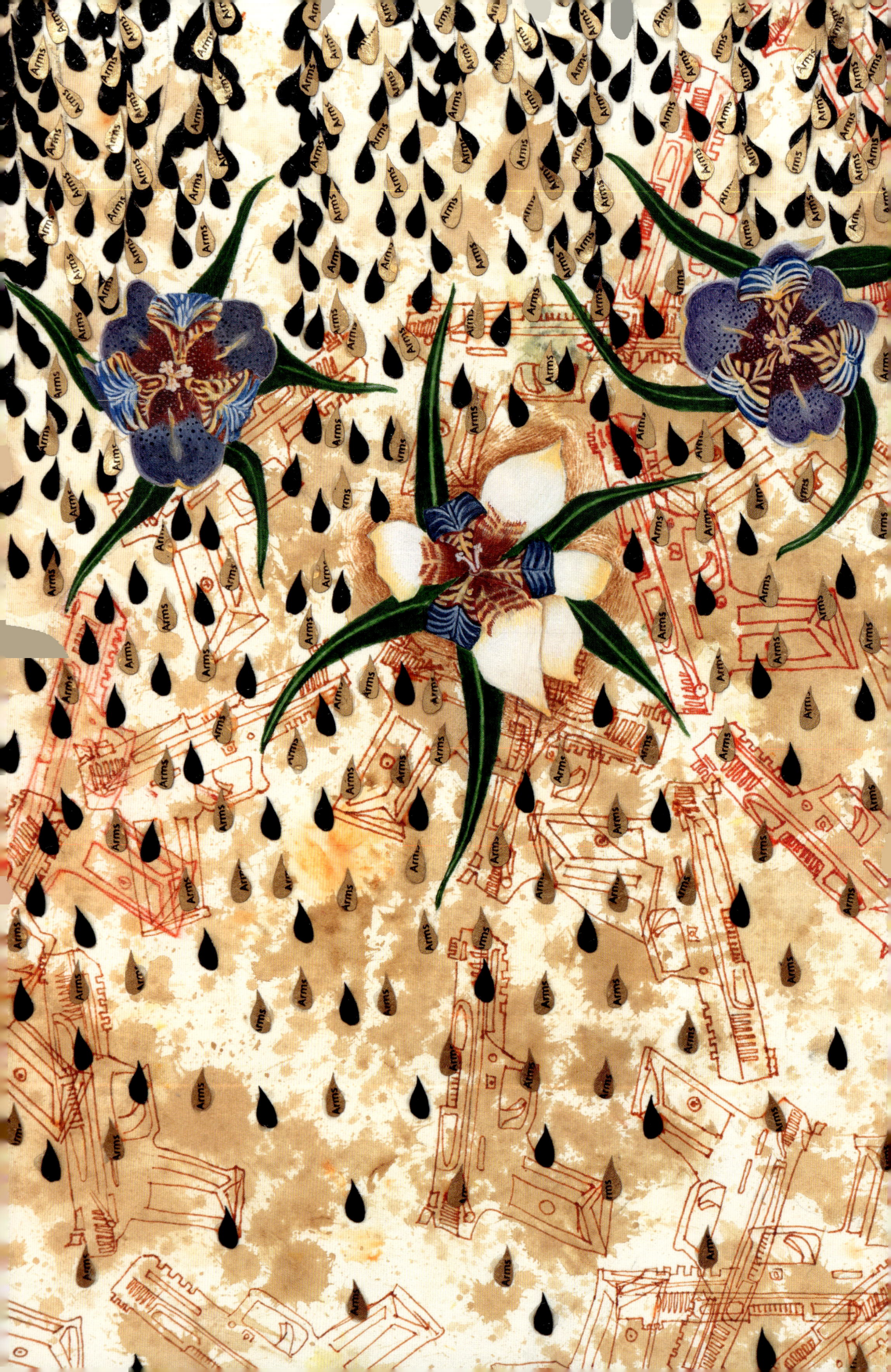

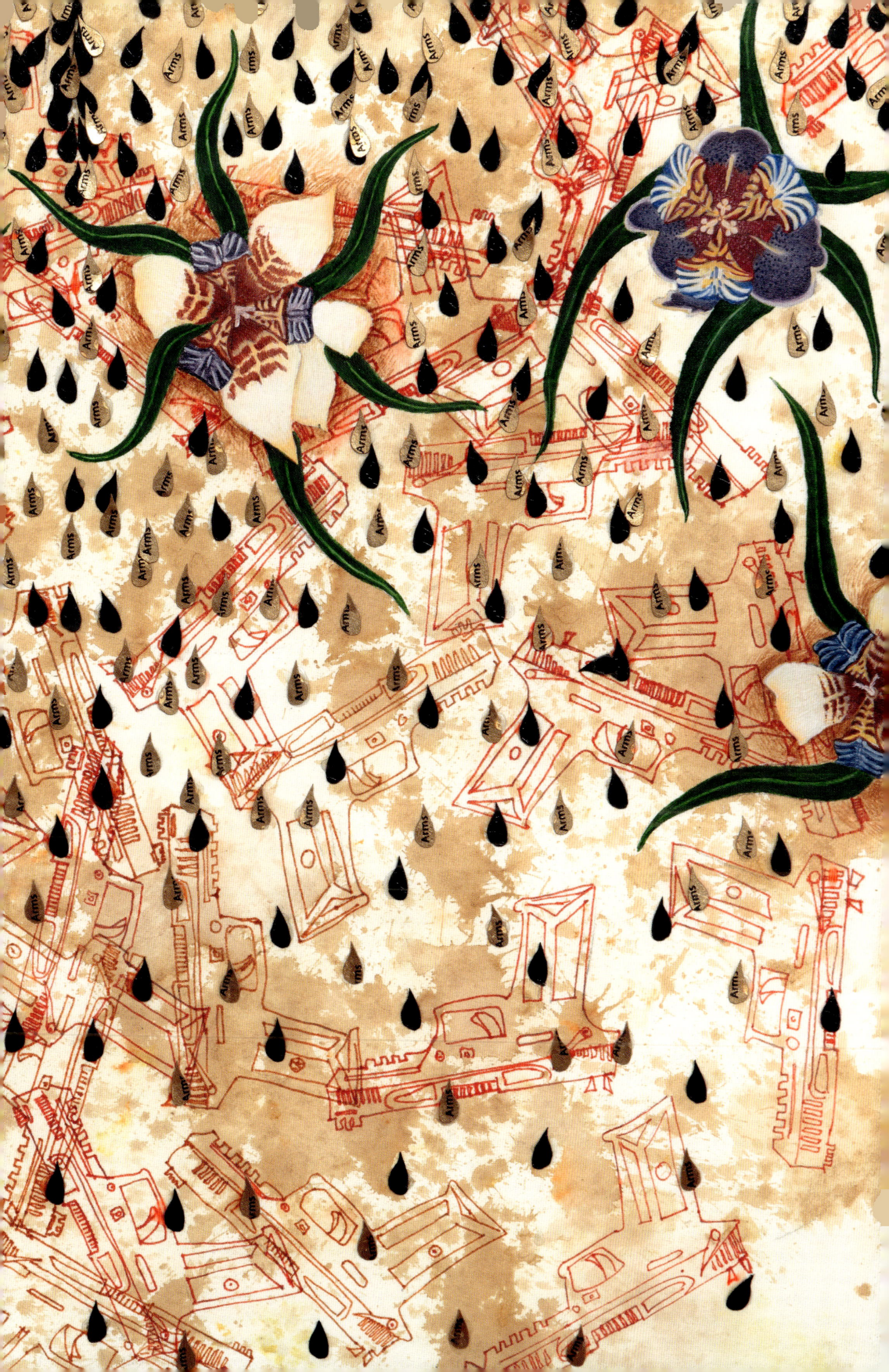

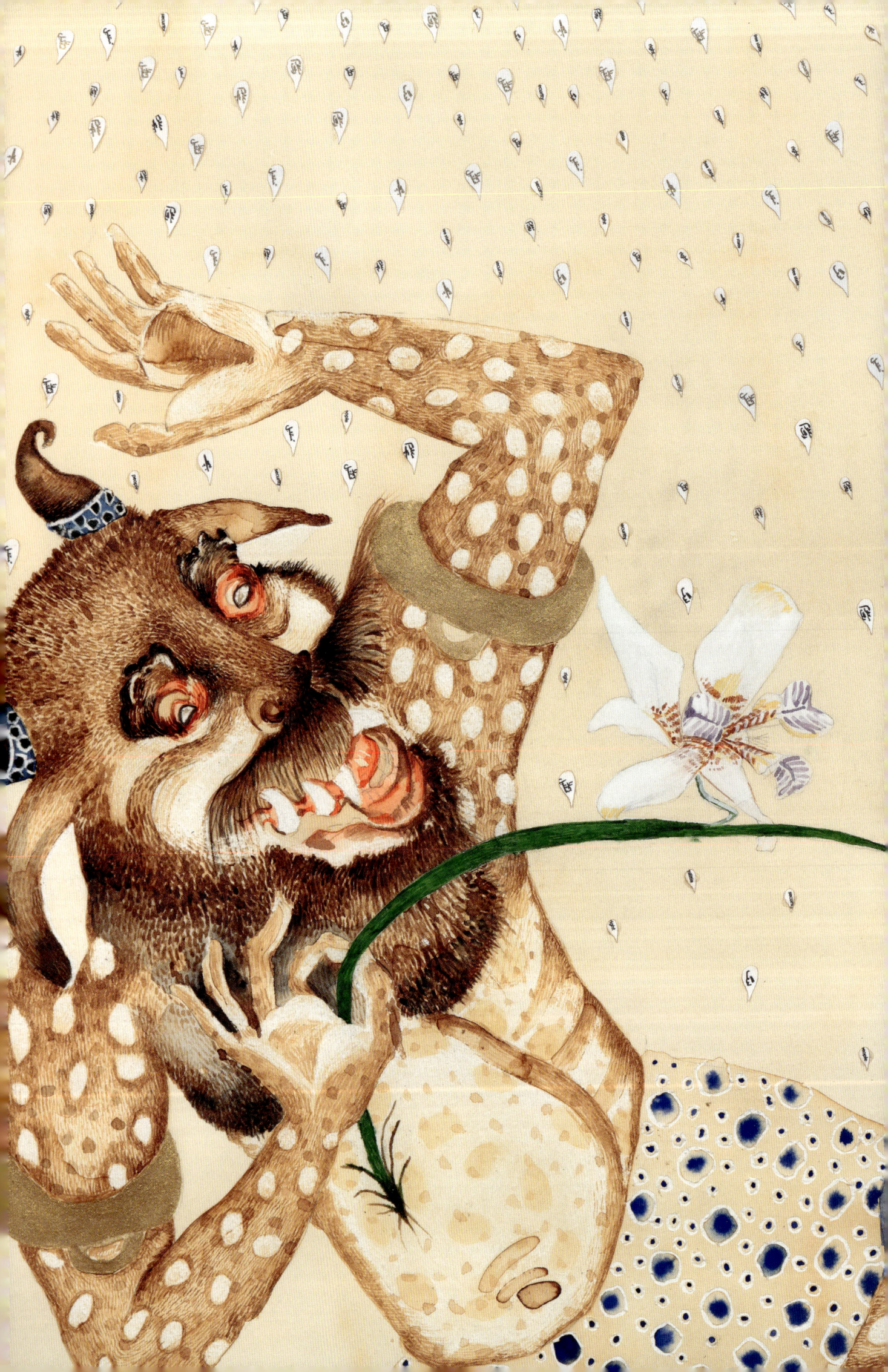

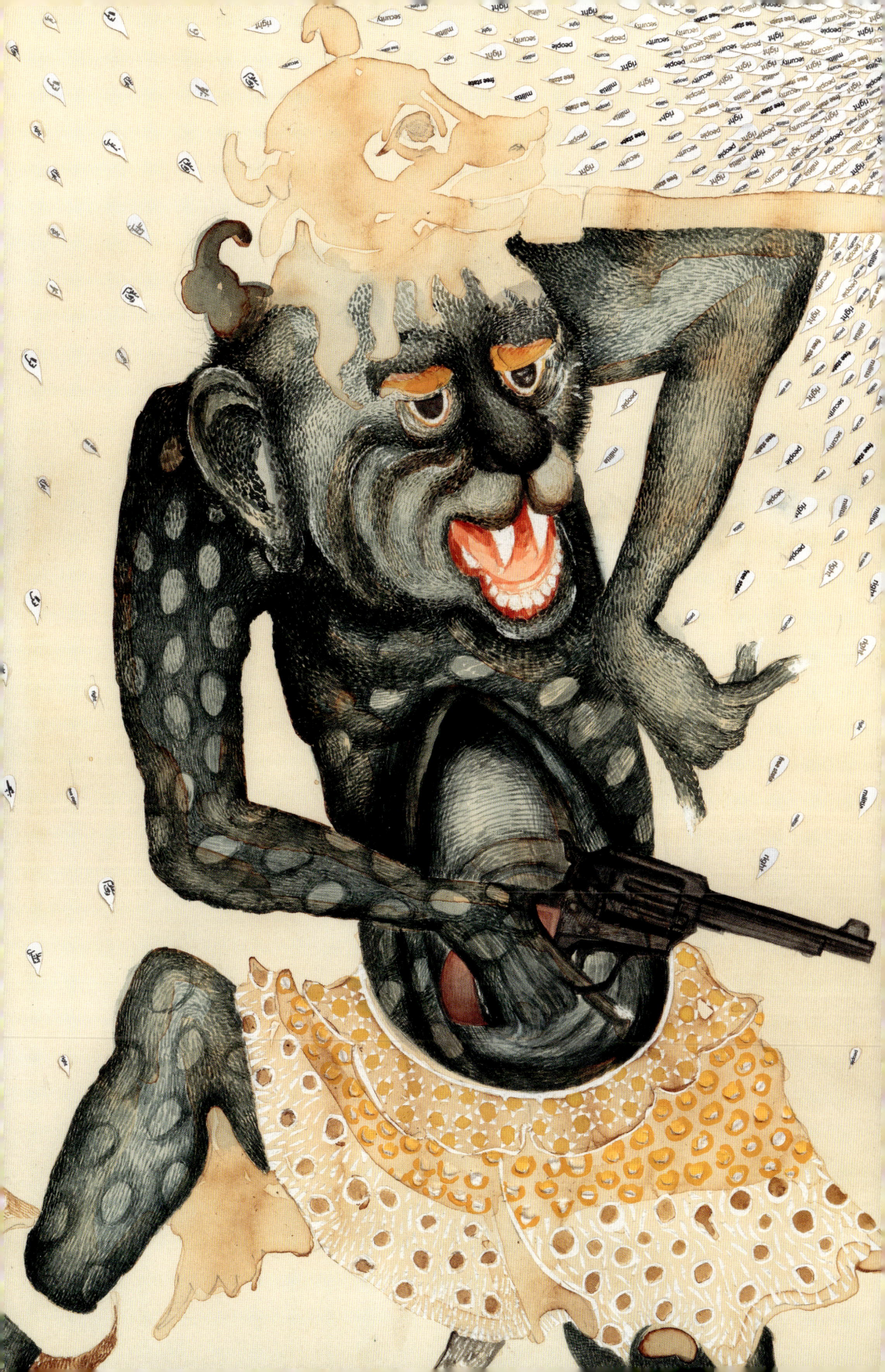

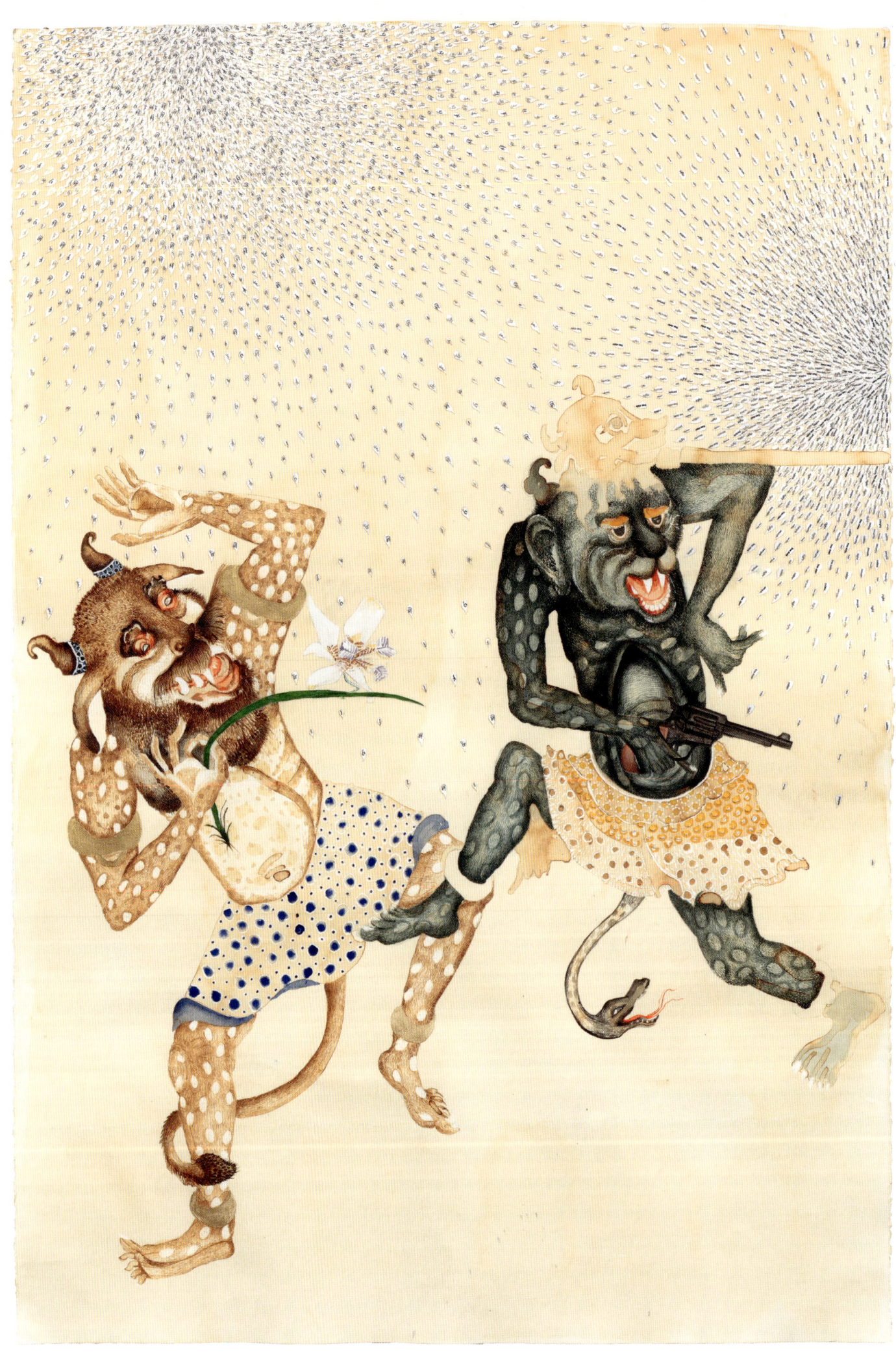

PREVIOUS PAGE (DETAIL)/ABOVE ***Untitled*** 2023
Collage of text, pen, water-based pigments and white
gouache on tea-stained paper, 46 × 31 inches

LIST OF WORKS

**All images courtesy the artist and Gallery Wendi Norris unless
otherwise stated**

BIOGRAPHIES AND ACKNOWLEDGMENTS

AMBREEN BUTT

Employing techniques rooted firmly in tradition, Ambreen Butt (b 1969 Lahore, Pakistan) creates works that explore the complexities of contemporary global politics, female identity and life as a Muslim person in the United States. Working through actions including staining, cutting, ripping, and tacking with repetitive urgency, Butt's painted and collaged works on paper and large-scale resin installations illuminate the radiant aesthetics of sacred geometries and Islamic ornamentation.

Butt's work has been the subject of solo exhibitions at institutions including the Dallas Contemporary, TX; Institute of Contemporary Art, Boston, MA; Isabella Stewart Gardner Museum, Boston, MA; Museum of Fine Arts, Boston, MA; National Museum of Women in the Arts, Washington, DC; and Worcester Art Museum, Worcester, MA.

The artist has been the recipient of numerous awards including the Brother Thomas Fellowship from the Boston Foundation; the Maud Morgan Prize from the Museum of Fine Arts, Boston; a Joan Mitchell Foundation grant; and a grant from the Canada Council for the Arts, Ontario. In 1999, she was the first recipient of the James and Audrey Foster Prize from the Institute of Contemporary Art in Boston, in addition to being an artist-in-residence at the Isabella Stewart Gardner Museum the same year.

Her work resides in numerous public institutions including the Institute of Contemporary Art, Boston; the Museum of Fine Arts, Boston; the Library of Congress, Washington DC; Minneapolis Institute of Art, Minnesota; National Museum of Women in the Arts, Washington DC; the Museum of Fine Arts, Houston; Worcester Art Museum, Massachusetts; the Hood Museum at Dartmouth College, New Hampshire; DeCordova Sculpture Park and Museum, Massachusetts; and the U.S. Art in Embassies.

Butt lives and works in Southlake, Texas. She received her BFA in traditional Indian and Persian miniature painting from the National College of Arts in Lahore. She earned her MFA in painting in 1997 from the Massachusetts College of Art and Design in Boston.

MARÍA MAGDALENA CAMPOS-PONS

María Magdalena Campos-Pons (b 1959, Matanzas, Cuba) is the Coneliuos Vanderbilt Endowed Chair Professor of Fine Arts, Drawing, Performance and Installation at Vanderbilt University. She is the founder of the Ríos Intermitentes International Biennale in Matanzas, Cuba, and the Awards Winning program Engine for Art, Democracy and Justice, EADJ. Campos-Pons is recipient of Columbia University Barnard College Medal of Distinction 2023 and elected a member of the American Academy of Arts and Science.

Campos-Pons graduated in 1980 from the National School of Art in Havana, Cuba. She went on to study painting at Higher Insitute of Art Havana's Universidad de las Artes (ISA). In 1988, she attended the MFA Program at Mass College of College of Art and Design where she focused on Interrelated Media and Painting. In the late 1980s, she taught at the Universidad de las Artes (ISA) in Havana. In 1991 she taught at the School of the Museum of Fine Arts at Tufts University and received numerous prizes and honors for both her teaching and her artistic practice. In 2017 she received a Dr Honoris Causa from Montserrat College of Art.

Campos-Pons' works are held by the Museum of Modern Art (New York); Princeton University Art Museum; Smithsonian American Art Museum (Washington, DC); Nasher Museum of Art at Duke University; J. Paul Getty Museum; Museum of Fine Arts (Boston); Institute of Contemporary Art (Boston); Whitney Museum of American Art (New York); Art Institute of Chicago; Victoria and Albert Museum (London); Pérez Art Museum (Miami); Harvard Art Museums (Cambridge), the Cuban National Museum of Fine Arts and other public and private collections. In addition, her work has appeared in "Thinking Historically in the Present" at the Sharjah Biennial 15 (United Arab Emirates). She has presented performances at venues including the Venice Biennale; documenta 14; Havana Biennial; Dakar Biennale; Johannesburg Biennale; Pacific Standard Time: LA/LA; and, at the Guggenheim Museum and National Portrait Gallery (Washington, DC).

SARA RAZA

Sara Raza (b 1979, London, U.K.) is an award-winning curator and writer specializing in global art and visual cultures from a postcolonial and post-Soviet perspective and the author of *Punk Orientalism: The Art of Rebellion* (Black Dog Press, London 2022). Raza has curated exhibitions and projects for international museums, biennials and festivals including the Solomon R Guggenheim Museum, New York; Galleria d'Arte Moderna, Milan; Rubin Museum of Art, New York; Mathaf: Modern Arab Art Museum, Doha, Qatar; the MacKenzie Art Gallery, Saskatchewan, Canada; Maraya Art Center, Sharjah; the Tashkent Biennale, Uzbekistan; the 55th Venice Biennale; and the 3rd Baku Public Art Festival, Azerbaijan, among others.

Formerly, she was the Guggenheim UBS MAP Curator for the Middle East and North Africa at the Guggenheim Museum, New York and Curator of Public Programs at Tate Modern, London. Raza is the West and Central Asia Desk Editor for *ArtAsiaPacific* magazine and has written for numerous artist monographs, books, and catalogues.

She is the recipient of the 11th ArtTable New Leadership Award for Women in the Arts and was honoured by Deutsche Bank and Apollo as one of "40 under 40" global art specialists in the "thinkers" category. She is a Walter Hopps Curatorial Excellence Award finalist and a recipient of the Arts Council of England Emerging Curator award (2004–05). Sara holds a BA (Hons) in English Literature and History of Art, and an MA in 20th-Century Art History and Theory, both from Goldsmiths College, University of London, and pursued studies towards her PhD at the Royal College of Art, London. She lives and works in New York City, where she teaches on the School of Visual Arts' MA Curatorial Practice programme and is a Red Burns Fellow at New York University's Interactive Telecommunications Program, where she also teaches on the programme's MA course.

QUDDUS MIRZA

Quddus Mirza (b 1961, Lahore, Pakistan) is a visual artist, art critic, and independent curator. He was the former Professor of Fine Art and the Head of the Fine Art Department at the National College of Arts, Lahore. Mirza has shown extensively in numerous group shows, along with several solo exhibitions, held in Pakistan and the UK. He has also curated a number of exhibitions in Pakistan, the U.K., and India.

Mirza is an art critic and writer for Pakistan's major newspaper *The News on Sunday* and for *Art India* magazine. He also contributes to publications including *Dawn, Herald, Himal, Depart, Libas, Contemporary* and *Flash Art*. He is the co-author of *50 Years of Visual Arts in Pakistan* (Sang-e-Meel Publications, Lahore, 1997) and has extensively written essays on Pakistani art in different international catalogues and other publications. He is the editor of online magazine *Art Now Pakistan*.

ACKNOWLEDGMENTS

I wish to express my gratitude to Gallery Wendi Norris and team for their contribution in bringing this publication to fruition. A special thanks to Wendi Norris for her exceptional leadership in overseeing this project and to Rachel Trout for being meticulously involved in the process from beginning to end. I am deeply grateful to the incredible writers who have contributed to this publication: Quddus Mirza, who has witnessed my artistic evolution from a young student to the artist I am today; curator Sara Raza, for her insightful and innovative contextualization of my work through the lens of Islamic sciences; artist Maria Magdalena Campos-Pons, my dear friend, mentor, and inspiration. To my Ustad, master miniaturist Bashir Ahmad, for gifting me the skills that I could not have received anywhere else in the world. To Justine Ludwig, for her unwavering support and friendship; Timothy Don, for often coming to my rescue in translating my visual language into words; Eram Bukhari, for her lifelong friendship and help in conceptualizing the cover of this publication; and Deama Khader, for being my right-hand in the studio, especially during the critical deadlines of this project. Lastly, and most importantly, to the two men in my life, Iqbal and Ali-Hamzah, for their unconditional love and support and for their patience during this time so that I could devote myself to this project.

This book is published by Black Dog Press Limited,
a company registered in England and Wales with company
number 11182259. Artifice Press Limited is an imprint within
the SJH Group. Copyright is owned by the SJH Group.
All rights reserved.

Black Dog Press Limited
The Maple Building
39–51 Highgate Road
London NW5 1RT
United Kingdom
—
+44 (0)20 8371 4047
office@blackdogonline.com
www.blackdogonline.com

Creative direction and design by Rachel Pfleger
Edited by Megan Jenkins Reagh
Printed in Lithuania by Kopa

ISBN 978-1-912165-51-3

British Library in Cataloguing Data. A CIP record for this
book is available from the British Library.

COVER IMAGE *Muhammed Yunus (16)* 2018
Watercolor, torn and collaged text on tea stained paper, 29 × 21 in

■□■□ black dog press